Hands-On Deep Learning for IoT

Train neural network models to develop intelligent
IoT applications

Mohammad Abdur Razzaque, PhD
Md. Rezaul Karim

BIRMINGHAM - MUMBAI

Hands-On Deep Learning for IoT

Copyright © 2019 Packt Publishing

Commissioning Editor: Pravin Dhandre
Acquisition Editor: Nelson Morris
Content Development Editor: Karan Thakkar
Senior Editor: Ayaan Hoda
Technical Editor: Sagar Sawant
Copy Editor: Safis Editing
Language Support Editors: Storm Mann, Sophie Rogers
Project Coordinator: Hardik Bhinde
Proofreader: Safis Editing
Indexer: Pratik Shirodkar
Graphics: Jisha Chirayil
Production Designer: Nilesh Mohite

First published: June 2019

Production reference: 1100619

Published by Packt Publishing Ltd.
Livery Place
35 Livery Street
Birmingham
B3 2PB, UK.

ISBN 978-1-78961-613-2

www.packtpub.com

Contributors

About the authors

Mohammad Abdur Razzaque, PhD, is a senior lecturer in the School of Computing and Digital Technologies, Teesside University, UK. He has more than 14 years of research and development and teaching experience on distributed systems (Internet of Things, P2P networking, and cloud computing) as well as experience in cybersecurity. He is an expert in end-to-end (sensors-to-cloud) IoT solutions. He offers consultancy in the areas of IoT solutions and the use of machine learning techniques in businesses. He has successfully published more than 65 research papers in these areas.

He holds a PhD in distributed systems (P2P wireless sensor networks, mobile ad hoc networks) from the School of Computer Science and Informatics, UCD, Dublin (2008).

Md. Rezaul Karim is a researcher, author, and data science enthusiast with a strong computer science background, coupled with 10 years of research and development experience in machine learning, deep learning, and data mining algorithms to solve emerging bioinformatics research problems by making them explainable. He is passionate about applied machine learning, knowledge graphs, and explainable artificial intelligence (XAI).

Currently, he is working as a research scientist at Fraunhofer FIT, Germany. He is also a PhD candidate at RWTH Aachen University, Germany. Before joining FIT, he worked as a researcher at the Insight Centre for Data Analytics, Ireland. Previously, he worked as a lead software engineer at Samsung Electronics, Korea.

About the reviewers

Vasilis Tzivaras is a self-motivated and enthusiastic computer engineer who works in a freelance capacity. He has strong communication and leadership skills gained at IEEE UOI SB, where he was chairman for approximately 4 years. He has over five years' experience in web development and penetration testing and has implemented several projects involving the latest technologies and frameworks. His enthusiasm for robotics has led to the development of a quadrotor and a mobile robot. He has also implemented a DIY autonomous home system capable of user interaction and autonomous procedures. Last but not least, with all this knowledge, he has authored books entitled *Building a Quadrotor with Arduino* and *Raspberry Pi Zero W Wireless Projects*.

Ruben Oliva Ramos is a computer systems engineer from Instituto Tecnológico de León, with a master's degree in computer and electronic systems engineering, teleinformatics, and networking specialization from the University of Salle Bajio in Leon, Guanajuato, Mexico. He has more than five years experience in developing web applications to control and monitor devices connected with Arduino and Raspberry Pi using web frameworks and cloud services to build IoT applications. He has written a book for Packt entitled *Internet of Things Programming with JavaScript, Raspberry Pi 3 Home Automation Projects*. He also has experience in the spheres of monitoring, controlling, and the acquisition of data using Arduino and Visual Basic .NET for Alfaomega.

I would like to thank my savior and lord, Jesus Christ, for giving me the strength and courage to pursue this project. I would also like to thank my dear wife, Mayte; our two lovely sons, Ruben and Dario; my dear father, Ruben;, my dear mom, Rosalia; my brother, Juan Tomas; and my sister, Rosalia; whom I love. I am very grateful to Packt Publishing for giving me the opportunity to collaborate as an author and reviewer and to be part of this honest and professional team.

Packt is searching for authors like you

If you're interested in becoming an author for Packt, please visit authors.packtpub.com and apply today. We have worked with thousands of developers and tech professionals, just like you, to help them share their insight with the global tech community. You can make a general application, apply for a specific hot topic that we are recruiting an author for, or submit your own idea.

Table of Contents

Preface

In the **Internet of Things (IoT)** era, a huge large number of sensing devices collect and generate various sensory data over time for a wide range of applications. This data is predominantly made up of big, fast, and real-time streams based on the applications. The use of analytics in relation to such big data or data streams is crucial for learning new information, predicting future insights, and making informed decisions, which makes IoT a worthy paradigm for businesses and a quality-of-life improving technology.

This book will provide you with a thorough overview of a class of advanced machine learning techniques called **deep learning (DL)**, to facilitate the analytics and learning in various IoT applications. A hands-on overview will take you through what each process is, from data collection, analysis, modeling, and a model's performance evaluation, to various IoT application and deployment settings.

You'll learn how to train **convolutional neural networks (CNN)** for developing applications for image-based road faults detection and smart garbage separation, followed by implementing voice-initiated smart light control and home access mechanisms powered by **recurrent neural networks (RNN)**.

You'll master IoT applications for indoor localization, predictive maintenance, and locating equipment in a large hospital using autoencoders, DeepFi, and LSTM networks. Furthermore, you'll learn IoT application development for healthcare with IoT security enhanced. After reading this book, you will have a good head start at developing more complex DL applications for IoT-enabled devices.

Last but not least, this book isn't meant to be read cover to cover. You can turn the pages to a chapter that looks like something you're trying to accomplish or that ignites your interest. If you notice any errors or glaring omissions, better an errata than never or let us know or file issues on GitHub repo of this book. Thank you! Happy reading!

Who this book is for

This book is intended for anyone who wants to use DL techniques to analyze and understand IoT generated big and real-time data streams with the power of TensorFlow, Keras, and Chainer. If you want to build your own extensive IoT applications that work, and that can predict smart decisions in the future, then this book is what you need! Hence, this book is dedicated to IoT application developers, data analysts, or DL enthusiasts who do not have much background in complex numerical computations, but who want to know what DL actually is.

What this book covers

Chapter 1, *End-to-End Life Cycle of IoT*, discusses the end-to-end life cycle of IoT and its related concepts and components, as well as the key characteristics and issues of IoT data that demands the use of DL in IoT. Furthermore, it also covers the importance of analytics in the IoT and the motivation to use DL in data analytics.

Chapter 2, *Deep Learning Architectures for IoT*, provides the basic concepts of DL architectures and platforms, which will be used in all subsequent chapters. We will start with a brief introduction to machine learning (ML) and move to DL, which is a branch of ML based on a set of algorithms that attempt to model high-level abstractions in data. We will briefly discuss some of the most well-known and widely used neural network architectures. Finally, various features of DL frameworks and libraries will be discussed, which will be used for developing DL applications on IoT-enabled devices.

Chapter 3, *Image Recognition in IoT*, covers hands-on image data processing application development in the IoT. First, it briefly describes different IoT applications and their image detection-based decision making. This chapter also briefly discusses two IoT applications and their image detection-based implementation in a real-world scenario. In the second part of the chapter, we shall present a hands-on image detection implementation of the applications using a DL algorithm.

Chapter 4, *Audio/Speech/Voice Recognition in IoT*, briefly describes different IoT applications and their speech/voice recognition-based decision making. In addition, it will briefly discuss two IoT applications and their speech/voice recognition-based implementations in a real-world scenario. In the second part of the chapter, we shall present a hands-on speech/voice detection implementation of the applications using DL algorithms.

Chapter 5, *Indoor localization in IoT,* discusses how the DL techniques can be used for indoor localization in IoT applications in general with the aid of a hands-on example. It will discuss how to collect data from those devices and technologies, such as analyzing Wi-Fi fingerprinting data through the use of DL models to predict the location of the device or users in indoor environments. We will also discuss some deployment settings of indoor localization services in IoT environments.

Chapter 6, *Physiological and Psychological State Detection in IoT,* presents DL-based human physiological and psychological state detection techniques for IoT applications in general. The first part of this chapter will briefly describe different IoT applications and their decision making abilities based on the detection of physiological and psychological states. In addition, it will briefly discuss two IoT applications and their physiological and psychological state detection-based implementations in a real-world scenario. In the second part of the chapter, we shall present a hands-on physiological and psychological state detection implementation of the applications using DL algorithms.

Chapter 7, *IoT Security,* presents DL-based networks and devices' behavioral data analysis, along with security incident detection techniques for IoT applications in general. The first part of this chapter will briefly describe different IoT security attacks and their potential detection techniques, including DL/ML-based ones. In addition, it will briefly discuss two IoT use cases where security attacks (such as a DoS attack and DDoS) can be detected intelligently and automatically through DL-based anomaly detection. In the second part of the chapter, we shall present a hands-on example of DL-based security incident detection implementations.

Chapter 8, *Predictive Maintenance for IoT,* describes how to develop a DL solution for predictive maintenance for IoT using the Turbofan Engine Degradation Simulation dataset. The idea behind predictive maintenance is to determine whether failure patterns of various types can be predicted. We will also discuss how to collect data from IoT-enabled devices for the purpose of predictive maintenance.

Chapter 9, *Deep Learning in Healthcare IoT,* presents DL-based IoT solutions for healthcare in general. The first part of this chapter will present an overview of different applications of IoT in healthcare, followed by a brief discussion of two use cases where healthcare services can be improved and/or automated through well-supported IoT solutions. In the second part of the chapter, we shall present hands-on experience of the DL-based healthcare incident and/or diseases detection part of the two use cases.

`Chapter 10`, *What's Next – Wrapping Up and Future Directions*, presents a summary of the earlier chapters, and then discusses the main challenges, together with examples, faced by existing DL techniques in their development and implementation for resource-constrained and embedded IoT environments. Finally, we summarize a number of existing solutions and point out some potential solution directions that can fill the existing gaps for DL-based IoT analytics.

To get the most out of this book

Readers will require the following hardware with an Intel Xenon CPU E5-1650 v3@3.5 GHz and 32 GB RAM with GPU support and Raspberry Pi 3. Additionally, some basic knowledge of Python and its libraries, such as pandas, NumPy, Keras, TensorFlow, scikit-learn, Matplotlib, Seaborn, OpenCV, and Beautiful Soup 4 will be helpful to grasp the concepts throughout the chapters.

Download the example code files

You can download the example code files for this book from your account at `www.packt.com`. If you purchased this book elsewhere, you can visit `www.packt.com/support` and register to have the files emailed directly to you. You can download the code files by following these steps:

1. Log in or register at `www.packt.com`.
2. Select the **SUPPORT** tab.
3. Click on **Code Downloads & Errata**.
4. Enter the name of the book in the **Search** box and follow the onscreen instructions.

Once the file is downloaded, please make sure that you unzip or extract the folder using the latest version of:

- WinRAR/7-Zip for Windows
- Zipeg/iZip/UnRarX for Mac
- 7-Zip/PeaZip for Linux

The code bundle for the book is also hosted on GitHub at https://github.com/ PacktPublishing/Hands-On-Deep-Learning-for-IoT. In case there's an update to the code, it will be updated on the existing GitHub repository. We also have other code bundles from our rich catalog of books and videos available at https://github.com/PacktPublishing/. Check them out!

Download the color images

We also provide a PDF file that has color images of the screenshots/diagrams used in this book. You can download it here: http://www.packtpub.com/sites/default/files/ downloads/9781789616132_ColorImages.pdf.

Conventions used

There are a number of text conventions used throughout this book. CodeInText: Indicates code words in text, database table names, folder names, filenames, file extensions, pathnames, dummy URLs, user input, and Twitter handles. Here is an example: "For the exploration, we can run image_explorer.py on the dataset as follows."

A block of code is set as follows:

```
# Import the required modules
import urllib
from bs4 import BeautifulSoup
from selenium import webdriver
import os, os.path
import simplejson
```

When we wish to draw your attention to a particular part of a code block, the relevant lines or items are set in bold:

```
import pandas as pd
import numpy as np
import tensorflow as tf
from sklearn.preprocessing import scale
from keras.models import Sequential
```

Any command-line input or output is written as follows:

```
$ mkdir css
$ cd css
```

Bold: Indicates a new term, an important word, or words that you see on screen. For example, words in menus or dialog boxes appear in the text like this. Here is an example: "**Google Chrome** | **More tools** | **Developer tools** (in Windows OS)."

 Warnings or important notes appear like this.

 Tips and tricks appear like this.

Get in touch

Feedback from our readers is always welcome.

General feedback: If you have questions about any aspect of this book, mention the book title in the subject of your message and email us at customercare@packtpub.com.

Errata: Although we have taken every care to ensure the accuracy of our content, mistakes do happen. If you have found a mistake in this book, we would be grateful if you would report this to us. Please visit www.packt.com/submit-errata, selecting your book, clicking on the Errata Submission Form link, and entering the details.

Piracy: If you come across any illegal copies of our works in any form on the internet, we would be grateful if you would provide us with the location address or website name. Please contact us at copyright@packt.com with a link to the material.

If you are interested in becoming an author: If there is a topic that you have expertise in, and you are interested in either writing or contributing to a book, please visit authors.packtpub.com.

Reviews

Please leave a review. Once you have read and used this book, why not leave a review on the site that you purchased it from? Potential readers can then see and use your unbiased opinion to make purchase decisions, we at Packt can understand what you think about our products, and our authors can see your feedback on their book. Thank you!

For more information about Packt, please visit packt.com.

1
Section 1: IoT Ecosystems, Deep Learning Techniques, and Frameworks

In this section, we will have an overview of IoT ecosystems, the key characteristics of IoT data (that is, real-time big data). We explain why analytics is necessary for data and why **deep learning** (**DL**) is important for analysis. We will also look into various techniques, their models and architectures, and their suitability in the IoT applications domain.

The following chapters are included in this section:

- Chapter 1, *End-to-End Life Cycle of IoT*
- Chapter 2, *Deep Learning Architectures for IoT*

The End-to-End Life Cycle of the IoT

1

By enabling easy access it, and interaction with, a wide variety of physical devices and their environments, the **Internet of Things (IoT)** will foster the development of various applications in various domains, such as health and medical care, intelligent energy management and smart grids, transportation, traffic management, and more. These applications will generate big and real-time/streaming data, which will require big data analysis tools, including advanced machine learning, that is, **deep learning (DL)**, to extract useful information and make informed decisions. We need to understand the **end-to-end (E2E)** life cycle of the IoT and its different components in order to apply advanced machine learning techniques on the generated data of IoT applications.

In this chapter, we will discuss the E2E life cycle of the IoT and its related concepts and components. We will explore its key characteristics and the IoT data issues that demand the use of DL in IoT. We will cover the following topics:

- The E2E life cycle of the IoT:
    - IoT application domains:
        - The importance of analytics in IoT
        - The motivation to use DL in IoT data analytics
- The key characteristics and requirements of IoT data

The E2E life cycle of the IoT

Different organizations and industries describe IoT differently. One way of defining it simply and tangibly is as a network of smart objects, which connects the physical and digital world together. Examining the E2E life cycle of the IoT solution or, more generally, of the IoT ecosystem, will help us to understand it further and show us how it is applicable to machine learning and DL.

Similar to the definition of IoT, there is no single consensus on the E2E life cycle or the IoT architecture that is agreed universally. Different architectures or layers have been proposed by different researchers. The most commonly proposed options are the three and five-layer life cycles or architectures, as shown in the following diagram:

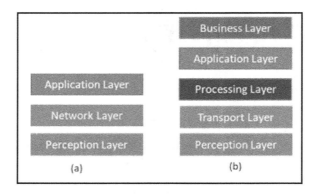

In the preceding diagram, **(a)** presents a three-layer IoT life cycle or architecture, and **(b)** presents a five-layer IoT life cycle or architecture.

The three-layer E2E IoT life cycle

This is the most basic and widely used IoT life cycle for IoT solutions. It consists of three layers: the perception, network, and application layers. These can be described as follows:

- **The perception layer**: This is the physical layer or sensing layer, which includes things or devices that have sensors to gather information about their environments. As shown in the following diagram, the perception layer of an E2E life cycle of the IoT solution in healthcare consists of patients, hospital beds, and wheelchairs that are deployed with sensors.
- **The network layer**: A network is responsible for connecting to other smart things, network devices, and servers. It is also responsible for transmitting and processing sensor data.
- **The application layer**: This layer is responsible for delivering application-specific services to users, based on the data from the sensor. It defines various applications in which IoT can be deployed, for example, smart homes, smart cities, and connected health.

The following diagram presents a three-layer E2E life IOT cycle in healthcare:

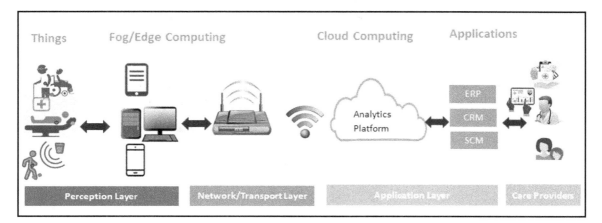

The three-layer E2E IoT life cycle or architecture defines the key ideas of IoT, but it may not be enough for research and development, as these often deal with the finer aspects of IoT. This is why other life cycles or architectures, such as the five-layer life cycle, have been proposed.

The five-layer IoT E2E life cycle

A five-layer IoT life cycle consists of the perception, transport, processing, application, and business layers. The role of the perception and application layers is the same as in the three-layer architecture. We outline the function of the remaining three layers as follows:

- **The transport layer**: This is similar to the network layer of the three-layer life cycle. It transfers the data gathered in the perception layer to the processing layer and vice versa through networks such as wireless, 3G, LAN, Bluetooth, RFID, and NFC.
- **The processing layer**: This is also known as the **middleware layer**. It stores, analyzes, and processes huge amounts of data that comes from the transport layer. It can manage and provide a diverse set of services to the lower layers. It employs many technologies, such as databases, cloud computing, and big data processing modules.
- **The business layer**: This layer manages the whole IoT system, including applications, business and profit models, and user privacy.

IoT system architectures

Understanding the architecture of the IoT system is important for developing an application. It is also important to consider our data processing requirements in different computing platform levels, including the fog level and the cloud level. Considering the criticality and latency-sensitiveness of many IoT applications (such as an IoT solution for the healthcare domain, as shown in the previous diagram), fog computing is essential for these applications. The following diagram, very briefly, presents how fog computing works:

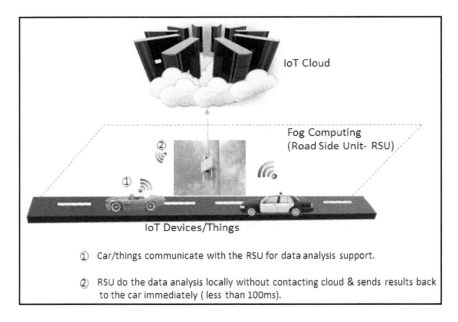

As we can see in the preceding diagram, in fog computing, a thing's (such as a car's) data does not move to the cloud for processing. In this way, fog computing addresses many challenges (such as high latency, downtime, security, privacy, and trust) faced by the cloud in IoT and offers many benefits, such as location awareness, low latency, support for mobility, real-time interactions, scalability, and business agility. The following diagram presents the protocol layer-wise architecture of fog computing:

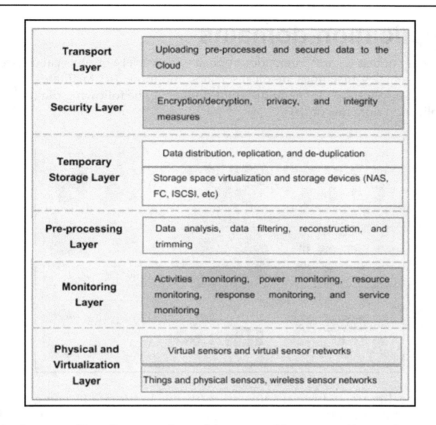

As shown in the preceding diagram, the architecture of fog computing or fog computing with IoT consists of six layers: physical and virtualization, monitoring, preprocessing, temporary storage, security, and transport. Notably, the preprocessing layer performs data management tasks by essentially analyzing, filtering, and trimming collected data from physical or virtual sensors.

IoT application domains

By enabling easy access to, and interaction with, a wide variety of physical devices or things such as vehicles, machines, medical sensors, and more, IoT facilitates the development of applications in many different domains. The following diagram highlights the key application domains of IoT:

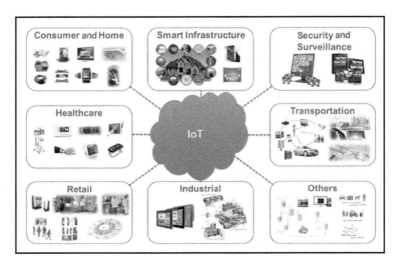

These include healthcare, industrial automation (that is, Industry 4.0), energy management and smart grids, transportation, smart infrastructure (such as the smart home and the smart city), retail, and many other areas that will transform our lives and societies for the better. These applications will have a global economic impact of $4 to $11 trillion per year by 2025. The key contributors (in order of their predicted contribution) of this quantity of money include the following:

- Factories or industries, including operation management and predictive maintenance
- Cities, including public safety, health, traffic control, and resource management
- Healthcare, including monitoring and managing illnesses and improving wellness
- Retail, including self-checkouts and inventory management
- Energy, including the smart grid

The tremendous demand for these applications implies the incredible and steep growth of IoT services and the big data that they generate.

The importance of analytics in IoT

The use of IoT in various application domains will only be effective if those applications can extract some business value from the data generated and collected by IoT devices. In this context, analysis of IoT data is essential in IoT solutions. Gartner identified IoT analytics as one of the two top technologies used in IoT.

IoT analytics is the application of data analysis tools and procedures to unlocking insights from the huge volumes of data generated by IoT devices in different ways. IoT analytics is essential for extracting insights from the data generated by IoT devices or things. More specifically, IoT business models analyze the information generated and collected by things in many ways – for example, to understand customer behavior, to deliver services, to improve products and services, and to identify and intercept business moments. The main element of most of these IoT business models or applications when it comes to understanding their data is an intelligent learning or machine learning mechanism for prediction, data mining, and pattern recognition. Traditional machine learning mechanisms or technologies work well with structured data, but they struggle with unstructured data.

An example of this is Google's Nest learning thermostat, which records temperature data in a structured way and then applies machine learning algorithms to understand the patterns of its user's temperature preferences and schedules. However, it does not understand unstructured data, such as multimedia data, which is audio signals and visual images. Additionally, the training of traditional machine learning algorithms relies on handcrafted and engineered feature sets that may not be easy in many IoT applications because of heterogeneity and the dynamics involved in the applications. In factories, for example, faults could be random and feature sets might be unavailable to classify them. For this reason, IoT demands new analytics approaches, including DL.

The motivation to use DL in IoT data analytics

In recent years, many IoT applications have been actively exploiting sophisticated DL technologies, which use neural networks to capture and understand their environments. Amazon Echo, for example, is considered to be an IoT application as it connects the physical and human world with the digital world; it can understand human voice commands using DL.

Additionally, Microsoft's Windows face-recognition security system (an IoT application) uses DL technology to perform tasks such as unlocking a door when it recognizes its user's face. DL and IoT are among the top three strategic technology trends for 2017, and were announced at the Gartner Symposium/ITxpo 2016. The intensive publicity around DL is due to the fact that traditional machine learning algorithms do not address the emerging analytic needs of IoT systems. On the contrary, DL algorithms or models, in general, bring two important improvements over traditional machine learning approaches. First, they reduce the need for handcrafted and engineered feature sets to be used for the training of a model. As a result, some features in IoT applications, which might not be apparent to humans, can be extracted easily by DL models. Moreover, DL models improve prediction accuracy.

However, enabling DL in IoT applications, especially in edge computing devices, fog computing devices, and end devices, is difficult because of their resource-constrained properties. Moreover, IoT data is different from general big data. We need to explore the properties of IoT data and how they are different from those of general big data in order to better understand the requirements for IoT data analytics.

The key characteristics and requirements of IoT data

The data from IoT applications exhibits two characteristics that require different treatment from the analytics approach. Many IoT applications, such as remote patient monitoring or autonomous vehicles, generate streams of data continuously, and this leads to a huge volume of continuous data. Many other applications, such as consumer product analysis for marketing or inhabitant monitoring in forests or underwater, produce data that accumulates as a source of big data. Streaming data is generated or captured within short intervals of time and need to be quickly analyzed to extract immediate and useful insights and make fast decisions.

On the contrary, the term big data refers to huge datasets that commonly used hardware and software platforms are not able to store, manage, process, and analyze. These two types of data need to be treated differently as their requirements for analytics response are different.

The results from big data analytics, such as business intelligence and transactional analysis, can be delivered after several days of data generation, but streaming data analytics results should be ready in anything from a few hundreds of milliseconds to a few seconds. For example, in driverless cars, the response time in the case of an emergency brake needs to be around 100 milliseconds. The following diagram highlights the key characteristics of IoT data and its analytics requirements:

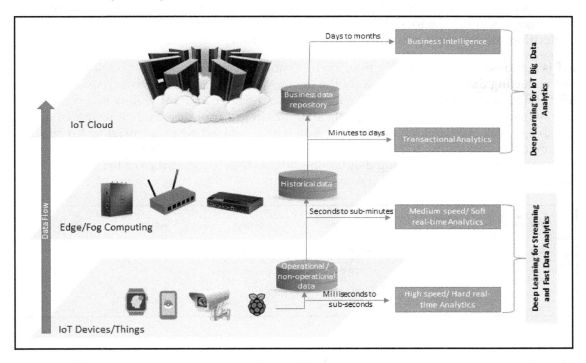

Many IoT applications, such as an application to monitor real-time average temperatures, rely on multiple sources of data. Data fusion, aggregation, and sharing play a critical role in these applications. This is even more critical for time-sensitive IoT applications, such as remote patient monitoring, or driverless cars, where the timely aggregation of data is needed to bring all pieces of data together for analysis and, subsequently, to provide reliable and accurate actionable insights.

In general, the analysis of streaming data is challenging, even in high-performance computing systems or cloud platforms. A potential solution for streaming data analytics is frameworks based on data parallelism and incremental processing. Although these techniques may reduce time latency and return a response from the streaming data analytics framework, they are not the optimal solution for real-time IoT applications. In this context, it is better to bring streaming data analytics closer to the source of data, through IoT devices or edge devices, with the support of fog or edge computing. However, adding data analytics to IoT devices or things introduces new challenges such as the limitation of computing, storage, and power resources at the source of the data.

IoT is responsible for generating big data by connecting billions of smart devices together and collecting data about the status of the devices and their environments frequently. Identifying and mining meaningful patterns from the huge amount of data that comes from raw sensors is the core utility of big data analytics in IoT applications, as it results in further insights for decision-making and trend prediction. By extracting these insights, IoT big data is of extreme importance to many businesses, as it enables them to gain an advantage over their competitors. The following diagram highlights the characteristics of IoT big data using the **six Vs** (**6Vs**):

Volume	Velocity	Variety	Veracity	Variability	Value
• How much data? - Billion devices will generate data in ZetaBytes.	• How fast can I access? -IoT data can be accessed in real time.	• What type of data? -Structured & unstructured IoT data - Heterogenous format of IoT data	•Is IoT data reliable? -Most IoT data are. - Crowdsensing data may not be.	•What are the rate of different IoT data flows? - Flow rate depends on applications, time, and space.	Usability and utility of data. -Most IoT data tremendously useful.

Real-life examples of fast and streaming IoT data

Remote patient monitoring is one of the most obvious and popular applications of IoT in healthcare. Through this application, which is sometimes known as **telehealth**, a patient will be connected to their care providers and get real-time feedback if necessary. The data generated by this application, such as variability in heart rate or blood pressure, is streaming data and needs to be processed quickly so that care providers can respond promptly to the patient's situation.

The following diagram presents a snapshot of a commercially available remote patient monitoring system:

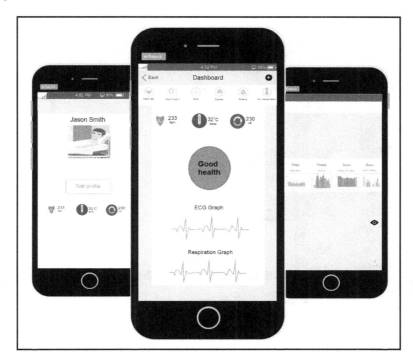

Real-life examples of IoT big data

The smart grid is an important source of IoT big data. Smart meters play an important role in the smart grid system by generating and gathering a precise measurement of the energy consumption of their users. At present, energy providers in many countries are interested in learning local energy consumption patterns, predicting the needs of their customers, and making appropriate decisions based on real-time analytics.

Another example of IoT big data is the data generated by smart devices. The following diagram presents the process of consumer product analysis for marketing using IoT data:

As shown in the preceding diagram, an IoT enabled remote patient monitoring system can produce a massive amount of data to be processed, stored, and analyzed. Nevertheless, smart devices such as smart coffee machines, smart fridges, and smart vending machines also can generate big data, which can be used for consumer product analysis.

Summary

In this chapter, we presented two different layered views of the E2E life cycle of the IoT. We also looked at the IoT system architecture and key application domains of IoT. Following this, we defined what is meant by IoT analytics and its importance in IoT applications, with special emphasis on DL. We discussed the key characteristics of IoT and their corresponding requirements in analytics. Finally, we presented a few real IoT examples, which generate fast and streaming data as well as big data. In the next chapter, you will be introduced to several common DL models and the most cutting-edge architectures that have been introduced in recent years, and learn how they can be useful in analyzing IoT streaming and big data.

It is essential to know the basics of different DL models and their different implementation frameworks in order to use them in different IoT applications. In the next chapter, we will present a list of popular DL models, including convolutional neural networks, long short-term memory, and autoencoders. In addition to this, we discuss a list of popular DL development frameworks, including TensorFlow and Keras.

Reference

- Pallavi Sethi and Smruti R. Sarangi, *Internet of Things: Architectures, Protocols, and Applications*, Journal of Electrical and Computer Engineering, vol. 2017, Article ID 9324035, 25 pages, 2017.
- Atlam, H.F.; Walters, R.J.; Wills, G.B. *Fog Computing and the Internet of Things: A Review*. Big Data Cogn. Comput. 2018, 2, 10.
- James Manyika, Michael Chui, Peter Bisson, Jonathan Woetzel, Richard Dobbs, Jacques Bughin, and Dan Aharon, *Unlocking the potential of the Internet of Things*, which is available at `https://www.mckinsey.com/business-functions/digital-mckinsey/our-insights/the-internet-of-things-the-value-of-digitizing-the-physical-world`.
- Stamford, Conn, *Gartner Identifies the Top 10 Internet of Things Technologies for 2017 and 2018*, which is available online at `https://www.gartner.com/newsroom/id/3221818`.
- J. Tang, D. Sun, S. Liu and J. Gaudiot, *Enabling Deep Learning on IoT Devices*, in Computer, vol. 50, no. 10, pp. 92-96, 2017.
- M. Mohammadi, A. Al-Fuqaha, S. Sorour, and M. Guizani, *Deep Learning for IoT Big Data and Streaming Analytics: A Survey*, in IEEE Communications Surveys and Tutorials, which is available at (DOI) 10.1109/COMST.2018.2844341.
- K. Panetta (2016), *Gartner's top 10 strategic technology trends for 2017*, which is available at `http://www:gartner:com/smarterwithgartner/gartners-top-10-technology-trends-2017/`.
- `https://www.napierhealthcare.com/lp/remote-patient-telehealth-monitoring?gclid=CjwKCAjwxILdBRBqEiwAHL2R865Aep4MKgFknoctRLDOk3VtSNQWiRdTFyRR-e2es-yaz_e6Dp6hNhoCmV4QAvD_BwE`.
- `https://www.softwareadvice.com/resources/iot-data-analytics-use-cases/`
  .

Deep Learning Architectures for IoT

2

In the era of the **Internet of Things (IoT)**, an enormous amount of sensory data for a wide range of fields and applications is being generated and collected from numerous sensing devices. Applying analytics over such data streams to discover new information, predict future insights, and make controlled decisions, is a challenging task, which makes IoT a worthy paradigm for business intelligence and quality-of-life improving technology. However, analytics on IoT—enabled devices requires a platform consisting of **machine learning (ML)** and **deep learning (DL)** frameworks, a software stack, and hardware (for example, a **Graphical Processing Unit (GPU)** and **Tensor Processing Unit (TPU)**).

In this chapter, we will discuss some basic concepts of DL architectures and platforms, which will be used in all subsequent chapters. We will start with a brief introduction to ML. Then, we will move onto DL, which is a branch of ML based on a set of algorithms that attempts to model high-level abstractions in data. We will briefly discuss some of the most well-known and widely used neural network architectures. Then, we will look at various features of DL frameworks and libraries that can be used for developing DL applications on IoT-enabled devices. Briefly, the following topics will be covered:

- A soft introduction to ML
- Artificial neural networks
- Deep neural network architectures
- DL frameworks

A soft introduction to ML

ML approaches are based on a set of statistical and mathematical algorithms carrying out tasks such as classification, regression analysis, concept learning, predictive modeling, clustering, and mining of useful patterns. Using ML, we aim to improve the whole learning process automatically so that we may not need complete human interactions, or so that we can at least reduce the level of such interactions as much as possible.

Working principle of a learning algorithm

Tom M. Mitchell explained what learning really means from a computer science perspective:

> *"A computer program is said to learn from experience E with respect to some class of tasks T and performance measure P, if its performance at tasks in T, as measured by P, improves with experience E."*

Based on this definition, we can conclude that a computer program or machine can do the following:

- Learn from data and histories
- Improve with experience
- Iteratively enhance a model that can be used to predict outcomes of questions

Since the preceding points are at the core of predictive analytics, almost every ML algorithm we use can be treated as an optimization problem. This is about finding parameters that minimize an objective function; for example, a weighted sum of two terms such as a cost function and regularization. Typically, an objective function has two components:

- A regularizer that controls the complexity of the model
- The loss that measures the error of the model on the training data

On the other hand, the regularization parameter defines the trade-off between minimizing the training error and the model's complexity in an effort to avoid overfitting problems. Now, if both of these components are convex, then their sum is also convex. So, when using an ML algorithm, the goal is to obtain the best hyperparameters of a function that return the minimum error when making predictions. Therefore, by using a convex optimization technique, we can minimize the function until it converges toward the minimum error.

Given that a problem is convex, it is usually easier to analyze the asymptotic behavior of the algorithm, which shows how fast it converges as the model observes more and more training data. The task of ML is to train a model so that it can recognize complex patterns from the given input data and can make decisions in an automated way. Thus, making predictions is all about testing the model against new (that is, unobserved) data and evaluating the performance of the model itself. However, in the process as a whole, and for making the predictive model a successful one, data acts as the first-class citizen in all ML tasks. In reality, the data that we feed to our ML systems must be made up of mathematical objects, such as vectors, so that they can consume such data.

Depending on the available data and feature types, the performance of your predictive model can vacillate dramatically. Therefore, selecting the right features is one of the most important steps before the model evaluation takes place. This is called **feature engineering,** where the domain knowledge pertaining to the data is used to create only selective or useful features that help prepare the feature vectors to be used so that an ML algorithm works.

For example, comparing hotels is quite difficult unless we already have a personal experience of staying in multiple hotels. However, with the help of an ML model, which is already trained with quality features out of thousands of reviews and features (for example, how many stars does a hotel have, the size of the room, the location, and room service, and so on), it is pretty feasible now. We'll see several examples throughout the chapters. However, before developing such an ML model, knowing a number of ML concepts is also important.

General ML rule of thumb

The general ML rule of thumb is that the more data there is, the better the predictive model. However, having more features often creates a mess, to the extent that the performance degrades drastically, especially if the dataset is multidimensional. The entire learning process requires input datasets that can be split into three types (or are already provided as such):

- A **training set** is the knowledge base coming from historical or live data that is used to fit the parameters of the ML algorithm. During the training phase, the ML model utilizes the training set to find optimal weights of the network and reach the objective function by minimizing the training error. Here, the backpropagation rule, or an optimization algorithm, is used to train the model, but all the hyperparameters are needed to be set before the learning process starts.

- A **validation set** is a set of examples used to tune the parameters of an ML model. It ensures that the model is trained well and generalizes toward avoiding overfitting. Some ML practitioners refer to it as a development set, or dev set as well.
- A **test set** is used for evaluating the performance of the trained model on unseen data. This step is also referred to as **model inferencing**. After assessing the final model on the test set (that is, when we're fully satisfied with the model's performance), we do not have to tune the model any further, but the trained model can be deployed in a production-ready environment.

A common practice is splitting the input data (after the necessary preprocessing and feature engineering) into 60% for training, 10% for validation, and 20% for testing, but it really depends on use cases. Sometimes, we also need to perform upsampling or downsampling on the data, based on the availability and quality of the datasets. This rule of thumb of learning on different types of training sets can differ across ML tasks, as we will cover in the next section. However, before that, let's take a quick look at a few common phenomena in ML.

General issues in ML models

When we use this input data for training, validation, and testing, usually, the learning algorithms cannot learn 100% accurately, which involves training, validation, and test error (or loss). There are two types of errors that you may encounter in an ML model:

- Irreducible error
- Reducible error

The irreducible error cannot be reduced even with the most robust and sophisticated model. However, the reducible error, which has two components, called bias and variance, can be reduced. Therefore, to understand the model (that is, prediction errors), we need to focus on bias and variance only. Bias means how far the predicted values are from the actual values. Usually, if the average predicted values are very different from the actual values (labels), then the bias is higher.

An ML model will have a high bias because it can't model the relationship between input and output variables (can't capture the complexity of data well) and becomes very simple. Thus, an overly simple model with high variance causes underfitting of the data. The following diagram gives some high-level insights, and also shows what a just-right fit model should look like:

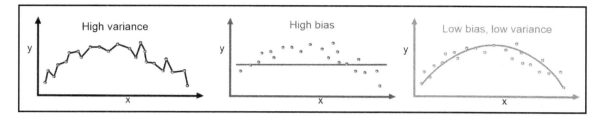

Variance signifies the variability between the predicted values and the actual values (how scattered they are). If the model has a high training error as well as the validation error or test error being the same as the training error, the model has a high bias. On the other hand, if the model has a low training error but has a high validation or high test error, the model has a high variance. An ML model usually performs very well on the training set, but doesn't work well on the test set (because of high error rates). Ultimately, it results in an underfit model. We can recap the overfitting and underfitting once more:

- **Underfitting**: If your training and validation errors are both relatively equal and very high, then your model is most likely underfitting your training data.
- **Overfitting**: If your training error is low and your validation error is high, then your model is most likely overfitting your training data. The just-right fit model learns very well and performs better on unseen data too.

 Bias-variance trade-off: the high bias and high variance issue is often called bias-variance trade-off, because a model cannot be too complex or too simple at the same time. Ideally, we strive for the best model that has both low bias and low variance.

Now we know the basic working principle of an ML algorithm. However, based on problem type and the method used to solve a problem, ML tasks can be different; for example, supervised learning, unsupervised learning, and reinforcement learning. We'll discuss these learning tasks in more detail in the next section.

ML tasks

Although every ML problem is more or less an optimization problem, the way in which they are solved can vary. In fact, learning tasks can be categorized into three types: supervised learning, unsupervised learning, and reinforcement learning.

Supervised learning

Supervised learning is the simplest and most well-known automatic learning task. It is based on a number of predefined examples, in which the category to which each of the inputs should belong is already known, as shown in the following diagram:

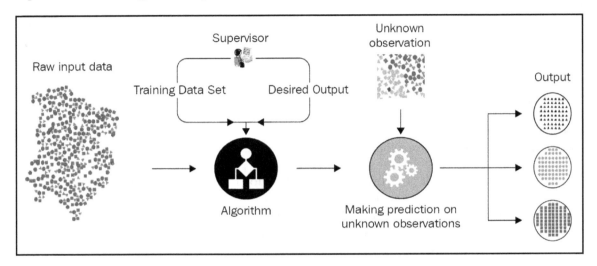

The preceding diagram shows a typical workflow of supervised learning. An actor (for example, a data scientist or data engineer) performs the **extraction, transformation, and load (ETL)** and the necessary feature engineering (including feature extraction, selection, and so on) to get the appropriate data with features and labels so that they can be fed into the model. Then, they split the data into training, development, and test sets. The training set is used to train an ML model, the validation set is used to validate the training against the overfitting problem and regularization, and then the actor would evaluate the model's performance on the test set (that is, unseen data).

However, if the performance is not satisfactory, the actor can perform additional tuning to get the best model based on hyperparameter optimization. Finally, they will deploy the best model in a production-ready environment. In the overall life cycle, there might be many actors involved (for example, a data engineer, data scientist, or an ML engineer), performing each step independently or collaboratively. The supervised learning context includes classification and regression tasks; classification is used to predict which class a data point is a part of (discrete value). It is also used for predicting the label of the class attribute. The following diagram summarizes these steps in a nutshell:

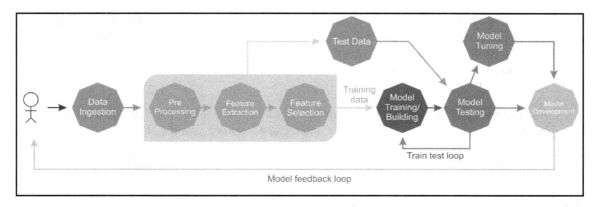

On the other hand, regression is used to predict continuous values and make a numeric prediction of the class attribute. In the context of supervised learning, the learning process required for the input dataset is split randomly into three sets; for example, 60% for the training set, 10% for the validation set, and the remaining 30% for the testing set.

Unsupervised learning

How would you summarize and group a dataset if the labels were not given? You'll probably try to answer this question by finding the underlying structure of a dataset and measuring the statistical properties, such as the frequency distribution, mean, and standard deviation. If the question is how would you effectively represent data in a compressed format, you'll probably reply saying that you'll use some software for doing the compression, although you might have no idea how that software would do it. The following diagram shows the typical workflow of an unsupervised learning task:

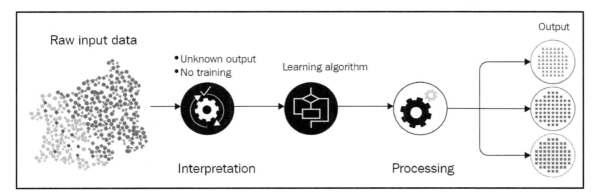

These are precisely two of the main goals of unsupervised learning, which is largely a data-driven process. We call this type of learning unsupervised because you will have to deal with unlabeled data. The following quote comes from Yann LeCun, director of AI research (source: *Predictive Learning*, NIPS 2016, Yann LeCun, Facebook Research):

> *"Most human and animal learning is unsupervised learning. If intelligence was a cake, unsupervised learning would be the cake, supervised learning would be the icing on the cake, and reinforcement learning would be the cherry on the cake. We know how to make the icing and the cherry, but we don't know how to make the cake. We need to solve the unsupervised learning problem before we can even think of getting to true AI."*

A few most widely used unsupervised learning tasks include the following:

- **Clustering**: Grouping data points based on similarity (or statistical properties), for example, a company such as Airbnb often groups its apartments and houses into neighborhoods so that customers can navigate the listed ones more easily
- **Dimensionality reduction**: Compressing the data with the structure and statistical properties preserved as much as possible, for example, often, the number of dimensions of the dataset needs to be reduced for the modelling and visualization
- **Anomaly detection**: Useful in several applications, such as identification of credit card fraud detection, identifying faulty pieces of hardware in an industrial engineering process, and identifying outliers in large-scale datasets
- **Association rule mining**: Often used in market basket analysis, for example, asking which items are bought together frequently

Reinforcement learning

Reinforcement learning is an artificial intelligence approach that focuses on the learning of the system through its interactions with the environment. In reinforcement learning, the system's parameters are adapted based on the feedback obtained from the environment, which, in turn, provides feedback on the decisions made by the system. The following diagram shows a person making decisions in order to arrive at their destination. Let's take an example of the route you take from home to work:

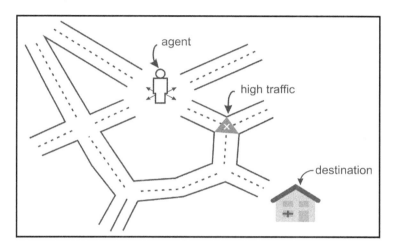

We can take a look at one more example in terms of a system modeling a chess player. In order to improve its performance, the system utilizes the result of its previous moves; such a system is said to be a system learning with reinforcement. In this case, you take the same route to work every day. However, out of the blue one day, you get curious and decide to try a different route with a view to finding the shortest path. Similarly, based on your experience and the time taken with the different route, you'll decide whether you should take that specific route more often. We can take a look at one more example in terms of a system modeling a chess player.

So far, we have learned the basic working principles of ML and different learning tasks. Let's have a look at each learning task with some example use cases in the next section.

Learning types with applications

We have seen the basic working principles of ML algorithms, and we have seen what the basic ML tasks are, and how they formulate domain-specific problems. However, each of these learning tasks can be solved using different algorithms. The following diagram provides a glimpse into this:

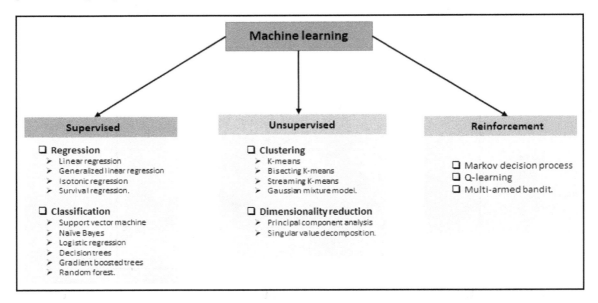

However, the preceding diagram lists only a few use cases and applications using different ML tasks. In practice, ML is used in numerous use cases and applications. We will try to cover a few of them throughout this book.

Delving into DL

Simple ML methods that were used in the normal-size data analysis are no longer effective and should be replaced by more robust ML methods. Although classical ML techniques allow researchers to identify groups or clusters of related variables, the accuracy and effectiveness of these methods diminish with large and multidimensional data.

How did DL take ML to the next level?

Simple ML methods used in small-scale data analysis are not effective when dealing with large and high-dimensional datasets. However, deep learning (DL), which is a branch of ML based on a set of algorithms that attempt to model high-level abstractions in data, can handle this issue. Ian Goodfellow defined DL in his book *"Deep Learning*, MIT Press, 2016" as follows:

> *"Deep learning is a particular kind of machine learning that achieves great power and flexibility by learning to represent the world as a nested hierarchy of concepts, with each concept defined in relation to simpler concepts, and more abstract representations computed in terms of less abstract ones."*

Similar to the ML model, a DL model also takes in an input, X, and learns high-level abstractions or patterns from it to predict an output of Y. For example, based on the stock prices of the past week, a DL model can predict the stock price for the next day. When performing training on such historical stock data, a DL model tries to minimize the difference between the prediction and the actual values. This way, a DL model tries to generalize to inputs that it hasn't seen before and makes predictions on test data.
Now, you might be wondering, if an ML model can do the same tasks, why do we need DL for this? Well, DL models tend to perform well with large amounts of data, whereas old ML models stop improving after a certain point. The core concept of DL, inspired by the structure and function of the brain, is called **artificial neural networks (ANNs)**.

Being at the core of DL, ANNs help you to learn the associations between sets of inputs and outputs in order to make more robust and accurate predictions. However, DL is not only limited to ANNs; there have been many theoretical advances, software stacks, and hardware improvements that bring DL to the masses. Let's look at an example in which we want to develop a predictive analytics model, such as an animal recognizer, where our system has to resolve two problems:

- To classify whether an image represents a cat or a dog
- To cluster images of dogs and cats.

If we solve the first problem using a typical ML method, we must define the facial features (ears, eyes, whiskers, and so on) and write a method to identify which features (typically non-linear) are more important when classifying a particular animal. However, at the same time, we cannot address the second problem because classical ML algorithms for clustering images (such as k-means) cannot handle nonlinear features. Take a look at the following diagram, which shows a workflow that we would follow to classify if the given image is of a cat:

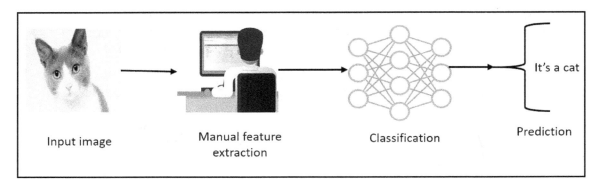

DL algorithms take these two problems one step further, and the most important features will be extracted automatically after determining which features are the most important for classification or clustering. In contrast, when using a classical ML algorithm, we would have to provide the features manually. A DL algorithm takes more sophisticated steps instead. For example, first, it identifies the edges that are the most relevant when clustering cats or dogs. It then tries to find various combinations of shapes and edges hierarchically, which is called ETL.

Then, after several iterations, it carries out the hierarchical identification of complex concepts and features. Following that, based on the features identified, the DL algorithm will decide which of the features are most significant for classifying the animal. This step is known as feature extraction. Finally, it takes out the label column and performs unsupervised training using **autoencoders** (**AEs**) to extract the latent features to be redistributed to k-means for clustering. Then, the **clustering assignment hardening loss** (**CAH loss**) and reconstruction loss are jointly optimized toward an optimal clustering assignment.

However, in practice, a DL algorithm is fed with a raw image representation, which doesn't see an image as we see it because it only knows the position of each pixel and its color. The image is divided into various layers of analysis. For example, at a lower level, there is the software analysis—a grid of a few pixels with the task of detecting a type of color or various nuances. If it finds something, it informs the next level, which, at this point, checks whether or not that given color belongs to a larger form, such as a line. The process continues to the upper levels until the algorithm understands what is shown in the following diagram:

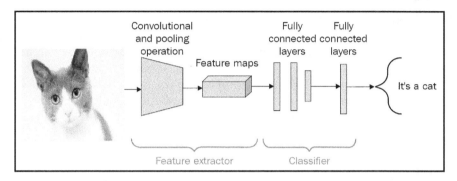

Although a dog versus a cat is an example of a very simple classifier, software that's capable of doing these types of things is now widespread and is found in systems for recognizing faces, or in those for searching an image on Google, for example. This kind of software is based on DL algorithms. By contrast, if we are using a linear ML algorithm we cannot build such applications, since these algorithms are incapable of handling non-linear image features.

Also, using ML approaches, we typically only handle a few hyperparameters. However, when neural networks are brought into the mix, things become too complex. In each layer, there are millions or even billions of hyperparameters to tune—so many that the cost function becomes non-convex. Another reason for this is that the activation functions that are used in hidden layers are non-linear, so the cost is non-convex. We will discuss this phenomenon in more detail in later chapters, but let's take a quick look at ANNs.

Artificial neural networks

ANNs, which are inspired by how a human brain works, form the core of DL and its true realization. Today's revolution around DL would not have been possible without ANNs. Thus, to understand DL, we need to understand how neural networks work.

ANN and the human brain

ANNs represent one aspect of the human nervous system, and how the nervous system consists of a number of neurons that communicate with each other using axons. The receptors receive the stimuli either internally or from the external world. Then, they pass this information to the biological neurons for further processing. There are a number of dendrites, in addition to another long extension called the axon. Toward the axon's extremities, there are minuscule structures called synaptic terminals, which are used to connect one neuron to the dendrites of other neurons. Biological neurons receive short electrical impulses called signals from other neurons, and, in response, they trigger their own signals.

We can, therefore, summarize that the neuron comprises a cell body (also known as the **soma**), one or more dendrites for receiving signals from other neurons, and an axon for carrying out the signals that are generated by the neurons. A neuron is in an active state when it is sending signals to other neurons. However, when it is receiving signals from other neurons, it is in an inactive state. In an idle state, a neuron accumulates all the signals that are received before reaching a certain activation threshold. This whole process motivated researchers to test out ANNs.

A brief history of ANNs

Inspired by the working principles of biological neurons, Warren McCulloch and Walter Pitts proposed the first artificial neuron model, in 1943, in terms of a computational model of nervous activity. This simple model of a biological neuron, also known as an **artificial neuron (AN)**, has one or more binary (on/off) inputs and one output only. An AN simply activates its output when more than a certain number of its inputs are active.

The example sounds too trivial, but even with such a simplified model, it is possible to build a network of ANs. Nevertheless, these networks can be combined to compute complex logical expressions too. This simplified model inspired John von Neumann, Marvin Minsky, Frank Rosenblatt, and many others to come up with another model called a **perceptron,** back in 1957. The perceptron is one of the simplest ANN architectures we have seen in the last 60 years. It is based on a slightly different AN called a **Linear Threshold Unit (LTU)**. The only difference is that the inputs and outputs are now numbers instead of binary on/off values. Each input connection is associated with a weight. The LTU computes a weighted sum of its inputs, then applies a step function (which resembles the action of an activation function) to that sum, and outputs the result.

One of the downsides of a perceptron is that its decision boundary is linear. Therefore, they are incapable of learning complex patterns. They are also incapable of solving some simple problems, such as **Exclusive OR (XOR)**. However, later on, the limitations of perceptrons were somewhat eliminated by stacking multiple perceptrons, called **MLP**. So, the most significant progress in ANNs and DL can be described in the following timeline. We have already discussed how the artificial neurons and perceptrons provided the base in 1943 and 1958, respectively. In 1969, Marvin *Minsky* and Seymour *Papert* formulated the XOR as a linearly non-separable problem, and later, in 1974, Paul *Werbos* demonstrated the backpropagation algorithm for training the perceptron.

However, the most significant advancement happened in 1982, when John Hopfield proposed the Hopfield Network. Then, one of the godfathers of the neural network and DL—Hinton and his team—proposed the Boltzmann Machine in 1985. However, in 1986 Geoffrey Hinton successfully trained the MLP and Jordan M.I. proposed RNNs. In the same year, Paul Smolensky also proposed the improved version of the Boltzmann Machine, called the **Restricted Boltzmann Machine (RBM)**. Then, in 1990, Lecun et al. proposed LeNet, which is a deep neural network architecture. For a brief glimpse, refer to the following diagram:

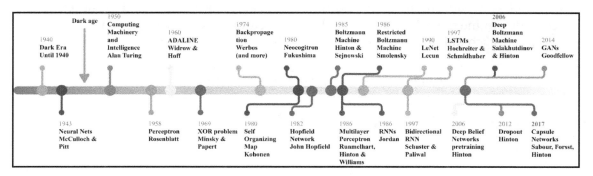

The most significant year of the 90's era was 1997, when Jordan et al. proposed a **recurrent neural network** (**RNN**). In the same year, Schuster et al. proposed the improved version of **long-short term memory** (**LSTM**) and the improved version of the original RNN called bidirectional RNN.

Despite significant advances in computing, from 1997 to 2005, we did not experience much advancement. Then, in 2006, Hinton struck again when, he and his team proposed a **deep belief network** (**DBN**) by stacking multiple RBMs. Then in 2012, Hinton invented the dropout that significantly improved the regularization and overfitting in the deep neural network. After that, Ian Goodfellow et al. introduced the GANs—a significant milestone in image recognition. In 2017, Hinton proposed CapsNet to overcome the limitation of regular CNNs, and this is so far one of the most remarkable milestones. We will discuss these architectures later in this chapter.

How does an ANN learn?

Based on the concept of biological neurons, the term and idea of ANNs arose. Similar to biological neurons, the artificial neuron consists of the following:

- One or more incoming connections that aggregate signals from neurons
- One or more output connections for carrying the signal to the other neurons
- An activation function, which determines the numerical value of the output signal

Besides the state of a neuron, synaptic weight is considered, which influences the connection within the network. Each weight has a numerical value indicated by W_{ij}, which is the synaptic weight connecting neuron i to neuron j. Now, for each neuron i, an input vector can be defined by $x_i = (x_1, x_2, ... x_n)$, and a weight vector can be defined by $w_i = (w_{i1}, x_{i2}, ... x_{in})$. Now, depending on the position of a neuron, the weights and the output function determine the behavior of an individual neuron. Then, during forward propagation, each unit in the hidden layer gets the following signal:

$$net_i = \sum_j W_{ij} X_j \ldots \ldots \ldots (a)$$

Nevertheless, among the weights, there is also a special type of weight called a bias unit, *b*. Technically, bias units aren't connected to any previous layer, so they don't have true activity. But still, the bias *b* value allows the neural network to shift the activation function to the left or right. By taking the bias unit into consideration, the modified network output is formulated as follows:

$$net_i = \sum_j W_{ij} X_j + b_j \ldots \ldots (b)$$

The preceding equation signifies that each hidden unit gets the sum of inputs, multiplied by the corresponding weight—this is known as the **Summing junction**. Then, the resultant output in the **Summing junction** is passed through the activation function, which squashes the output, as depicted in the following diagram:

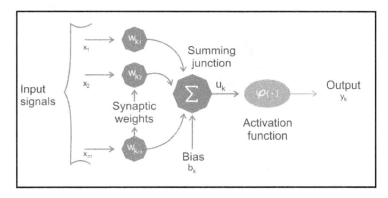

A practical neural network architecture, however, is composed of input, hidden, and output layers that are composed of nodes that make up a network structure. It still follows the working principle of an artificial neuron model, as shown in the preceding diagram. The input layer only accepts numeric data, such as features in real numbers, and images with pixel values. The following diagram shows a neural network architecture for solving a multiclass classification (that is, 10 classes) problem based on a data having 784 features:

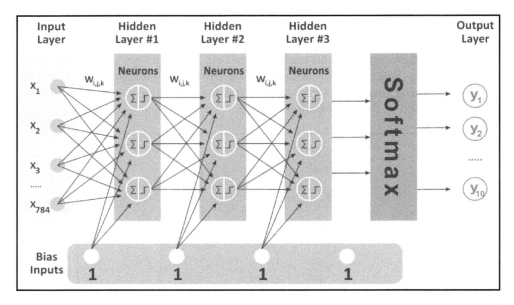

A neural network with one input layer, three hidden layers, and an output layer

Here, the hidden layers perform most of the computation to learn the patterns, and the network evaluates how accurate its prediction is compared to the actual output using a special mathematical function called the loss function. It could be a complex one or a very simple mean squared error, which can be defined as follows:

$$MSE = \frac{1}{n} \sum_{i=1}^{n} \left(Y_i - \hat{Y}_i \right)^2$$

In the preceding equation, $\hat{Y}$ is the prediction made by the network, while Y represents the actual or expected output. Finally, when the error is no longer being reduced, the neural network converges and makes a prediction through the output layer.

Training a neural network

The learning process for a neural network is configured as an iterative process of the optimization of the weights. The weights are updated in each epoch. Once the training starts, the aim is to generate predictions by minimizing the loss function. The performance of the network is then evaluated on the test set. We already know about the simple concept of an artificial neuron. However, generating only some artificial signals is not enough to learn a complex task. As such, a commonly used supervised learning algorithm is the backpropagation algorithm, which is very often used to train a complex ANN.

Ultimately, training such a neural network is an optimization problem, too, in which we try to minimize the error by adjusting network weights and biases iteratively, by using backpropagation through **gradient descent (GD)**. This approach forces the network to backtrack through all its layers to update the weights and biases across nodes in the opposite direction of the loss function.

However, this process using GD does not guarantee that the global minimum is reached. The presence of hidden units and the non-linearity of the output function means that the behavior of the error is very complex and has many local minima. This backpropagation step is typically performed thousands or millions of times, using many training batches, until the model parameters converge to values that minimize the cost function. The training process ends when the error on the validation set begins to increase, because this could mark the beginning of a phase of overfitting:

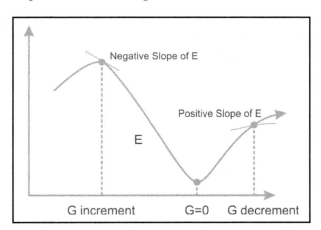

Searching for the minimum for the error function E, we move in the direction in which the gradient G of E is minimal

The downside of using GD is that it takes too long to converge, which makes it impossible to meet the demand of handling large-scale training data. Therefore, a faster GD, called **stochastic gradient descent** (**SGD**) was proposed, which is also a widely used optimizer in DNN training. In SGD, we use only one training sample per iteration from the training set to update the network parameters, which is a stochastic approximation of the true cost gradient.

 There are other advanced optimizers nowadays such as Adam, RMSProp, ADAGrad, and Momentum. Each of them is either a direct or indirect optimized version of SGD.

Weight and bias initialization

Now, here's a tricky question: how do we initialize the weights? Well, if we initialize all the weights to the same value (for example, 0 or 1), each hidden neuron will get the same signal. Let's try to break it down:

- If all weights are initialized to 1, then each unit gets a signal equal to the sum of the inputs.
- If all weights are 0, which is even worse, then every neuron in a hidden layer will get zero signal.

For network weight initialization, Xavier initialization is used widely. It is similar to random initialization, but often turns out to work much better, since it can identify the rate of initialization depending on the total number of input and output neurons by default. You may be wondering whether you can get rid of random initialization while training a regular DNN.

Well, recently, some researchers have been talking about random orthogonal matrix initializations that perform better than just any random initialization for training DNNs. When it comes to initializing the biases, we can initialize them to zero. But setting the biases to a small constant value, such as 0.01 for all biases, ensures that all **rectified linear units** (**ReLU**) can propagate a gradient. However, it neither performs well nor shows consistent improvement. Therefore, sticking with zero is recommended.

Activation functions

To allow a neural network to learn complex decision boundaries, we apply a non-linear activation function to some of its layers. Commonly used functions include Tanh, ReLU, softmax, and variants of these. More technically, each neuron receives a signal of the weighted sum of the synaptic weights and the activation values of the neurons that are connected as input. One of the most widely used functions for this purpose is the so-called sigmoid logistic function, which is defined as follows:

$$Out_i = \frac{1}{(1 + e^{-x})}$$

The domain of this function includes all real numbers, and the co-domain is (0, 1). This means that any value obtained as an output from a neuron (as per the calculation of its activation state) will always be between zero and one. The Sigmoid function, as represented in the following diagram, provides an interpretation of the saturation rate of a neuron, from not being active (equal to 0) to complete saturation, which occurs at a predetermined maximum value (equal to 1):

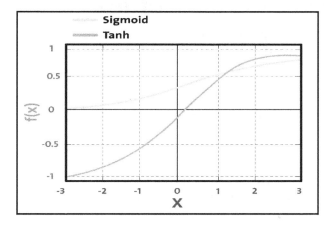

Sigmoid versus Tanh activation function

On the other hand, a hyperbolic tangent, or **Tanh**, is another form of activation function. **Tanh** flattens a real-valued number between **-1** and **1**. The preceding graph shows the difference between the **Tanh** and **Sigmoid** activation functions. In particular, mathematically, speaking the *tanh* activation function can be expressed as follows:

$$\tanh(x) = 2\sigma(2x) - 1$$

In general, in the last level of a **feedforward neural network (FFNN)**, the softmax function is applied as the decision boundary. This is a common case, especially when solving a classification problem. The softmax function is used for the probability distribution over the possible classes in a multiclass classification problem. To conclude, choosing proper activation functions and network weight initializations are two problems that make a network perform at its best and help to obtain good training. Now that we know the brief history of neural networks, let's deepdive into different architectures in the next section, which will give us an idea of their usage.

Neural network architectures

Up to now, numerous neural network architectures have been proposed and are in use. However, more or less all of them are based on a few core neural network architectures. We can categorize DL architectures into four groups:

- Deep neural networks
- Convolutional neural networks
- Recurrent neural networks
- Emergent architectures

However, DNNs, CNNs, and RNNs have many improved variants. Although most of the variants are proposed or developed for solving domain-specific research problems, the basic working principles still follow the original DNN, CNN, and RNN architectures. The following subsections will give you a brief introduction to these architectures.

Deep neural networks

DNNs are neural networks that have a complex and deeper architecture with a large number of neurons in each layer, and many connections between them. Although DNN refers to a very deep network, for simplicity, we consider MLP, **stacked autoencoder (SAE)**, and **deep belief networks (DBNs)** as DNN architectures. These architectures mostly work as an FFNN, meaning information propagates from input to output layers.

Multiple perceptrons are stacked together as MLPs, where layers are connected as a directed graph. Fundamentally, an MLP is one of the most simple FFNNs since it has three layers: an input layer, a hidden layer, and an output layer. This way, the signal propagates one way, from the input layer to the hidden layers to the output layer, as shown in the following diagram:

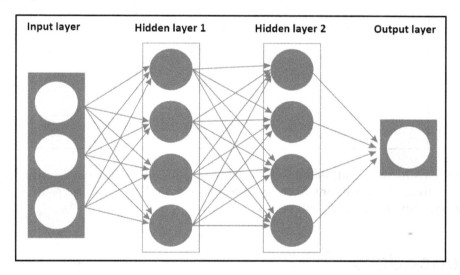

Autoencoders and RBMs are the basic building blocks for SAEs and DBNs, respectively. Unlike MLP, which is an FFNN that's trained in a supervised way, both SAEs and DBNs are trained in two phases: unsupervised pretraining and supervised fine-tuning. In unsupervised pretraining, layers are stacked in order and trained in a layer-wise manner with used unlabeled data.

In supervised fine-tuning, an output classifier layer is stacked and the complete neural network is optimized by retraining with labeled data. One problem with MLP is that it often overfits the data, so it doesn't generalize well. To overcome this issue, DBN was proposed by Hinton et al. It uses a greedy, layer-by-layer, pretraining algorithm. DBNs are composed of a visible layer and multiple hidden unit layers. The building blocks of a DBN are RBMs, as shown in the following diagram, where several RBMs are stacked one after another:

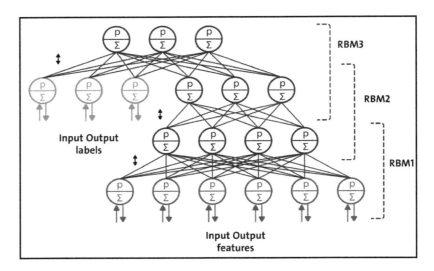

The top two layers have undirected, symmetric connections in-between, but the lower layers have directed connections from the preceding layer. Despite numerous successes, DBNs are now being replaced with AEs.

Autoencoders

AEs are also special types of neural networks that learn automatically from the input data. AEs consist of two components: the encoder and the decoder. The encoder compresses the input into a latent-space representation. Then, the decoder part tries to reconstruct the original input data from this representation:

- **Encoder**: Encodes or compresses the input into a latent-space representation using a function known as $h = f(x)$
- **Decoder**: Decodes or reconstructs the input from the latent space representation using a function known as $r = g(h)$

So, an AE can be described by a function of $g(f(x)) = 0$, where we want 0 as close to the original input of x. The following diagram shows how an AE typically works:

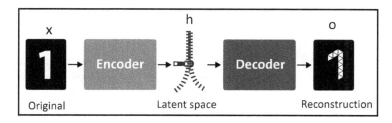

AEs are very useful for data denoising and dimensionality reduction for data visualization because they can learn data projections called representations more effectively than PCA.

Convolutional neural networks

CNNs have achieved much and have been widely adopted in computer vision (for example, image recognition). In CNN networks, the connection schemes are significantly different compared to an MLP or DBN. A few of the convolutional layers are connected in a cascade style. Each layer is backed up by an ReLU layer, a pooling layer, additional convolutional layers (+ReLU), and another pooling layer, which is followed by a fully connected layer and a softmax layer. The following diagram is a schematic of the architecture of a CNN that's used for facial recognition, which takes facial images as input and predicts emotions such as anger, disgust, fear, happy, and sad:

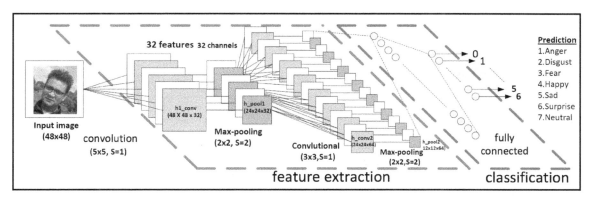

A schematic architecture of a CNN used for facial recognition

Importantly, DNNs have no prior knowledge of how the pixels are organized because they do not know that nearby pixels are close. CNNs embed this prior knowledge using lower layers by using feature maps in small areas of the image, while the higher layers combine lower-level features into larger features.

This setting works well with most of the natural images, giving CNN a decisive head start over DNNs. The output from each convolutional layer is a set of objects, called feature maps, that are generated by a single kernel filter. Then, the feature maps can be used to define a new input to the next layer. Each neuron in a CNN network produces an output, followed by an activation threshold, which is proportional to the input and not bound.

Recurrent neural networks

In RNNs, connections between units form a directed cycle. The RNN architecture was originally conceived by Hochreiter and Schmidhuber in 1997. RNN architectures have standard MLPs, plus added loops so that they can exploit the powerful nonlinear mapping capabilities of the MLP. They also have some form of memory. The following diagram shows a very basic RNN that has an input layer, two recurrent layers, and an output layer:

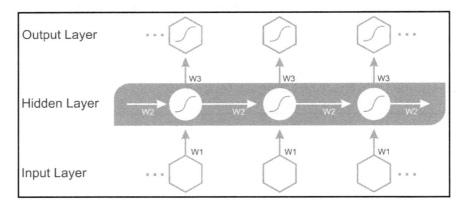

However, this basic RNN suffers from gradient vanishing and the exploding problem, and cannot model long-term dependencies. These architectures include LSTM, **gated recurrent units (GRUs)**, bidirectional-LSTM, and other variants. Consequently, LSTM and GRU can overcome the drawbacks of regular RNNs: the gradient vanishing/exploding problem and long-short term dependency.

Emergent architectures

Many other emergent DL architectures have been suggested, such as **Deep SpatioTemporal Neural Networks (DST-NNs)**, **Multi-Dimensional Recurrent Neural Networks (MD-RNNs)**, and **Convolutional AutoEncoders (CAEs)**. Nevertheless, there are a few more emerging networks, such as **CapsNets** (which is an improved version of a CNN, designed to remove the drawbacks of regular CNNs), RNN for image recognition, and **Generative Adversarial Networks (GANs)** for simple image generation. Apart from these, factorization machines for personalization and deep reinforcement learning are also being used widely.

Residual neural networks

Since there are sometimes millions and millions of hyperparameters and other practical aspects, it's really difficult to train deeper neural networks. To overcome this limitation, Kaiming H. et al. (https://arxiv.org/abs/1512.03385v1) proposed a residual learning framework to ease the training of networks that are substantially deeper than those used previously.

They also explicitly reformulated the layers as learning residual functions with reference to the layer inputs, instead of learning non-referenced functions. This way, these residual networks are easier to optimize and can gain accuracy from considerably increased depth. The downside is that building a network by simply stacking residual blocks inevitably limits the optimization ability. To overcome this limitation, Ke Zhang et al. also proposed using a multilevel residual network (https://arxiv.org/abs/1608.02908).

Generative adversarial networks

GANs are deep neural net architectures that consist of two networks pitted against each other (hence the name *adversarial*). Ian Goodfellow et al. introduced GANs in a paper (see more at https://arxiv.org/abs/1406.2661v1). In GANs, the two main components are the **generator and discriminator**:

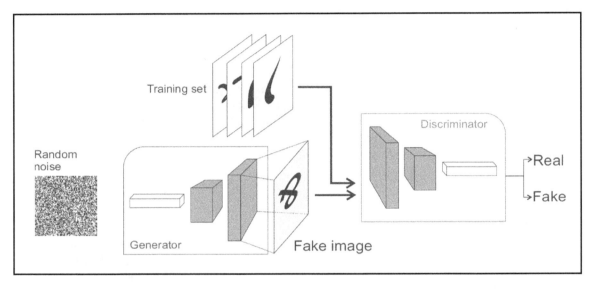

Working principle of generative adversarial networks

In a GAN architecture, a generator and a discriminator are pitted against each other—hence the name, adversarial:

- The generator tries to generate data samples out of a specific probability distribution and is very similar to the actual object.
- The discriminator will judge whether its input is coming from the original training set or from the generator part.

Many DL practitioners think that GANs were one of the most important advancements because GANs can be used to mimic any distribution of data, and, based on the data distribution, they can be taught to create robot artist images, super-resolution images, text-to-image synthesis, music, speech, and more. For example, because of the concept of adversarial training, Facebook's AI research director, Yann LeCun, suggested that GANs are the most interesting idea in the last 10 years of ML.

Capsule networks

In CNNs, each layer understands an image at a much more granular level through a slow receptive field or max pooling operations. If the images have rotation, tilt, or very different shapes or orientation, CNNs fail to extract such spatial information and show very poor performance at image processing tasks. Even the pooling operations in CNNs cannot be much help against such positional invariance. This issue in CNNs has led us to the recent advancement of CapsNet through the paper entitled *Dynamic Routing Between Capsules* (see more at `https://arxiv.org/abs/1710.09829`) by Geoffrey Hinton et al:

> *"A capsule is a group of neurons whose activity vector represents the instantiation parameters of a specific type of entity, such as an object or an object part."*

Unlike a regular DNN, where we keep on adding layers, in CapsNet, the idea is to add more layers inside a single layer. This way, a CapsNet is a nested set of neural layers. In CapsNet, the vector inputs and outputs of a capsule are computed using the routing algorithm used in physics, which iteratively transfers information and processes the **self-consistent field** (**SCF**) procedure:

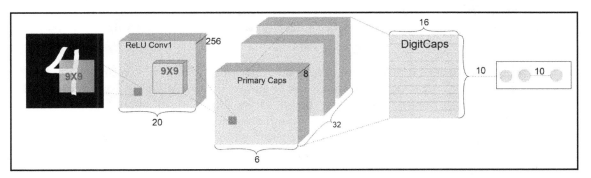

The preceding diagram shows a schematic diagram of a simple three-layer CapsNet. The length of the activity vector of each capsule in the DigiCaps layer indicates the presence of an instance of each class, which is used to calculate the loss. Now that we have learned about the working principles of neural networks and the different neural network architectures, implementing something hands-on would be great. However, before that, let's take a look at some popular DL libraries and frameworks, which come with the implementation of these network architectures.

Neural networks for clustering analysis

Several variants of k-means have been proposed to address issues with higher-dimensional input spaces. However, they are fundamentally limited to linear embedding. Hence, we cannot model non-linear relationships. Nevertheless, fine-tuning in these approaches is based on only cluster assignment hardening loss (see later in this section). Therefore, a fine-grained clustering accuracy cannot be achieved. Since the quality of the clustering results is dependent on the data distribution, deep architecture can help the model learn mapping from the data space to a lower-dimensional feature space in which it iteratively optimizes a clustering objective. Several approaches have been proposed over the last few years, trying to use the representational power of deep neural networks for preprocessing clustering inputs.

A few notable approaches include deep embedded clustering, deep clustering networks, discriminatively boosted clustering, clustering CNNs, deep embedding networks, convolutional deep embedded clustering, and joint unsupervised learning of deep representation for images. Other approaches include DL with non-parametric clustering, CNN-based joint clustering and representation learning with feature drift compensation, learning latent representations in neural networks for clustering, clustering using convolutional neural networks, and deep clustering with convolutional autoencoder embedding.

Most of these approaches follow more or less the same principle: that is, representation learning using a deep architecture to transform the inputs into a latent representation and using these representations as input for a specific clustering method. Such deep architectures include MLP, CNN, DBN, GAN, and variational autoencoders. The following diagram shows an example of how to improve the clustering performance of a DEC network using convolutional autoencoders and optimizing both reconstruction and CAH losses jointly. The latent space out of the encoder layer is fed to K-means for soft clustering assignment. Blurred genetic variants signify the existence of reconstruction errors:

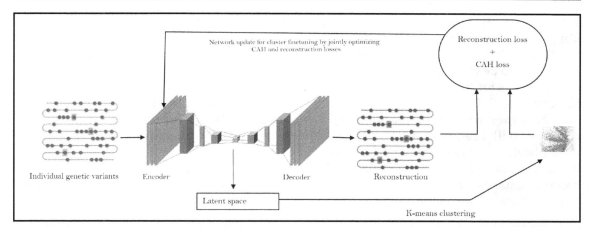

DL based clustering (source: Karim et al., Recurrent Deep Embedding Networks for Genotype Clustering and Ethnicity Prediction, arXiv:1805.12218)

In summary, in these approaches, there are three important steps involved—extracting cluster-friendly deep features using deep architectures, combining clustering and non-clustering losses, and, finally, network updates to optimize clustering and non-clustering losses jointly.

DL frameworks and cloud platforms for IoT

There are several popular DL frameworks. Each of them comes with some pros and cons. Some of them are desktop-based, and some of them are cloud-based platforms, where you can deploy/run your DL applications. However, most of the libraries that are released under an open license help when people are using graphics processors, which can ultimately help in speeding up the learning process. Such frameworks and libraries include TensorFlow, PyTorch, Keras, Deeplearning4j, H2O, and the **Microsoft Cognitive Toolkit (CNTK)**. Even a few years back, other implementations, including Theano, Caffee, and Neon, were used widely. However, these are now obsolete.

Deeplearning4j (**DL4J**) is one of the first commercial-grade, open source, distributed DL libraries that was built for Java and Scala. This also provides integrated support for Hadoop and Spark. DL4J is built for use in business environments on distributed GPUs and CPUs. DL4J aims to be cutting-edge and *Plug and Play*, with more convention than configuration, which allows for fast prototyping for non-researchers. Its numerous libraries can be integrated with DL4J and will make your JVM experience easier, regardless of whether you are developing your ML application in Java or Scala. Similar to NumPy for JVM, ND4J comes up with basic operations of linear algebra (matrix creation, addition, and multiplication). However, ND4S is a scientific computing library for linear algebra and matrix manipulation. It also provides n-dimensional arrays for JVM-based languages. The following diagram shows last year's Google Trends, illustrating how popular TensorFlow is:

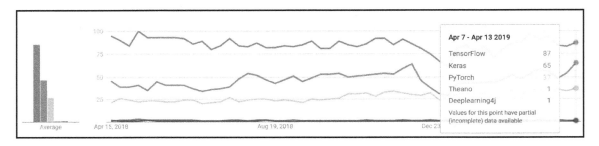

As well as these frameworks, Chainer is a powerful, flexible, and intuitive DL framework, which supports CUDA computation. It only requires a few lines of code to leverage a GPU. It also runs on multiple GPUs with little effort. Most importantly, Chainer supports various network architectures, including feed-forward nets, convnets, recurrent nets, and recursive nets. It also supports per-batch architectures. One more interesting feature in Chainer is that it supports forward computation, by which any control flow statements of Python can be included without lacking the ability of backpropagation. It makes code intuitive and easy to debug.

The DL framework power scores 2018 also shows that TensorFlow, Keras, and PyTorch are far ahead of other frameworks (see https://towardsdatascience.com/deep-learning-framework-power-scores-2018-23607ddf297a). Scores were calculated based on usage, popularity, and interest in DL frameworks through the following sources. Apart from the preceding libraries, there are some recent initiatives for DL in the cloud. The idea is to bring DL capability to big data with billions of data points and high-dimensional data. For example, **Amazon Web Services** (**AWS**), Microsoft Azure, Google Cloud Platform, and **NVIDIA GPU Cloud** (**NGC**) all offer machine and DL services that are native to their public clouds.

In October 2017, AWS released **Deep Learning AMIs (DLAMIs)** for **Amazon Elastic Compute Cloud (Amazon EC2)** P3 instances. These AMIs come preinstalled with DL frameworks, such as TensorFlow, Gluon, and Apache MXNet, which are optimized for the NVIDIA Volta V100 GPUs within Amazon EC2 P3 instances. The DL service currently offers three types of AMIs: Conda AMI, Base AMI, and AMI with source code.The CNTK is Azure's open source DL service. Similar to the AWS offering, it focuses on tools that can help developers build and deploy DL applications. Azure also provides a model gallery that includes resources, such as code samples, to help enterprises get started with the service.

On the other hand, NGC empowers AI scientists and researchers with GPU-accelerated containers (see `https://www. nvidia. com/en-us/data-center/gpu-cloud-computing/`). The NGC features containerized DL frameworks, such as TensorFlow, PyTorch, MXNet, and more that are tuned, tested, and certified by NVIDIA to run on the latest NVIDIA GPUs on participating cloud-service providers. Nevertheless, there are also third-party services available through their respective marketplaces.

When it comes to cloud-based IoT system-development markets, currently it forks into three obvious routes: off-the-shelf platforms (for example, AWS IoT Core, Azure IoT Suite, and Google Cloud IoT Core), which trade off vendor lock-in and higher-end volume pricing against cost-effective scalability and shorter lead times; reasonably well-established MQTT configurations over the Linux stack (example: Eclipse Mosquitto); and the more exotic emerging protocols and products (for example, Nabto's P2P protocol) that are developing enough uptake, interest, and community investment to stake a claim for strong market presence in the future.

As a DL framework, Chainer Neural Network is a great choice for all devices powered by Intel Atom, NVIDIA Jetson TX2, and Raspberry Pi. Therefore, using Chainer, we don't need to build and configure the ML framework for our devices from scratch. It provides prebuilt packages for three popular ML frameworks, including TensorFlow, Apache MXNet, and Chainer. Chainer works in a similar fashion, which depends on a library on the Greengrass and a set of model files generated using Amazon SageMaker and/or stored directly in an Amazon S3 bucket. From Amazon SageMaker or Amazon S3, the ML models can be deployed to AWS Greengrass to be used as a local resource for ML inference. Conceptually, AWS IoT Core functions as the managing plane for deploying ML inference to the edge.

Summary

In this chapter, we introduced a number of fundamental DL themes. We started our journey with a basic, but comprehensive, introduction to ML. Then, we gradually moved on to DL and different neural architectures. We then had a brief overview of the most important DL frameworks that can be utilized to develop DL-based applications for IoT-enabled devices.

IoT applications, such as smart home, smart city, and smart healthcare, heavily rely on video or image data processing for decision making. In the next chapter, we will cover DL-based image processing for IoT applications, including image recognition, classification, and object detection. Additionally, we will cover hands-on video data processing in IoT applications.

2
Section 2: Hands-On Deep Learning Application Development for IoT

In this section, we will get familiar with how to use deep learning to create applications for various use cases, such as image recognition, audio/speech/voice recognition, indoor localization, and physiological and psychological state detection. We'll also look at how to create applications through examples using clustering algorithms for anomaly detection in IoT.

This section includes the following chapters:

- Chapter 3, *Image Recognition in IoT*
- Chapter 4, *Audio/Speech/Voice Recognition in IoT*
- Chapter 5, *Indoor localization in IoT*
- Chapter 6, *Physiological and Psychological State Detection in IoT*
- Chapter 7, *IoT Security*

Image Recognition in IoT 3

Many IoT applications, including smart homes, smart cities, and smart healthcare, will extensively use image recognition-based decision-making (such as facial recognition for a smart door or lock) in the future. **Machine learning (ML)** and **deep learning (DL)** algorithms are useful for image recognition and decision-making. Consequently, they are very promising for IoT applications. This chapter will cover hands-on DL-based image data processing for IoT applications.

The first part of this chapter will briefly describe different IoT applications and their image detection-based decision-making. Furthermore, it will briefly discuss an IoT application and its image detection-based implementation in a real-world scenario. In the second part of the chapter, we shall present a hands-on image detection implementation of an application using a DL algorithm. In this chapter, we will cover the following topics:

- IoT applications and image recognition
- Use case one: Image-based road fault detection
- Use case two: Image-based smart solid waste separation
- Implementing the use cases
- Transfer learning for image recognition in IoT
- CNNs for image recognition in IoT applications
- Collecting data
- Data pre-processing
- Model training
- Evaluating the models

IoT applications and image recognition

The image recognition landscape in IoT applications is rapidly changing. Significant advances in mobile processing power, edge computing, and machine learning are paving the way for the widespread use of image recognition in many IoT applications. For example, omnipresent mobile devices (which are a key components in many IoT applications) equipped with high-resolution cameras facilitate the generation of images and videos by everyone, everywhere.

Moreover, intelligent video cameras, such as IP cameras and Raspberry Pis with cameras, are used in many places, such as smart homes, campuses, and factories, for different applications. Many IoT applications—including smart cities, smart homes, smart health, smart education, smart factories, and smart agriculture—make decisions using image recognition/classification. As shown in the following diagram, these applications use one or more of the following image recognition services:

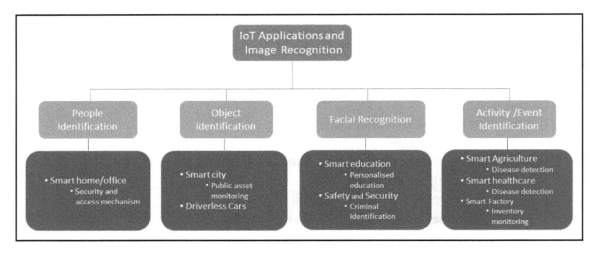

Let's us discuss the previous image in detail:

- **People Identification**: Generally, secure and friendly access to home, office, and any other premises is a challenging task. The use of smart devices, including IoT solutions, can offer secure and friendly access to many premises. Let's consider the example of office or home access. We use one or more keys access to our homes or offices. If we lose these keys, this could not only inconvenience us but put our security at risk if somebody else finds them. In this context, image recognition-based people identification can be used as a keyless access method for a smart home or office.

- **Object Identification**: IoT-based automated object identification is highly desirable in many domains, including driverless cars, smart cities, and smart factories. For example, smart city applications, such as smart vehicle license plate recognition and vehicle detection, as well as city-wide public asset monitoring, can use image recognition-based object detection services. Similarly, a smart factory can use the object detection service for inventory management.

- **Facial Recognition**: The image processing-based facial detection and recognition landscape is changing so rapidly that it will be a commodity soon. Smartphones with biometrics will then be the norm. Smartphones and IoT-based facial recognition can be used in many applications, such as safety and security, and smart education. For example, in a smart class (education), a face recognition system can be used to identify the response to a lecture.

- **Event Detection**: Symptoms of many human diseases (such as hand foot mouth), animal diseases (such as, foot and mouth, and poultry diseases), and plant diseases are explicit and visible. These diseases can be digitally detected using IoT solutions integrated with DL-based image classification.

Use case one – image-based automated fault detection

Public assets (such as roads, public buildings, and tourist places) in a city are heterogeneous and distributed within the city. Most cities in the world face challenges in monitoring, fault detection, and reporting these assets. For example, in many UK cities, citizens often report faults, but the accuracy and efficiency of the reporting is an issue in many cases. In a smart city, these assets can be monitored, and their faults can be detected and reported through an IoT application. For example, a vehicle (such as a city council vehicle) attached with one or more sensors (such as a camera or a mic) can be used for the road fault monitoring and detection.

Roads are important assets in a city, and they have many faults. Potholes, bumps, and road roughness are some of the most frustrating hazards and anomalies experienced by commuters and vehicles. Importantly, vehicles may frequently face suspension problems, steering misalignment, and punctures, which could also lead to accidents. The cost of road-fault-related damages is significant. For example, pothole-related damage alone cost UK drivers £1.7 billion a year. An IoT application with the support of an appropriate DL algorithm can be used to automatically detect these faults and report them appropriately. This reduces the number of road-fault-related damage in a cost-effective way.

Implementing use case one

As shown in the following diagram, the implementation of the use case consists of three main elements:

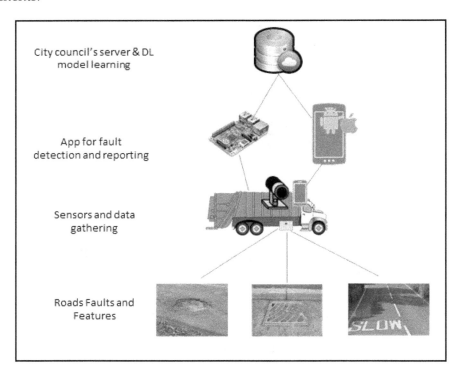

Let us learn about the components in detail:

- **Sensors and data gathering**: The selection of sensors for data gathering depends on the assets and fault types. If we use a smartphone as the edge-computing device, its camera can be used for sensing and data gathering about road faults. On the contrary, if we use Raspberry Pi as the edge-computing device, we need to use an external camera, as there is no built-in camera within the Raspberry Pi. The preceding diagram shows the Raspberry Pi and camera used for the use case implementation. We used a Raspberry Pi 3 model B+ with 1 GB RAM and a 5-megapixel sensor with an Omnivision OV5647 sensor in a fixed-focus lens. The sampling or photographic rate of the camera will depend on the vehicle's speed and the availability of a road's faults. For example, if the smartphone camera or the camera installed on the vehicle can capture one picture a second, the phone or Raspberry Pi will be able to detect the faults within two seconds if the speed of the vehicle is 40 km/h or less. Once the image is sensed and captured, it will be sent to the detection method.

- **Fault detection and reporting**: In this phase, the edge-computing device will be installed with one app. The installed app in a smartphone or Raspberry Pi will be loaded with pre-trained fault detection and a classification model. Once the vehicle's smartphone or Raspberry Pi camera takes a picture (following a sampling rate), these models will detect and classify a potential fault and report to the application server (local council).

- **Council's server and Fault Detection Model**: The council's server is responsible for the following:
    - Learning the model for fault detection and classification using reference datasets
    - Disseminating and updating the models for the edge-computing device
    - Receiving and storing the fault data

Image-based model learning and validation of road's fault detection is at the heart of the implementation. The second part (covered in the sections starting from *Transfer learning for image recognition in IoT*) of the chapter will describe the implementation of the DL-based anomaly detection of the previous use case. All the necessary codes are available in the chapter's code folder.

Use case two – image-based smart solid waste separation

Solid waste is a global challenge. The management of solid waste is expensive, and improper waste management is also seriously impacting the global economy, public health, and the environment. Generally, solid waste, such as plastic, glass bottles, and paper, are recyclable, and they need an effective recycling method to become economically and environmentally beneficial. However, in most countries, the existing recycling processes are done manually. In addition, citizens or consumers often become confused about the recycling method.

In this context, IoT with the support of machine learning and deep learning, especially image-based object recognition, can identify the type of waste and help sort it accordingly without any human intervention.

Implementing use case two

The implementation of image-based smart solid waste separation includes two key components:

- A bin with an individual chamber with a controllable lid for each type of solid waste
- An IoT infrastructure with a DL model for image recognition

The first component of the implementation is not within the scope of this book, and we are considering the component as available for this implementation. As shown in the following diagram, the IoT implementation of the use case consists of two main elements:

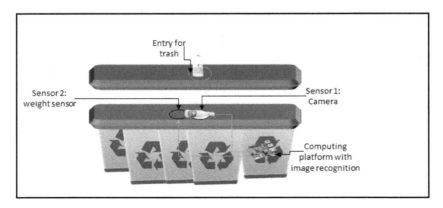

- **Sensors and data gathering**: Selection of sensors for data gathering depends on the types of solid waste and their features. For example, many glass and plastic bottles are very similar in color and appearance. However, their weights are generally distinctly different. For the use case, we are considering two sensors:
  - One or more cameras to capture an image of trash when it enters into a bin through the entry point
  - A weight sensor to get the weight of the trash

  We use Raspberry Pi as the computing platform. The use case was tested using a Raspberry Pi 3 model B+ with 1 GB RAM and a 5 megapixel sensor with an Omnivision OV5647 sensor in a fixed-focus lens. Once the image and weight are sensed and captured, they are sent to the sorting method.

- **Trash detection and sorting**: This is the key element of the implementation. The Raspberry Pi will be loaded with a pretrained trash detection and sorting model using DL. Once the detection algorithm detects trash and sorts it, it will actuate the control system to open the appropriate lid and move it into the bin.

The use case scenario is focusing on waste management in urban public areas, including parks, tourist attractions, landscaping, and other recreational areas. Generally, citizens and/or visitors in these areas individually dispose of their waste. Importantly, they dispose of items in small numbers, from single items to just a few items.

All of the following sections will describe the implementation of the DL-based image recognition needed for the aforementioned use cases. All the necessary codes are available in the chapter's code folder.

Transfer learning for image recognition in IoT

Generally, transfer learning means transferring pre-trained machine learning model representations to another problem. In recent years, this is becoming a popular means of applying DL models to a problem, especially in image processing and recognition, as it enables training a DL model with comparatively little data.

The following diagram shows two models:

- An architecture for a standard DL model (a)
- An architecture for a transfer-learning DL model (b):

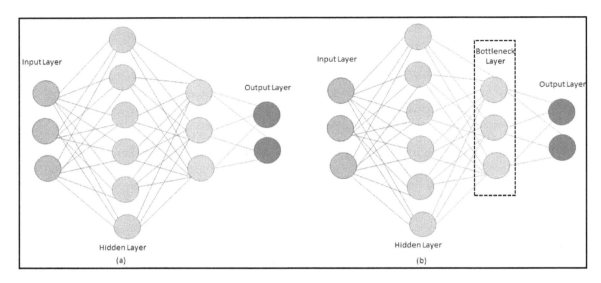

As shown in the figure of an architecture for a standard DL model, a fully trained neural net takes input values in an initial layer and then sequentially feeds this information forward with necessary transformation until the second-to-last layer (which is also known as the **bottleneck layer**) has constructed a high-level representation of the input that can more easily be transformed into a final output. The complete training of the model involves the optimization of weight and bias terms used in each connection (labeled in blue). In large and heterogeneous datasets, the number of these weight and bias terms could be in the millions.

In transfer learning, we can use the early and middle layers and only re-train the latter layers. One popular approach to transfer learning is to reuse the pre-trained weights for the whole network other than the last layer and relearn the weights of the last layer or classification part by retraining the network using the new dataset. As shown in the diagram of an architecture for a transfer-learning DL model, we reused the orange connections and retrained the network using the new dataset to learn the last layer's green connections.

Many pre-trained DL models, including the Inception-v3 and MobileNets models, are available to be used for transfer learning. The Inception-v3 model, which was trained for the ImageNet *Large Visual Recognition Challenge*, classifies images into 1,000 classes, such as *Zebra*, *Dalmatian*, and *Dishwasher*. Inception-v3 consists of two parts:

- A feature extraction part with a convolutional neural network, which extracts features from the input
- A classification part with fully connected and softmax layers, which classifies the input data based on the features identified in part one

If we want to use Inception-v3, we can reuse the feature extraction part and re-train the classification part with our dataset.

Transfer learning offers two benefits:

- Training on new data is faster.
- The ability to solve a problem with less training data rather than learning from scratch.

These features of transfer learning are especially useful for the implementation of DL models in IoT's resource-constrained edge devices, as we do not need to train the resource-hungry feature extraction part. Thus, the model can be trained using less computational resources and time.

CNNs for image recognition in IoT applications

A **Convolutional Neural Network** (**CNN**) has different implementations. **AlexNet** is one such implementation, and it won the ImageNet Challenge: ILSVRC 2012. Since then, CNNs have become omnipresent in computer vision and image detection and classification. Until April 2017, the general trend was to make deeper and more complicated networks to achieve higher accuracy. However, these deeper and complex networks offered improved accuracy but did not always make the networks more efficient, particularly in terms of size and speed. In many real-world applications, especially in IoT applications, such as a self-driving car and patient monitoring, recognition tasks need to be accomplished in a timely fashion on a resource-constrained (processing, memory) platform.

In this context, MobileNet V1 was introduced in April 2017. This version of Mobilenet was an improvement on its second version (MobileNetV2) in April 2018. **Mobilenets** and their variants are the efficient CNN DL model's IoT applications, especially for image recognition-based IoT applications. In the following paragraphs, we present a brief overview of MobileNets.

MobileNets are the implementations of most popular and widely used DL models, namely CNNs. They are especially designed for resource-constrained mobile devices to support classification, detection, and prediction. Personal mobile devices, including smartphones, wearable devices, and smartwatches, installed with DL models improve user experience, offering any time, anywhere access, with the additional benefits of security, privacy, and energy consumption. Importantly, new emerging applications in mobile devices will need ever-more efficient neural networks to interact with the real world in real time.

The following diagram shows how the standard convolutional filters (figure a) are replaced by two layers in Mobilenet V1. It uses a depthwise convolution (figure b) and a pointwise convolution (figure c) to build a depthwise separable filter:

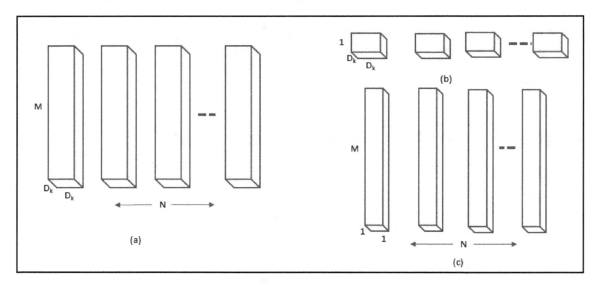

The main motivation of MobileNet V1 is that convolutional layers are expensive to compute, and they can be replaced by so-called **depthwise separable convolutions**. In MobileNet V1, the depthwise convolution process uses a single filter to every input channel, and the pointwise convolution then uses a 1 x 1 convolution process to the outputs of the earlier depthwise convolution. As shown in the diagram of a standard convolution filter, a standard convolution both filters and combines inputs into a new set of outputs in one step. Unlike standard CNNs, the depthwise separable convolution (factorized) in MobileNets splits this into two layers (as shown in the diagram of Mobilenet V1): a layer for filtering and a separate layer for combining.

The following diagram presents the factorized architecture of Mobilenet V1. This factorization drastically reduces computation and model size as the model needs to calculate a significantly smaller number of parameters. For example, MobileNet V1 needs to calculate 4.2 million parameters, whereas a full convolution network needs to calculate 29.3 million parameters:

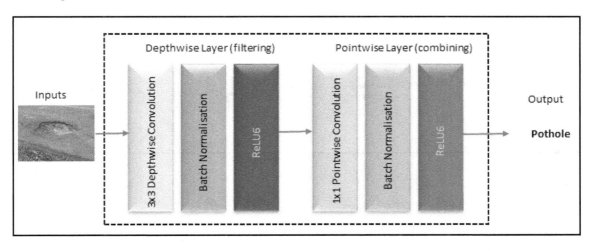

MobileNet V2 is an updated and significantly improved version of MobileNet V1. It has greatly improved and pushes existing mobile visual recognition, including classification, detection, and semantic segmentation. Like MobileNet V1, the MobileNet V2 was released as part of the TensorFlow-Slim Image Classification Library. If needed, you can explore this in Google's Colaboratory. In addition, MobileNet V2 is available as modules on TF-Hub, and pre-trained checkpoints or saved models can be found at `https://github.com/ tensorflow/models/tree/master/research/slim/nets/mobilenet and can be used as transfer learning.`

The following diagram presents a simple architecture of MobileNet V2. MobileNet V2 has been developed as an extension of MobileNet V1. It uses depth-wise separable convolution as efficient building blocks. In addition, MobileNet V2 includes two new features in the architecture. One is the linear bottlenecks between the layers, and the other one is shortcut connections between the bottlenecks:

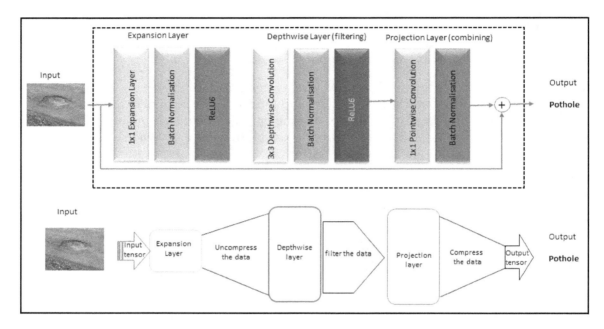

Collecting data for use case one

We can collect data using a smartphone camera or a Raspberry Pi camera and prepare the dataset by ourselves, or download existing images from the internet (that is, via Google, Bing, and so on) and prepare the dataset. Alternatively, we can use an existing open source dataset. For use case one, we have used a combination of both. We have downloaded an existing dataset on pothole images (one of the most common road faults) from and updated the dataset with more images from Google images. The open source dataset (PotDataset) for pothole recognition was published by Cranfield University, UK. The dataset includes images of pothole objects and non-pothole objects, including manholes, pavements, road markings, and shadows. The images were manually annotated and organized into the following folders:

- Manhole
- Pavement
- Pothole
- Road markings
- Shadow

Exploring the dataset from use case one

It is essential to explore the dataset before applying DL algorithms to the data. For the exploration, we can run image_explorer.py on the dataset as follows:

```
python image_explorer.py datset_original
```

The following diagram presents a snapshot of the data exploration process:

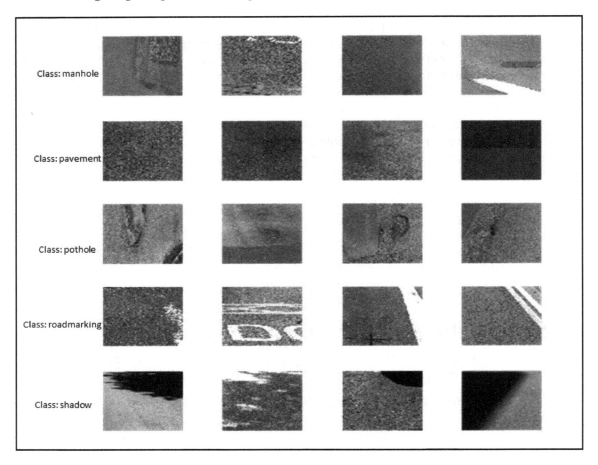

As shown in the diagram of data exploration, the differences between pothole and non-pothole objects are not always obvious if we are using only the smartphone camera. A combination of an IR and smartphone camera can improve the situation. In addition, we found that the pothole images we have used here might not be enough to cover a wide range of potholes such as the following:

- Many images in the used dataset show that the potholes are already maintained/fixed.
- There are a few images of a large-sized pothole in the used dataset.

In this context, we decided to update the pothole images dataset by collecting more images from the internet. Next, we briefly discuss the data collection process:

1. **Search**: Use any browser (we used Chrome), go to Google, and search for *pothole images* in Google Images. Your search window will look like the following screenshot:

 You can select copyright-free images by clicking on *Tools* and changing the usage rights to *Labeled for reuse with modification*.

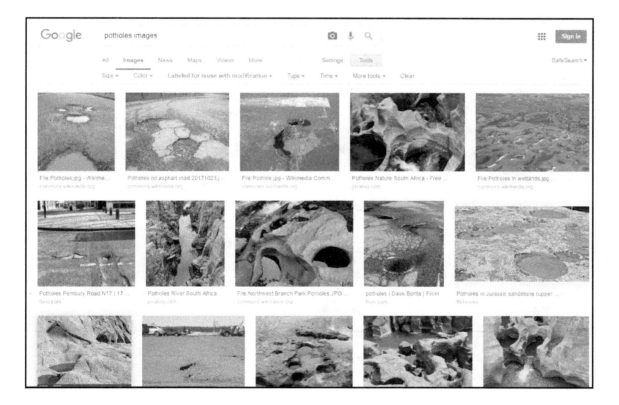

2. **Gathering Images URLs**: This step is to use a few lines of JavaScript code to gather the image URLs. The gathered URLs can be used in Python to download the images. As shown in the following screenshot, select the JavaScript console (assuming you use the Chrome web browser, but you can use Firefox as well) by clicking **View** | **Developer** | **JavaScript Console** (in macOS) and customize and control **Google Chrome** | **More tools** | **Developer tools** (in Windows OS):

Once you have selected the JavaScript console, you will see a browser window such as the following screenshot, and this will enable you to execute JavaScript in a REPL-like manner:

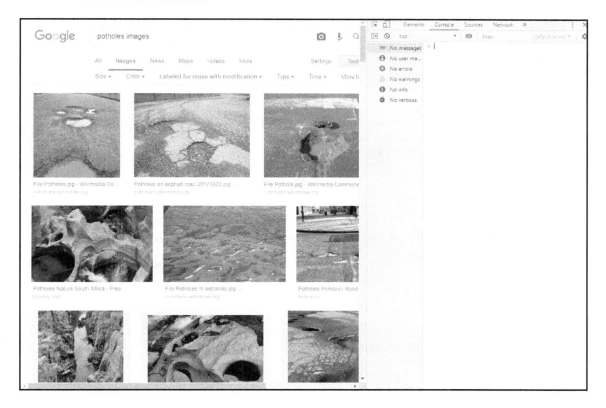

3. Now do the following in order:

- Scroll the page and go down until you have found all useful images (note: please use images that are not subject to copyright) for your dataset. After that, you need to collect the URLs for the selected images.

- Now move to the JavaScript console and then copy and paste the following JavaScript codes into the console:

```
// Get the jquery into the JavaScript console
var scriptJs = document.createElement('scriptJs');
scriptJs.src =
"https://ajax.googleapis.com/ajax/libs/jquery/2.2.0/jquery.
min.js";
document.getElementsByTagName('head')[0].appendChild(script
Js)
```

- The preceding line of code will pull the jQuery JavaScript library. Now you can use a CSS selector to collect a list of URLs using the following lines of code:

```
// Collect the selected URLs
var urls_images = $('.rg_di .rg_meta').map(function() {
return JSON.parse($(this).text()).ou; });
```

4. Finally, write the URLs to a file (one per line) using the following lines of code:

```
// write the URls to a file
var text_url_Save = urls_images.toArray().join('\n');
var hiddenComponents = document.createElement('a');
hiddenComponents.href = 'data:attachment/text,' +
encodeURI(text_url_Save);
hiddenComponents.target = '_blank';
hiddenComponents.download = 'imageurls.txt';
hiddenComponents.click();
```

Once you execute the preceding lines of code, you will have a file named `imageurls.txt` in your default download directory. If you want to download them into a specific folder, then write `hiddenComponents.download = 'your fooler/imageurls.txt` instead of `hiddenComponents.download = 'imageurls.txt'` in the preceding code.

5. **Downloading the images**: Now you are ready to download the running the images `download_images.py` (available in code folder of the chapter) in the previously downloaded `imageurls.txt`:

```
python download_images.py  imageurls.txt
```

6. **Exploration**: Once we have downloaded the images, we need to explore them in order delete the irrelevant images. We can do this through a bit of manual inspection. After this, we need to resize and convert them into grayscale images to match the previously downloaded dataset:

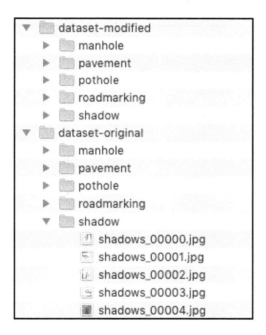

The preceding screenshot shows the folder structure of the pothole and non-pothole images datasets.

Collecting data for use case two

As is the case with use case one, we can collect data through digital cameras or use an existing open source or a combination of both. We are using an existing and open source dataset for the implementation of the sorting algorithm. The dataset was collected from urban environments of the USA . As solid waste types may vary by country, it is better to update the dataset based on the country the use case will be used for. The dataset consists of six types of solid wastes: glass, paper, cardboard, plastic, metal, and trash. The dataset consists of 2,527 images, and they were annotated and organized into the following folders, as shown in the following screenshot:

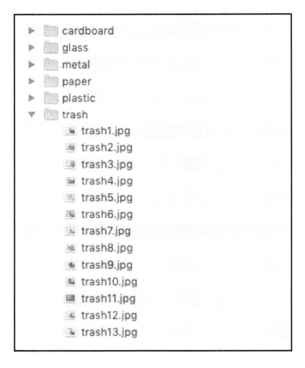

Data exploration of use case two

The following presents a snapshot of the data exploration for use case two. As we can see, glass and plastic images could be confusing to the sorting algorithm. In this context, weight sensor data can be useful for fixing this issue:

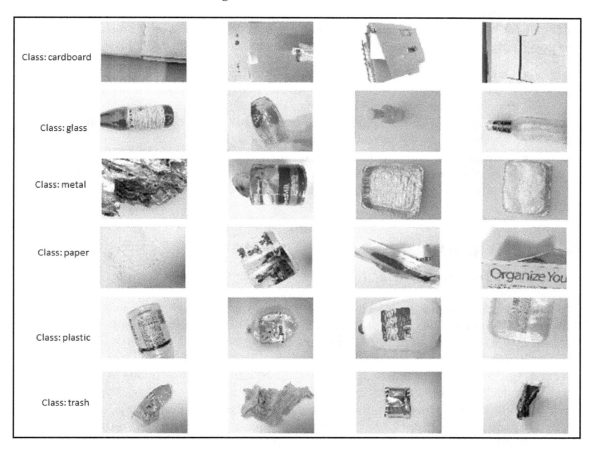

Data pre-processing

This is an essential step for a DL pipeline. The existing datasets on pothole images and the solid waste images used in the use cases are pre-processed and are ready to be used for training, validation, and testing. As shown in the following diagram, both the original and modified (additional images downloaded for the pothole class) are organized as sub-folders, each named after one of the five categories and containing only images from that category. There are a few issues to be noted during the training image set preparation:

- **Data size**: We need to collect at least a hundred images for each class to train a model that works well. The more we can gather, the better the accuracy of the trained model is likely to be. Each of the five categories in the used dataset has more than 1,000 sample images. We also made sure that the images are a good representation of what our application will actually face in real implementation.
- **Data heterogeneity**: Data collected for training should be heterogeneous. For example, images about potholes need to be taken in as wide a variety of situations as we can, at different times, and with different devices.

Models training

As we mentioned earlier, we are using transfer learning that does not require training from scratch; retraining of the models with a new dataset will sufficiently work in many cases. We retrained two popular architectures or models of CNN, namely Incentive V3 and Mobilenet V1, on a desktop computer, which is replicating the city council's server. In both models, it took less than an hour to retrain the models, which is an advantage of the transfer learning approach. We need to understand the list of key arguments before running the `retrain.py`file, which is in the code folder. If we type in our Terminal (in Linux or macOS) or Command Prompt (Windows) `python retrain.py -h`, we shall see a window like the following screenshot with additional information (that is, an overview of each argument). The compulsory argument is the image directory, and it is one of the dataset directories shown in the preceding figures on the folder view of the datasets:

```
usage: retrain.py [-h] [--image_dir IMAGE_DIR] [--output_graph OUTPUT_GRAPH]
                  [--intermediate_output_graphs_dir INTERMEDIATE_OUTPUT_GRAPHS_DIR]
                  [--intermediate_store_frequency INTERMEDIATE_STORE_FREQUENCY]
                  [--output_labels OUTPUT_LABELS]
                  [--summaries_dir SUMMARIES_DIR]
                  [--how_many_training_steps HOW_MANY_TRAINING_STEPS]
                  [--learning_rate LEARNING_RATE]
                  [--testing_percentage TESTING_PERCENTAGE]
                  [--validation_percentage VALIDATION_PERCENTAGE]
                  [--eval_step_interval EVAL_STEP_INTERVAL]
                  [--train_batch_size TRAIN_BATCH_SIZE]
                  [--test_batch_size TEST_BATCH_SIZE]
                  [--validation_batch_size VALIDATION_BATCH_SIZE]
                  [--print_misclassified_test_images] [--model_dir MODEL_DIR]
                  [--bottleneck_dir BOTTLENECK_DIR]
                  [--final_tensor_name FINAL_TENSOR_NAME] [--flip_left_right]
                  [--random_crop RANDOM_CROP] [--random_scale RANDOM_SCALE]
                  [--random_brightness RANDOM_BRIGHTNESS]
                  [--architecture ARCHITECTURE]
```

In the following, we are presenting two examples of command: one to retrain the Incentive model V3 and the other to retain Mobilenet V1 on the modified dataset (dataset-modified). To retrain Incentive V3, we did not pass the architecture argument value as it is the default architecture included in `retrain.py`. For the rest of the arguments, including data split ratio among training, validation, and test, we used the default values. In this use case, we are using the split rule of the data that put 80% of the images into the main training set, keeping 10% separate for validation during training, and the final 10% of the data as a testing set. The testing set is to test the real-world classification performance of the classifier:

```
python retrain.py \
--output_graph=trained_model_incentive-modified-dataset/retrained_graph.pb \
--output_labels=trained_model_incentive-modified-dataset/retrained_labels.txt \
--image_dir=dataset-modified
```

To run the training and validation of the Mobilenet V1 model, use the following command:

```
python retrain.py \
--output_graph=trained_model_mobilenetv1-modified-dataset/retrained_graph.pb \
--output_labels=trained_model_mobilenetv1-modified-dataset/retrained_labels.txt \
--architecture mobilenet_1.0_224 \
--image_dir=dataset-modified
```

Once we run the preceding commands, it will generate the retrain models
(`retrained_graph.pb`), labels text (`retrained_labels.txt`) in the given directory and
summary directory consists of train and validation summary information of the models.
The summary information (`--summaries_dir` argument with default value
`retrain_logs`) can be used by TensorBoard to visualize different aspects of the models,
including the networks, and their performance graphs. If we type the following command
in the terminal or Command Prompt, it will run TensorBoard:

```
tensorboard --logdir retrain_logs
```

Once TensorBoard is running, navigate your web browser to `localhost:6006` to view the
TensorBoard and view the network of the corresponding model. The following diagrams
(a) and **(b)** show the network for Incentive V3 and Mobilenet V1 respectively. The diagram
demonstrates the complexity of Incentive V3 compared to Mobilenet V1:

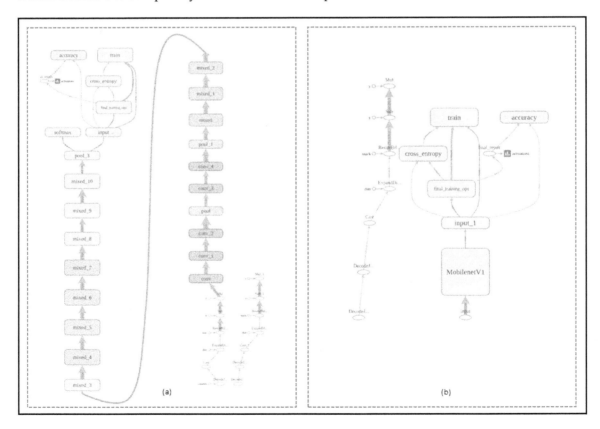

In the second use case, we have retrained only the Mobilenet V1 on the solid waste dataset. You can retrain the model as mentioned by only providing an image or dataset directory as follows:

```
--image_dir=dataset-solidwaste
```

Evaluating models

Firstly, we have identified the size of the retrain models. As shown in the following screenshot, Mobilenet V1 requires only 17.1 MB (for both use cases), which is than one-fifth of Incentive V3 (92.3 MB), and this model can be easily deployed in resource-constrained IoT devices, including Raspberry Pi or smartphones. Secondly, we have evaluated the performance of the models. Two levels of performance evaluation have been done for the use cases: (i) dataset-wide evaluation or testing has been done during the retraining phase on the desktop PC platform/server, and (ii) an individual image or sample (real-life image) was tested or evaluated in the Raspberry Pi 3 environment:

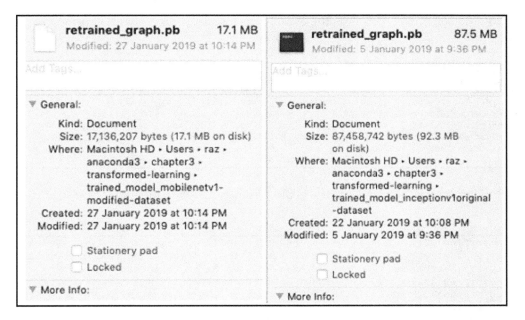

Model performance (use case one)

All the evaluation performances of use case one are presented in the following screenshots. The following six screenshots present the training, validation, and testing performances of Incentive V3 and Mobilenet V1 models on the two sets of data. The first three screenshots present the results generated in the terminal after retraining the models, and the last three screenshots are generated from the TensorBoard.

The following screenshot presents the evaluation results of Incentive V3 on the original dataset:

```
INFO:tensorflow:2019-01-27 18:48:59.149569: Step 3990: Train accuracy = 95.0%
INFO:tensorflow:2019-01-27 18:48:59.149738: Step 3990: Cross entropy = 0.139672
INFO:tensorflow:2019-01-27 18:48:59.284896: Step 3990: Validation accuracy = 93.0% (N=100
INFO:tensorflow:2019-01-27 18:49:00.564238: Step 3999: Train accuracy = 95.0%
INFO:tensorflow:2019-01-27 18:49:00.564402: Step 3999: Cross entropy = 0.131412
INFO:tensorflow:2019-01-27 18:49:00.698488: Step 3999: Validation accuracy = 97.0% (N=100
INFO:tensorflow:Final test accuracy = 94.5% (N=1035)
INFO:tensorflow:Froze 2 variables.
INFO:tensorflow:Converted 2 variables to const ops.
```

The following screenshot presents the evaluation results of Incentive V3 on the modified dataset:

```
INFO:tensorflow:2019-01-27 21:49:07.512191: Step 3990: Train accuracy = 97.0%
INFO:tensorflow:2019-01-27 21:49:07.512365: Step 3990: Cross entropy = 0.122777
INFO:tensorflow:2019-01-27 21:49:07.729347: Step 3990: Validation accuracy = 96.0% (N=100)
INFO:tensorflow:2019-01-27 21:49:09.603333: Step 3999: Train accuracy = 98.0%
INFO:tensorflow:2019-01-27 21:49:09.603515: Step 3999: Cross entropy = 0.122347
INFO:tensorflow:2019-01-27 21:49:09.814565: Step 3999: Validation accuracy = 94.0% (N=100)
INFO:tensorflow:Final test accuracy = 94.0% (N=1073)
INFO:tensorflow:Froze 2 variables.
INFO:tensorflow:Converted 2 variables to const ops.
```

The following screenshot presents the evaluation results of Mobilenet V1 on the original dataset:

```
INFO:tensorflow:2019-01-27 19:44:50.069255: Step 3990: Train accuracy = 99.0%
INFO:tensorflow:2019-01-27 19:44:50.069425: Step 3990: Cross entropy = 0.035808
INFO:tensorflow:2019-01-27 19:44:50.158899: Step 3990: Validation accuracy = 99.0% (N=
INFO:tensorflow:2019-01-27 19:44:50.926383: Step 3999: Train accuracy = 99.0%
INFO:tensorflow:2019-01-27 19:44:50.926563: Step 3999: Cross entropy = 0.046513
INFO:tensorflow:2019-01-27 19:44:51.006902: Step 3999: Validation accuracy = 96.0% (N=
INFO:tensorflow:Final test accuracy = 95.7% (N=1035)
INFO:tensorflow:Froze 2 variables.
INFO:tensorflow:Converted 2 variables to const ops.
```

The following screenshot presents the evaluation results of Mobilenet V1 on the modified dataset:

```
INFO:tensorflow:2019-01-27 20:28:24.273400: Step 3990: Train accuracy = 100.0%
INFO:tensorflow:2019-01-27 20:28:24.273570: Step 3990: Cross entropy = 0.063349
INFO:tensorflow:2019-01-27 20:28:24.383185: Step 3990: Validation accuracy = 95.0% (N=1
INFO:tensorflow:2019-01-27 20:28:25.607641: Step 3999: Train accuracy = 99.0%
INFO:tensorflow:2019-01-27 20:28:25.607888: Step 3999: Cross entropy = 0.028579
INFO:tensorflow:2019-01-27 20:28:25.759702: Step 3999: Validation accuracy = 92.0% (N=1
INFO:tensorflow:Final test accuracy = 96.0% (N=1073)
INFO:tensorflow:Froze 2 variables.
INFO:tensorflow:Converted 2 variables to const ops.
```

The following screenshot presents the evaluation results of Incentive V3 on the original dataset generated by TensorBoard:

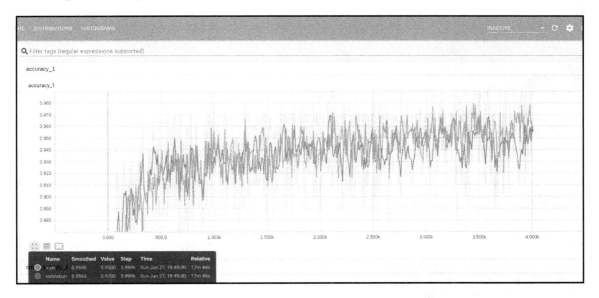

The following screenshot presents the evaluation results of Mobilenet V1 on the original dataset generated by TensorBoard:

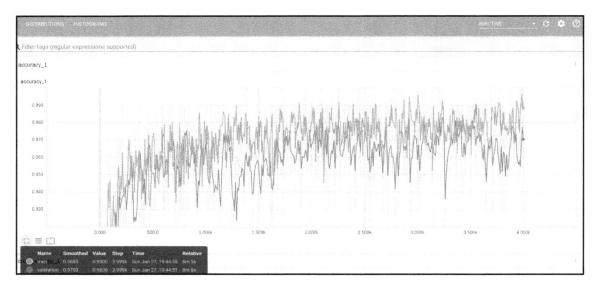

From all the previous model performance screenshots, it is clear that both training and validation accuracies are well above 90%, which is enough for fault detection.

The following diagrams show the classification or object detection performances on individual samples. For these, we have used two different sets of classification code (available in the chapter's code folder).

The first screenshot is showing the snapshot of running the classifier for Mobilenet V1 on two samples. As we can see from all results, test or evaluation accuracy is well above 94%, and with such accuracy, the DL models (CNNs) have the potential to detect objects, including potholes, manholes, and other objects on the road. However, object detection time on the Pi 3 was in the range of three to five seconds, which needs to be improved if we want to use them in real-time detection and actuation. In addition, results show that models trained on the modified dataset have a good chance to provide high detection or testing accuracy in a real environment (shown in the preceding screenshots), especially in detecting potholes, as this class of data has been improved by adding diverse images from the googled images:

```
Mohammads-MacBook-Air:transformed-learning raz$ python label_image.py --graph=trained_model_mobilenetv1-modified-dataset/retrained_graph.pb --labels=trained_model_mobilenetv1-modi
bels.txt --input_layer=input --output_layer=final_result --input_height=224 --input_width=224 --image=test/pothole2.jpg
/Users/raz/anaconda3/lib/python3.6/site-packages/h5py/__init__.py:36: FutureWarning: Conversion of the second argument of issubdtype from `float` to `np.floating` is deprecated. I
ted as `np.float64 == np.dtype(float).type`.
  from ._conv import register_converters as _register_converters
2019-01-28 18:02:16.108124: I tensorflow/core/platform/cpu_feature_guard.cc:141] Your CPU supports instructions that this TensorFlow binary was not compiled to use: AVX2 FMA
pothole 0.99144566
shadow 0.006273513
roadmarking 0.0022471682
manhole 2.2895005e-05
pavement 1.0783568e-05
Mohammads-MacBook-Air:transformed-learning raz$ python label_image.py --graph=trained_model_mobilenetv1-original-dataset/retrained_graph.pb --labels=trained_model_mobilenetsv1-or
labels.txt --input_layer=input --output_layer=final_result --input_height=224 --input_width=224 --image=test/pothole2.jpg
/Users/raz/anaconda3/lib/python3.6/site-packages/h5py/__init__.py:36: FutureWarning: Conversion of the second argument of issubdtype from `float` to `np.floating` is deprecated. I
ted as `np.float64 == np.dtype(float).type`.
  from ._conv import register_converters as _register_converters
2019-01-28 18:08:00.364422: I tensorflow/core/platform/cpu_feature_guard.cc:141] Your CPU supports instructions that this TensorFlow binary was not compiled to use: AVX2 FMA
pothole 0.9827071
shadow 0.014883991
roadmarking 0.0023621535
manhole 3.5012974e-05
pavement 1.1739314e-05
Mohammads-MacBook-Air:transformed-learning raz$ ▌
```

The following screenshot presents the evaluation results of pothole detection with the Incentive V3 model trained on the original dataset (Pi 3 B+):

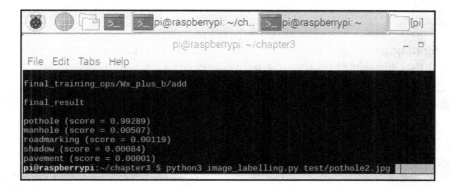

The following diagram presents the evaluation results of manhole detection with the Incentive V3 model trained on the original dataset (Pi 3 B+):

The following diagram presents the evaluation results of pothole detection with the Mobilenet V1 model trained on the original dataset (Pi 3 B+):

The following diagram presents the evaluation results of manhole detection with the Mobilenet V1 model trained on the original dataset (Pi 3 B+):

Model performance (use case two)

All the evaluation performances of use case two are presented in the following screenshots. For this use case, we are presenting only the results for Mobilenet V1 .The following diagrams present the training, validation, and testing performances of the Mobilenet V1 models on the two datasets. As we can see from the following screenshot, the test accuracy is not that high (77.5%) but good enough for solid waste detection and sorting:

```
INFO:tensorflow:2019-02-16 15:22:41.199519: Step 3980: Train accuracy = 100.0%
INFO:tensorflow:2019-02-16 15:22:41.199691: Step 3980: Cross entropy = 0.014032
INFO:tensorflow:2019-02-16 15:22:41.252618: Step 3980: Validation accuracy = 81.0% (N=100)
INFO:tensorflow:2019-02-16 15:22:41.787808: Step 3990: Train accuracy = 100.0%
INFO:tensorflow:2019-02-16 15:22:41.787986: Step 3990: Cross entropy = 0.016459
INFO:tensorflow:2019-02-16 15:22:41.846011: Step 3990: Validation accuracy = 87.0% (N=100)
INFO:tensorflow:2019-02-16 15:22:42.326762: Step 3999: Train accuracy = 100.0%
INFO:tensorflow:2019-02-16 15:22:42.326932: Step 3999: Cross entropy = 0.015315
INFO:tensorflow:2019-02-16 15:22:42.392484: Step 3999: Validation accuracy = 87.0% (N=100)
INFO:tensorflow:Final test accuracy = 77.5% (N=271)
```

The following screenshot presents the evaluation results of Mobilenet V1 on the dataset generated by TensorBoard:

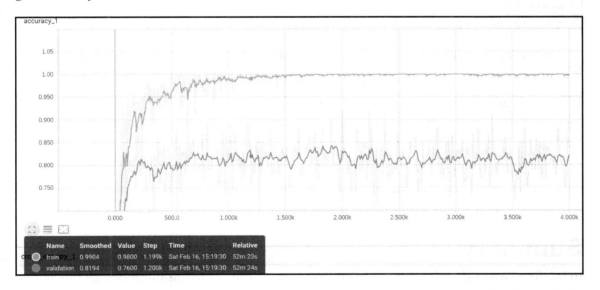

The following three screenshots show the classification or object (solid waste) detection performances on individual samples. The first screenshot presents the evaluation results of glass detection:

```
Mohammads-MacBook-Air:transformed-learning raz$ python label_image.py --graph=trained_model_mobilenetv1-garbage-dataset/retr
ls.txt --input_layer=input --output_layer=final_result --input_height=224 --input_width=224 --image=test-garbage/glass3.jpeg
/Users/raz/anaconda3/lib/python3.6/site-packages/h5py/__init__.py:36: FutureWarning: Conversion of the second argument of is
ted as `np.float64 == np.dtype(float).type`.
  from ._conv import register_converters as _register_converters
2019-02-16 16:05:37.535686: I tensorflow/core/platform/cpu_feature_guard.cc:141] Your CPU supports instructions that this Te
glass 0.9997981
plastic 0.0001634804
trash 1.3350626e-05
paper 8.399338e-06
cardboard 8.345092e-06
Mohammads-MacBook-Air:transformed-learning raz$ python label_image.py --graph=trained_model_mobilenetv1-garbage-dataset/retr
ls.txt --input_layer=input --output_layer=final_result --input_height=224 --input_width=224 --image=test-garbage/glass3.jpeg
```

The following screenshot presents the evaluation results of plastic detection:

```
Mohammads-MacBook-Air:transformed-learning raz$ python label_image.py --graph=trained_model_mobilenetv1-garbage-dataset/retra
ls.txt --input_layer=input --output_layer=final_result --input_height=224 --input_width=224 --image=test-garbage/glass2.jpeg
/Users/raz/anaconda3/lib/python3.6/site-packages/h5py/__init__.py:36: FutureWarning: Conversion of the second argument of issu
ted as `np.float64 == np.dtype(float).type`.
  from ._conv import register_converters as _register_converters
2019-02-16 15:59:45.588410: I tensorflow/core/platform/cpu_feature_guard.cc:141] Your CPU supports instructions that this Tens
plastic 0.9916095
paper 0.0070591657
cardboard 0.000957468
glass 0.0002852132
metal 8.8677225e-05
```

The following screenshot presents the evaluation results of metal detection using Mobilenet V1:

```
ls.txt --input_layer=input --output_layer=final_result --input_height=224 --input_width=224 --image=test-garbage/tin1.jpeg
/Users/raz/anaconda3/lib/python3.6/site-packages/h5py/__init__.py:36: FutureWarning: Conversion of the second argument of iss
ted as `np.float64 == np.dtype(float).type`.
  from ._conv import register_converters as _register_converters
2019-02-16 15:59:01.822456: I tensorflow/core/platform/cpu_feature_guard.cc:141] Your CPU supports instructions that this Ten
metal 0.9152763
paper 0.07105696
cardboard 0.013308621
plastic 0.00035772196
glass 2.888089e-07
```

Summary

In the first part of this chapter, we briefly described different IoT applications and their image detection-based decision-making. In addition, we briefly discussed two use cases: image detection-based road fault detection, and image detection-based solid waste sorting. The first application can detect potholes on the road using a smartphone camera or a Raspberry Pi camera. The second application detects different types of solid waste and sorts them according to smart recycling.

In the second part of the chapter, we briefly discussed transfer learning with a few example networks, and examined its usefulness in resource-constrained IoT applications. In addition, we discussed the rationale behind selecting a CNN, including two popular implementations, namely Inception V3 and Mobilenet V1. The rest of the chapter described all the necessary components of the DL pipeline for the Inception V3 and Mobilenet V1 models.

In many IoT applications, image recognition alone may not be enough for object and/or subject detection. In this context, sometimes, audio/speech/voice recognition can be useful. Chapter 3, Audio/Speech/Voice Recognition in IoT, will present DL-based speech/voice data analysis and recognition in IoT applications.

References

- *Smart patrolling: An efficient road surface monitoring using smartphone sensors and crowdsourcing*, Gurdit Singh, Divya Bansal, Sanjeev Sofat, Naveen Aggarwal, *Pervasive and Mobile Computing*, volume 40, 2017, pages 71-88
- *Road Damage Detection Using Deep Neural Networks with Images Captured Through a Smartphone*, Hiroya Maeda, Yoshihide Sekimoto, Toshikazu Seto, Takehiro Kashiyama, Hiroshi Omata, arXiv:1801.09454
- *Potholes cost UK drivers £1.7 billion a year: Here's how to claim if you car is damaged*, Luke John Smith: https://www.express.co.uk/life-style/cars/938333/pothole-damage-cost-how-to-claim-UK
- *What a Waste: A Global Review of Solid Waste Management*, D Hoornweg and P Bhada-Tata, World Bank, Washington, DC, USA, 2012
- *Efficient Convolutional Neural Networks for Mobile Vision Applications*, Andrew G Howard, Menglong Zhu, Bo Chen, Dmitry Kalenichenko, Weijun Wang, Tobias Weyand, Marco Andreetto, Hartwig Adam, *MobileNets*: arXiv:1704.04861
- *Imagenet classification with deep convolutional neural networks*, A Krizhevsky, I Sutskever, G E Hinton, in *Advances in Neural Information Processing Systems*, pages 1,097–1,105, 2012. 1, 6.
- *MobileNetV2: Inverted Residuals and Linear Bottlenecks*, Mark Sandler, Andrew Howard, Menglong Zhu, Andrey Zhmoginov, Liang-Chieh Chen, arXiv:1801.04381.
- Pothole dataset: https://cord.cranfield.ac.uk/articles/PotDataset/5999699
- Trashnet: https://github.com/garythung/trashnet

4
Audio/Speech/Voice Recognition in IoT

Automatic audio/speech/voice recognition is becoming a common, convenient way for people to interact with their devices, including smartphones, wearables, and other smart devices. Machine learning and DL algorithms are useful for audio/speech/voice recognition and decision making. Consequently, they are very promising for IoT applications, which rely on audio/speech/voice recognition for their activity and decisions. This chapter will present DL-based speech/voice data analysis and recognition in IoT applications in general.

The first part of this chapter will briefly describe different IoT applications and their speech/voice recognition-based decision making. In addition, it will briefly discuss two IoT applications and their speech/voice recognition-based implementations in a real-world scenario. In the second part of the chapter, we will present a hands-on speech/voice detection implementation of the applications using DL algorithms. We will cover the following topics:

- IoT applications and audio/speech recognition
- Use case one – voice-controlled smart light
- Implementing a voice-controlled smart light
- Use case two – voice-controlled home access
- Implementing voice-controlled home access
- DL for audio/speech recognition in IoT
- DL algorithms for audio/speech recognition in IoT applications
- Different deployment options for DL-based audio/speech recognition in IoT
- Data collection and preprocessing
- Model training
- Evaluating models

Speech/voice recognition for IoT

Like image recognition, the speech/voice recognition landscape in IoT applications is rapidly changing. In recent years, consumers have become depending on voice command features and this has been fueled by Amazon, Google, Xiomi, and other companies' voice-enabled search and/or devices. This technology is becoming an extremely useful technology for users. Statistics show that around 50% of households (`https://techcrunch.com/2017/11/08/voice-enabled-smart-speakers-to-reach-55-of-u-s-households-by-2022-says-report/`) in the United States use voice-activated commands for accessing online content. Thus, IoT, machine learning, and DL-supported speech/voice recognition has revolutionized the focus of businesses and consumer expectations. Many industries—including home automation, healthcare, automobiles, and entertainment—are adopting voice-enabled IoT applications. As shown in the following diagram, these applications use one or more of the following speech/voice recognition services:

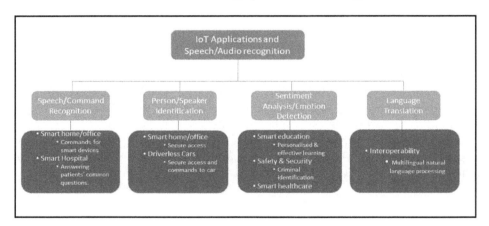

- **Speech/command Recognition:** Voice-controlled IoT applications are gaining popularity in many application domains, such as smart home/office, smart hospital, and smart cars, because of their convenience. For example, a mobility disabled person may find difficulty in switching on their TV or light. A voice-controlled/commanded TV/light can ease this difficulty by turning on the TV/light simply by listening to a voice. This will offer independent living to many disabled individuals and/or people with special needs. Voice-activated smart microwave ovens can revolutionize cooking. Moreover, a voice enabled smart speaker can assist with and answer many common questions in many public service areas, such as hospitals, airports, and train stations. For example, a smart voice-enabled speaker can answer patients' common questions in hospital, such as when the visiting time is and who the ward doctor is.

- **Person/Speaker Identification:** Speaker/person recognition is the second important service provided by IoT applications that has received the spotlight in recent years. The key applications that are utilizing DL/machine learning-based speaker recognition services include personalized voice-controlled assistants, smart home appliances, biometric authentication in security services, criminal investigations, and smart cars [1,2]. Voice-controlled home/office access is an example of biometric authentication.
- **Sentiment Analysis/Emotion Detection:** User emotion detection or sentiment analysis can be useful in providing personalized and effective services to the user. IoT applications, such as smart healthcare [3], smart education, and security and safety, can improve their services through DL-based emotion detection or sentiment analysis. For example, in a smart classroom, a teacher can analyze the students' sentiments in real time or quasi real time to offer personalized and/or group-wise teaching. This will improve their learning experience.
- **Language Translation:** There are 6,500 (`https://www.infoplease.com/askeds/how-many-spoken-languages`) active spoken languages worldwide, and this is a challenge to effective communication and interoperability. Many public services, such as the immigration office, can use a translator instead of a paid interpreter. Tourists can use smart devices, such as **ILI** (`https://iamili.com/us/`), to effectively communicate with others.

Use case one – voice-controlled smart light

According to the **World Health Organisation** (**WHO**), more than one billion people in the world live with some form of disability. Almost 20% of them are experiencing considerable difficulties in functioning and living independently. In the future, disability will be an even bigger concern because of its increasing prevalence. IoT applications, such as smart home, with the support of machine learning/DL, can offer support to this community and improve their quality of life through independence. One of these applications is a voice-activated smart light/fan control.

An individual facing a disability such as mobility impairment faces various difficulties in living their day-to-day life. One of these difficulties is switching on/off home or office lights/fans/other devices. Voice-activated smart control of home/office lights/fans/other devices is an IoT application. However, voice recognition and the correct detection of a given command is not an easy job. A person's accent, pronunciation, and ambient noises can make the person's voice recognition difficult. An appropriate DL algorithm trained on a significantly large voice dataset can be useful in addressing these issues and can make a working voice-controlled smart light application.

Implementing use case one

The following diagram presents the key components needed for the implementation of a voice-activated light (in a room):

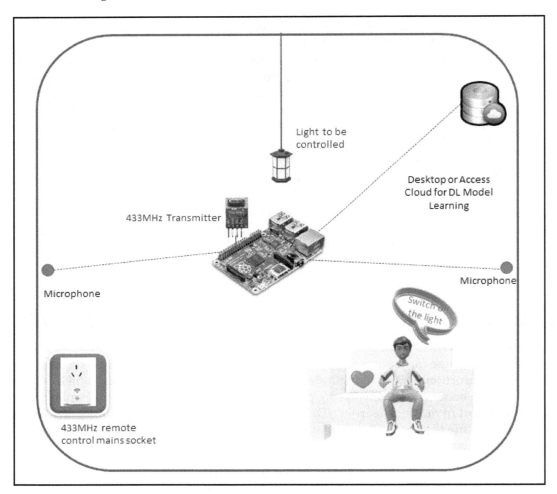

As shown in the preceding diagram, the implementation of the use case will need the following components:

- **Sensors and a Computing Platform**: For this use case, we are considering two omnidirectional microphones that are installed on the walls of the room. These microphones are wirelessly connected to a computing platform. In this use case, we are using a Raspberry Pi 3 as the computing platform, and this can work as the smart home's edge-computing device to control the IoT devices deployed in the home. We need two more devices: a 433 MHz wireless transmitter, connected to the Raspberry Pi, to transmit the processed commands to the switch, and a 433 MHz remote control or wirelessly controlled mains socket to control the light or target device.

- **Voice-Activated Command Detection and Control**: In this phase, the edge-computing device will be installed with one app. The installed app on the Raspberry Pi will be loaded with a pre-trained voice command detection and classification model. Once one of the microphones receives a "switch off the light" command or similar, it sends the received commands to the Raspberry Pi for processing and detection using the DL model. Finally, the Raspberry Pi transmits detected commands to the wirelessly controlled mains socket for the necessary action to be taken on the light.

- **Desktop or Server for Model Learning**: We also need a desktop/server or access to a cloud computing platform in order to learn the model for voice detection and classification using reference datasets. This learned model will be preinstalled in the Raspberry Pi.

The second part (in the sections starting from *DL for Sound/Audio Recognition in IoT*) of the chapter will describe the implementation of the DL-based anomaly detection of the preceding use case. All the necessary code is available in the chapter's code folder.

Use case two – voice-controlled home access

Creating secure and friendly access to homes, offices, and any other premises is a challenging task, as it may need keys or an access card (such as a hotel room access card) that a user may not always remember to carry with them. The use of smart devices, including IoT solutions, can offer secure and friendly access to many premises. A potential approach to smart and secure access to homes/offices is image recognition-based identification of people and the opening of a door/gate accordingly. However, one problem with this approach is that any intruder can collect a photograph of one or more permitted persons and present the photo to the installed camera to access the office/home. One solution to this problem is to use a combination of image recognition and voice recognition or only voice recognition to allow access to the home/office.

A voice biometric (or voiceprint) is unique to every individual, and mimicking this is a challenging task. However, detection of this unique property is not an easy job. DL-based speech recognition can identify unique properties and the corresponding person, and allow access only to that person.

Implementing use case two

As shown in the following diagram, the implementation of the voice-activated light (in a room) use case consists of three main elements:

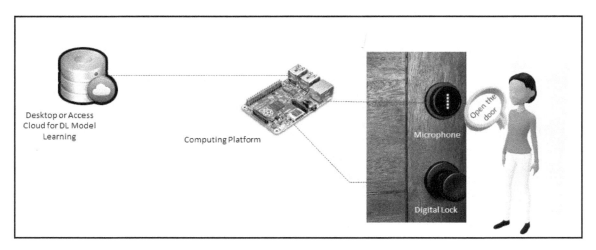

- **Sensors and computing platform**: For this use case, we are considering one omnidirectional microphone installed in the entrance of the home and connected to the computing platform wirelessly or concealed in the walls. For the computing platform, we are using a Raspberry Pi , and this will work as the smart home's edge-computing device to control the IoT devices deployed in the home. Also, the door is installed with a digital lock system that can be controlled through a computer.
- **Voice-activated command detection and control**: In this phase, the edge-computing device will be installed with one app. The installed app on the Raspberry Pi will be loaded with a pre-trained speaker or person detection and classification model. Once an authentic user talks to the door microphone, it gathers the audio signals and sends the received speech signal to the Raspberry Pi for processing and person detection using the DL model. If the detected person is on the **white list** (the list of occupants of the home) of the smart home controller (Raspberry Pi, in this case), the controller will command the door to be unlocked, otherwise it won't.
- **Desktop or server for model learning:** We also need a desktop/server or access to a cloud computing platform in order to learn the model for voice detection and classification using reference datasets. This learned model will be preinstalled in the Raspberry Pi.

All the following sections describe the implementation of the DL-based command/speaker recognition needed for the aforementioned use cases. All the necessary code is available in the chapter's code folder.

DL for sound/audio recognition in IoT

It is important to understand the working principle of an **Automatic Speech Recognition** (**ASR**) system before discussing the useful DL models.

ASR system model

An **Automatic Speech Recognition (ASR)** system needs three main sources of knowledge. These sources are known as an **acoustic model**, a **phonetic lexicon**, and a **language model** [4]. Generally, an acoustic model deals with the sounds of language, including the phonemes and extra sounds (such as pauses, breathing, background noise, and so on). On the other hand, a phonetic lexicon model or dictionary includes the words that can be understood by the system, with their possible pronunciations. Finally, a language model includes knowledge about the potential word sequences of a language. In recent years, DL approaches have been extensively used in acoustic and language models of ASR.

The following diagram presents a system model for **automatic speech recognition (ASR)**. The model consists of three main stages:

- Data gathering
- Signal analysis and feature extraction (also known as **preprocessing**)
- Decoding/identification/classification. As shown in the following diagram, DL will be used in the identification stage:

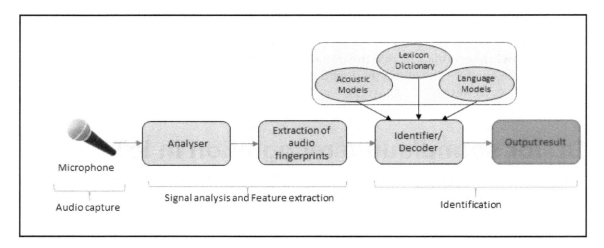

Features extraction in ASR

Features extraction is an important preprocessing stage in a DL pipeline of ASR. This stage consists of an analyzer and the extraction of audio fingerprints or features. This stage also mainly computes a sequence of feature vectors, which provides a compact representation of a gathered speech signal. Generally, this task can be performed in three key steps. The first step is known as speech analysis. This step carries out a spectra-temporal analysis of the speech signal and generates raw features describing the envelope of the power spectrum of short speech intervals. The second step extracts an extended feature vector that consists of static and dynamic features. The final step converts these extended feature vectors into more compact and robust vectors. Importantly, these vectors are the input for a DL-based command/speaker/language recognizer.

A number of feature extraction methods are available for ASR, and **Linear Predictive Codes (LPC)**, **Perceptual Linear Prediction (PLP)**, and **Mel Frequency Cepstral Coefficients (MFCC)** are widely used ones. MFCC is the most widely used method for feature extraction. The following diagram presents the key components of MFCC:

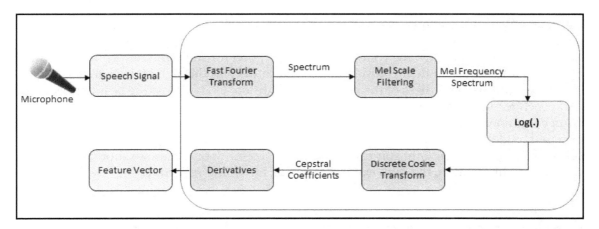

The key steps of the MFCC are as follows:

1. Inputting sound files and converting them to original sound data (a time domain signal).
2. Converting time domain signals into frequency domain signals through short-time Fourier transforms, windowing, and framing.
3. Turning frequency into a linear relationship that humans can perceive through Mel spectrum transformation.

4. Separating the DC component from the sine component by adopting DCT Transform through Mel cepstrum analysis.

5. Extracting sound spectrum feature vectors and converting them into images.

DL models for ASR

A number of DL algorithms or models have been used in ASR. A **Deep Belief Network** (**DBN**) is one of the early implementations of DL in ASR. Generally, it has been used as a pre-training layer with a single supervised layer of a **Deep Neural Network** (**DNN**). **Long Short-Term Memory** (**LSTM**) has been used for large-scale acoustic modeling. **Time Delay Neural Network** (**TDNN**) architectures have been used for audio signal processing. CNN, which has popularized DL, is also used as DL architecture for ASR. Use of DL architectures has significantly improved the speech recognition accuracy of ASRs. However, not all DL architectures have shown improvements, especially in different types of audio signals and environments, such as noisy and reverberant environments. CNNs can be used to reduce spectral variations and model the spectral correlation that exists in a speech signal.

Recurrent Neural Networks (**RNNs**) and LSTM are widely used in continuous and/or natural language processing because of the capability to incorporate temporal features of input during evolution. On the contrary, CNNs are good for short and non-continuous audio signals because of their translation invariance, such as the skill of discovering structure patterns, regardless of the position. In addition, CNNs show the best performance for speech recognition in noisy and reverberant environments, and LSTMs are better in clean conditions. The reason for this could be CNNs' emphasis on local correlations as opposed to global ones. In this context, we will use CNNs for the implementation of use cases, as voices used for light control and speech used for door access are short and non-continuous. In addition, their environments can be noisy and reflective.

CNNs and transfer learning for speech recognition in IoT applications

A CNN is a very widely used DL algorithm for image recognition. Recently, this has become popular in audio/speech/speaker recognition, as these signals can be converted into images. A CNN has different implementations, including two versions of Mobilenets, and Incentive V3. An overview of Mobilenets and Incentive V3 are presented in Chapter 3, *Image Recognition in IoT*.

Collecting data

Data collection for ASR is a challenging task for many reasons, including privacy. Consequently, open source datasets are limited in number. Importantly, these datasets may not be easy to access, may have insufficient data/speakers, or may be noisy. In this context, we decided to use two different datasets for the two use cases. For the voice-driven controlled smart light, we are using Google's speech command datasets, and for use case two, we can scrap data from one of three popular open data sources, LibriVox, LibriSpeech ASR, corpus, voxceleb, and YouTube.

Google's speech command dataset includes 65,000 one-second long utterances of 30 short words, contributed to by thousands of different members of the public through the AIY website. The dataset offers basic audio data on common words such as On, Off, Yes, digits, and directions, but this can be useful in testing the first use case. For example, the switch on the light command can be represented by On while switch off the light can be represented by Off data in the dataset. Similarly, data gathered on an individual's speech through scrapping can represent the occupants of a home. The second use case will consider a typical home with three to five occupants. These occupants will be the white list for the home and will be granted access if they are identified. Any people other than the listed ones will not be granted automated access to the home. We tested CNN on Google's speech commands dataset and a smaller version of it. The following screenshots show a hierarchical view of the smaller dataset used for use case one:

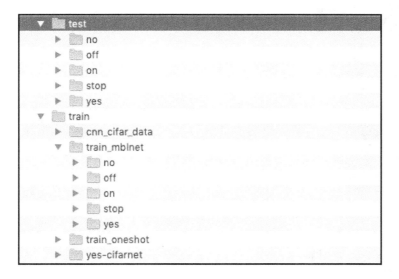

For use case two, we scrapped data from LibriVox and also downloaded audio files from the LibriSpeech ASR corpus. We wrote a web scrapper using BeautifulSoup and Selenium for the scrapping. You can write a similar scrapper using other Python modules or even other languages, such as Node.js, C, C++, and PHP. The scrapper will parse the LibriVox website or any other given link and download the listed audio books/files we want. In the following code, we briefly present the scrapper's script, which consists of three main parts:

Part 1: Import the necessary Python modules for audio file scrapping:

```
# Import the required modules
import urllib
from bs4 import BeautifulSoup
from selenium import webdriver
import os, os.path
import simplejson
from selenium.webdriver.common.by import By
from selenium.webdriver.support.ui import WebDriverWait
from selenium.webdriver.support import expected_conditions as EC
```

Part 2: Prepare the links for the audio books to be downloaded. Please note that the links may include repeated readers, which will be cleaned up to produce a non-repeated reader/speaker/home occupants dataset:

```
# Create links book for the audio data to be downloaded: this may include
repeated readers
book_links = []
browser = webdriver.PhantomJS(executable_path = '/usr/local/bin/phantomjs')

for i in range(1): ## testing first 0-1 (2) pages of the site : to minimise
the time require to downloads
    url =
("https://librivox.org/search?title=&author=&reader=&keywords=&genre_id=0&s
tatus=all&project_type=solo&recorded_language=&sort_order=catalog_date&sear
ch_page={}&search_form=advanced").format(i)
    print(url)
    browser.get(url)
    element = WebDriverWait(browser, 100).until(
    EC.presence_of_element_located((By.CLASS_NAME , "catalog-result")))
    html = browser.page_source
    soup = BeautifulSoup(html, 'html.parser')
    ul_tag = soup.find('ul', {'class': 'browse-list'})
    for li_tag in ul_tag.find_all('li', {'class': 'catalog-result'}):
        result_data = li_tag.find('div', {'class': 'result-data'})
        book_meta = result_data.find('p', {'class': 'book-meta'})
        link = result_data.a["href"]
        print(link)
        if str(book_meta).find("Complete") and link not in book_links:
```

```
        book_links.append(link)
    print(len(book_links)) # links per page could be different from regular
browsers
browser.quit()
```

Part 3: Download the audio files from the listed books and form a dataset of non-repeatable readers/speakers:

```
#  List of Links or pages for the audio books to be downloaded
f = open('audiodownload_links.txt', 'w')
simplejson.dump(download_links, f)
f.close()

# Record the file size of each reader's file
f = open('audiodownload_sizes.txt', 'w')
simplejson.dump(download_sizes, f)
f.close()

# Download the audio files and save them in local directory
 def count_files():
     dir = 'audio_files_downloaded'
     list = [file for file in os.listdir(dir) if file.endswith('.zip')] #
dir is your directory path
     number_files = len(list)
     return number_files
counter = 100 # this is for naming each downloaded file
for link, size in zip(download_links, download_sizes):
     if size >= 50 and size <= 100:
         localDestination =
'audio_files_downloaded/audio{}.zip'.format(counter)
         resultFilePath, responseHeaders = urllib.request.urlretrieve(link,
localDestination)
         counter += 1
cnt2 =  0
num = count_files()
if num < 200:
     for link, size in zip(download_links, download_sizes):
         if size > 100 and size <= 150:
             localDestination =
'audio_files_downloaded/audio{}.zip'.format(counter)
             resultFilePath, responseHeaders =
urllib.request.urlretrieve(link, localDestination)
             counter += 1
         cnt2 += 1
num = count_files()
if num < 200:
     for link, size in zip(download_links, download_sizes):                  if size >
150 and size <= 200:
```

```
            localDestination =
'audio_files_downloaded/audio{}.zip'.format(counter)
            resultFilePath, responseHeaders =
urllib.request.urlretrieve(link, localDestination)
            counter += 1
num = count_files()
if num < 200:
    for link, size in zip(download_links, download_sizes):
        if size > 200 and size <= 250:
            localDestination =
'audio_files_downloaded/audio{}.zip'.format(counter)
            resultFilePath, responseHeaders =
urllib.request.urlretrieve(link, localDestination)
            counter += 1
num = count_files()
if num < 200:
    for link, size in zip(download_links, download_sizes):
        if size > 250 and size <= 300:
            localDestination =
'audio_files_downloaded/audio{}.zip'.format(counter)
            resultFilePath, responseHeaders =
urllib.request.urlretrieve(link, localDestination)
            counter += 1
num = count_files()
if num < 200:
    for link, size in zip(download_links, download_sizes):
        if size > 300 and size <= 350:
            localDestination =
audio_files_downloaded/audio{}.zip'.format(counter)
            resultFilePath, responseHeaders =
urllib.request.urlretrieve(link, localDestination)
            counter += 1
num = count_files()
if num < 200:
    for link, size in zip(download_links, download_sizes):
        if size > 350 and size <= 400:
            localDestination =
'audio_files_downloaded/audio{}.zip'.format(counter)
            resultFilePath, responseHeaders =
urllib.request.urlretrieve(link, localDestination)
            counter += 1
```

After downloading the desired number of reader's/speaker's audio files or .mp3 files (such as five speakers or home occupants), we process the .mp3 files and convert them into fixed-size five-second audio files (.wav). We can do this through a shell script using tools such as ffmpeg, sox, and mp3splt, or we can do it manually (if there are not many readers/occupants and files).

As the implementations are based on CNNs, we need to convert the WAV audio files into images. The process of converting audio files into images varies according to the input data format. We can use `convert_wav2spect.sh` (available in the Chapter 4, *Audio/Speech/Voice Recognition in IoT* code folder) to convert the WAV files into fixed-size (503 x 800) spectrogram color images:

```bash
#!/bin/bash
#for file in test/*/*.wav
for file in train/*/*.wav
do
    outfile=${file%.*}
        sox "$file" -n spectrogram -r -o ${outfile}.png
done
```

Generally, sox, the tool in the preceding script, supports the `.png` format, and if we need to convert the images, we can do this through the batch renaming of the files from Windows or Command Prompt. The following screenshot shows a hierarchical view of the dataset used for use case 2:

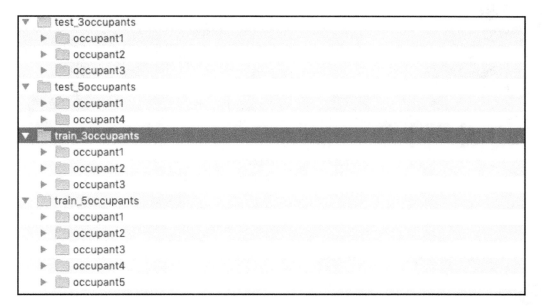

Exploring data

It is essential to explore a dataset before applying DL algorithms on the data. To explore, firstly, we can run the audio signal (.wav) to the image converter, wav2image.py (available in Chapter 4, *Audio/Speech/Voice Recognition in IoT* code directory), to see how the spectrum image looks. This will produce images, as shown. The following screenshot shows converted images for an on command:

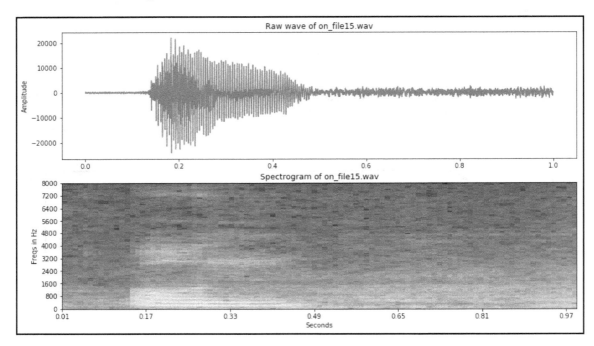

The following screenshot shows converted images for an `off` command. As we can see from the screenshots, their color distributions are different, which will be exploited by the DL algorithms in order to recognize them:

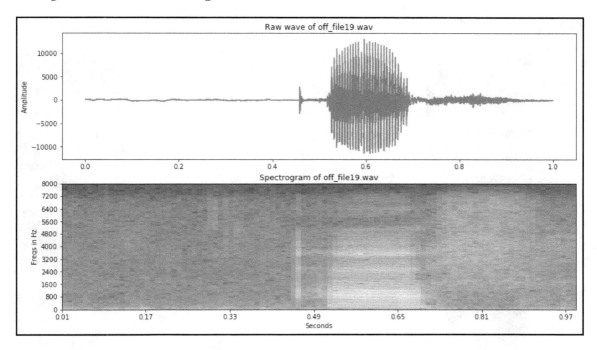

We can also carry out group-wise exploration of data, and for this we can run `image_explorer.py` on the dataset we want to explore, as shown:

```
python image_explorer.py
```

The following screenshot presents a snapshot of the data exploration process of the spectrum image data in the speech commands dataset. Interestingly, the colors of the images are different than the individual images presented earlier. This could be because of the tools we used for them. For the group ones, we used the sox tool; while we used `ffmpegf` for the individual ones:

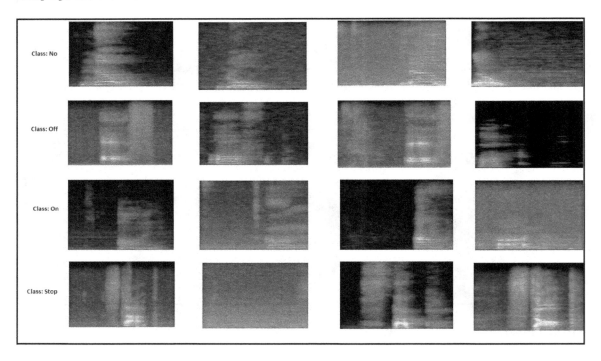

As shown in the preceding screenshot of data exploration, the differences between four different speech commands in spectrum images may not always be significant. This is a challenge in audio signal recognition.

The following screenshot presents a snapshot of the data exploration process of the spectrum image data based on a speaker's/occupant's speech (5-second) dataset:

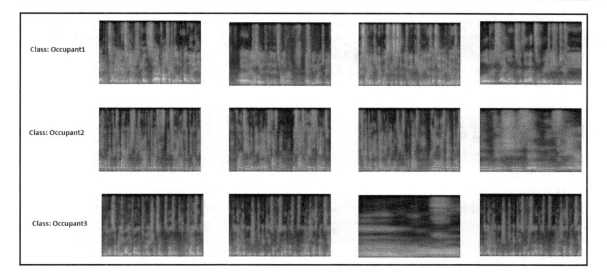

Class: Occupant1
Class: Occupant2
Class: Occupant3

As shown in the preceding screenshot, each occupant's short speech spectrum images present a pattern that will help to classify the occupants and grant access accordingly.

Data preprocessing

Data preprocessing is an essential step for a DL pipeline. The speech commands dataset consists of 1-second .wav files for each short speech command, and these files only need to be converted into a spectrum image. However, the downloaded audio files for the second use case are not uniform in length; hence, they require two-step preprocessing:

- .mp3 to uniform length (such as a 5-second length) WAV file conversion
- .wav file to spectrum image conversion.

The preprocessing of the datasets is discussed in the data collection section. A few issues to be noted during the training image set preparation are as follows:

- **Data Size**: We need to collect at least a hundred images for each class in order to train a model that works well. The more we can gather, the better the accuracy of the trained model is likely to be. Each of the categories in the use case one dataset has more than 3,000 sample images. However, one-shot learning (learning with fewer samples) works well with fewer than 100 training samples. We also made sure that the images are a good representation of what our application will actually face in a real implementation.

- **Data heterogeneity**: Data collected for training should be heterogeneous. For example, audio or speech signals about a speaker need to be taken in as wide a variety of situations as possible, at different conditions of their voice, and with different devices.

Models training

As mentioned earlier, we are using transfer learning for both use cases, which does not require training from scratch; retraining the models with a new dataset will sufficiently work in many cases. In addition, in `Chapter 3`, *Image Recognition in IoT* , we found that Mobilenet V1 is a lightweight (low-memory footprint and lower training time) CNN architecture. Consequently, we are implementing both uses using the Mobilenet V1 network. Importantly, we will use TensorFlow's `retrain.py` module as it is specially designed for CNNs (such as Mobilenet V1) based transfer learning).

We need to understand the list of key arguments of `retrain.py` before retraining Mobilenet V1 on the datasets. For the retraining, if we type in our Terminal (in Linux or macOS) or Command Prompt (Windows) `python retrain.py -h`, we will see a window like the following screenshot with additional information (such as an overview of each argument):

```
usage: retrain.py [-h] [--image_dir IMAGE_DIR] [--output_graph OUTPUT_GRAPH]
                  [--intermediate_output_graphs_dir INTERMEDIATE_OUTPUT_GRAPHS_DIR]
                  [--intermediate_store_frequency INTERMEDIATE_STORE_FREQUENCY]
                  [--output_labels OUTPUT_LABELS]
                  [--summaries_dir SUMMARIES_DIR]
                  [--how_many_training_steps HOW_MANY_TRAINING_STEPS]
                  [--learning_rate LEARNING_RATE]
                  [--testing_percentage TESTING_PERCENTAGE]
                  [--validation_percentage VALIDATION_PERCENTAGE]
                  [--eval_step_interval EVAL_STEP_INTERVAL]
                  [--train_batch_size TRAIN_BATCH_SIZE]
                  [--test_batch_size TEST_BATCH_SIZE]
                  [--validation_batch_size VALIDATION_BATCH_SIZE]
                  [--print_misclassified_test_images] [--model_dir MODEL_DIR]
                  [--bottleneck_dir BOTTLENECK_DIR]
                  [--final_tensor_name FINAL_TENSOR_NAME] [--flip_left_right]
                  [--random_crop RANDOM_CROP] [--random_scale RANDOM_SCALE]
                  [--random_brightness RANDOM_BRIGHTNESS]
                  [--architecture ARCHITECTURE]
```

As shown in the preceding screenshot, the compulsory argument is the `--image directory`, and it needs to be a dataset directory in which we want to train or retrain the models. In the case of Mobilenet V1, we must explicitly mention the CNN architecture, such as `--architecture mobilenet_1.0_224`. For the rest of the arguments, including data split ratio among training, validation, and test, we used the default values. The default split of data is to put 80% of the images into the main training set, keep 10% aside to run frequently as validation during training, and the final 10% of the data is for testing the real-world performance of the classifier.

The following is the command for running the retraining model for the Mobilenet v1 model:

```
python retrain.py \
--output_graph=trained_model_mobilenetv1/retrained_graph.pb \
--output_labels=trained_model_mobilenetv1/retrained_labels.txt   \
--architecture mobilenet_1.0_224 \
--image_dir= your dataset directory
```

Once we run the preceding commands, they will generate the retrain models (`retrained_graph.pb`) and labels text (`retrained_labels.txt`) in the given directory and the summary directory consists of training and validation summary information for the models. The summary information (`--summaries_dir argument with default value retrain_logs`)) can be used by TensorBoard to visualize different aspects of the models, including the networks and their performance graphs. If we type the following command in the Terminal or Command Prompt, it will run `tensorboard`:

```
tensorboard --logdir retrain_logs
```

Once TensorBoard is running, navigate your web browser to `localhost:6006` to view TensorBoard and view the network of the corresponding model. The following diagram presents the network of the Mobilnet V1 used:

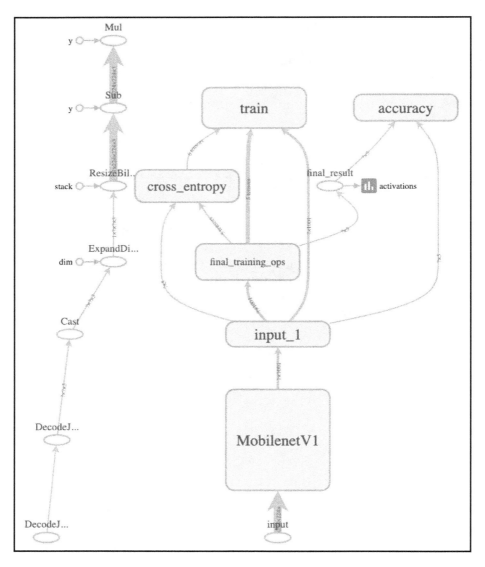

Evaluating models

We can evaluate the models from three different aspects:

- Learning/(re)training time
- Storage requirement
- Performance (accuracy)

The Mobilnet V1's retraining and validation process using the `retrain.py` module took less than an hour on a desktop (Intel Xenon CPU E5-1650 v3@3.5GHz and 32 GB RAM) with GPU support.

The storage/memory requirement of a model is an essential consideration for resource-constrained IoT devices. To evaluate the storage/memory footprint of the Mobilenet V1, we compared its storage requirement to another two similar networks' (the Incentive V3 and CIFAR-10 CNN) storage requirements. The following screenshot presents the storage requirements for the three models. As shown, Mobilenet V1 requires only 17.1 MB, less than one-fifth of the Incentive V3 (87.5 MB) and CIFAR-10 CNN (91.1 MB). In terms of storage requirements, Mobilenet V1 is a better choice for many resource-constrained IoT devices, including the Raspberry Pi and smartphones:

Finally, we have evaluated the performance of the models. Two levels of performance evaluation have been carried out for the use cases:

- Dataset-wide evaluation or testing has been done during the retraining phase on the desktop PC platform/server side
- Individual audio and a group of home occupants, samples were tested or evaluated in the Raspberry Pi 3 environment. All the evaluation performances are presented in the following figures.

Model performance (use case 1)

The following screenshots present the evaluation results of Mobilenet V1 on a speech command dataset (customized to only five commands, including `on`, `no`, `off`, `yes`, and `stop`). Note that `on` is considered to be *switch on the light* for use case one due to the lack of a real dataset:

```
Command Prompt
INFO:tensorflow:2019-05-19 15:11:02.719906: Step 3920: Validation accuracy = 67.0% (N=100)
INFO:tensorflow:2019-05-19 15:11:03.547944: Step 3930: Train accuracy = 69.0%
INFO:tensorflow:2019-05-19 15:11:03.547944: Step 3930: Cross entropy = 1.082193
INFO:tensorflow:2019-05-19 15:11:03.626063: Step 3930: Validation accuracy = 77.0% (N=100)
INFO:tensorflow:2019-05-19 15:11:04.516587: Step 3940: Train accuracy = 84.0%
INFO:tensorflow:2019-05-19 15:11:04.516587: Step 3940: Cross entropy = 0.712184
INFO:tensorflow:2019-05-19 15:11:04.594707: Step 3940: Validation accuracy = 73.0% (N=100)
INFO:tensorflow:2019-05-19 15:11:05.408637: Step 3950: Train accuracy = 85.0%
INFO:tensorflow:2019-05-19 15:11:05.408637: Step 3950: Cross entropy = 0.566925
INFO:tensorflow:2019-05-19 15:11:05.518001: Step 3950: Validation accuracy = 77.0% (N=100)
INFO:tensorflow:2019-05-19 15:11:06.318512: Step 3960: Train accuracy = 78.0%
INFO:tensorflow:2019-05-19 15:11:06.318512: Step 3960: Cross entropy = 0.747383
INFO:tensorflow:2019-05-19 15:11:06.396632: Step 3960: Validation accuracy = 70.0% (N=100)
INFO:tensorflow:2019-05-19 15:11:07.193423: Step 3970: Train accuracy = 79.0%
INFO:tensorflow:2019-05-19 15:11:07.193423: Step 3970: Cross entropy = 0.794154
INFO:tensorflow:2019-05-19 15:11:07.271541: Step 3970: Validation accuracy = 74.0% (N=100)
INFO:tensorflow:2019-05-19 15:11:08.084003: Step 3980: Train accuracy = 68.0%
INFO:tensorflow:2019-05-19 15:11:08.084003: Step 3980: Cross entropy = 1.074563
INFO:tensorflow:2019-05-19 15:11:08.220279: Step 3980: Validation accuracy = 73.0% (N=100)
INFO:tensorflow:2019-05-19 15:11:09.063962: Step 3990: Train accuracy = 71.0%
INFO:tensorflow:2019-05-19 15:11:09.063962: Step 3990: Cross entropy = 0.928895
INFO:tensorflow:2019-05-19 15:11:09.142080: Step 3990: Validation accuracy = 62.0% (N=100)
INFO:tensorflow:2019-05-19 15:11:09.954521: Step 3999: Train accuracy = 77.0%
INFO:tensorflow:2019-05-19 15:11:09.954521: Step 3999: Cross entropy = 0.845275
INFO:tensorflow:2019-05-19 15:11:10.032663: Step 3999: Validation accuracy = 69.0% (N=100)
INFO:tensorflow:Final test accuracy = 72.0% (N=3702)
INFO:tensorflow:Froze 2 variables.
INFO:tensorflow:Converted 2 variables to const ops.

(tf-gpu) C:\Anaconda3\Book-DL-IoT\chapter4\DL-for-Speech&Speaker\use-case-1new>cd ..
```

The following screenshot was generated from the TensorBoard log files. The orange line represents the training and the blue one represents the validation accuracy of the Mobilenet V1 on the command dataset:

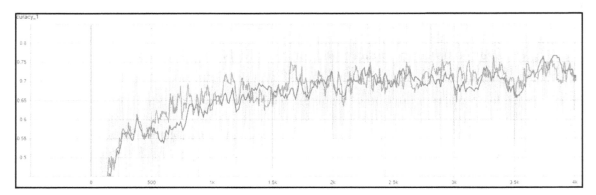

As we can see from the preceding two screenshots, the performance of the Mobilenet V1 is not great, but it will be sufficient for detecting commands by adding more information to the commands, such as *switch on the main light* instead of only *on*. Furthermore, we can use a better audio file to image converter to improve the image quality and recognition accuracy.

Model performance (use case 2)

The following screenshots represents the evaluation results of Mobilenet V1 on a `three occupants` dataset. As we can see, the performance of the dataset is reasonably good. It can successfully detect occupants more than 90% of the time:

```
INFO:tensorflow:2019-05-19 15:37:30.206873: Step 3900: Validation accuracy = 91.0% (N=100)
INFO:tensorflow:2019-05-19 15:37:31.238052: Step 3910: Train accuracy = 100.0%
INFO:tensorflow:2019-05-19 15:37:31.238052: Step 3910: Cross entropy = 0.002250
INFO:tensorflow:2019-05-19 15:37:31.347420: Step 3910: Validation accuracy = 91.0% (N=100)
INFO:tensorflow:2019-05-19 15:37:32.237980: Step 3920: Train accuracy = 100.0%
INFO:tensorflow:2019-05-19 15:37:32.237980: Step 3920: Cross entropy = 0.001900
INFO:tensorflow:2019-05-19 15:37:32.316100: Step 3920: Validation accuracy = 95.0% (N=100)
INFO:tensorflow:2019-05-19 15:37:33.206647: Step 3930: Train accuracy = 100.0%
INFO:tensorflow:2019-05-19 15:37:33.206647: Step 3930: Cross entropy = 0.001575
INFO:tensorflow:2019-05-19 15:37:33.300417: Step 3930: Validation accuracy = 96.0% (N=100)
INFO:tensorflow:2019-05-19 15:37:34.102219: Step 3940: Train accuracy = 100.0%
INFO:tensorflow:2019-05-19 15:37:34.102219: Step 3940: Cross entropy = 0.001931
INFO:tensorflow:2019-05-19 15:37:34.175381: Step 3940: Validation accuracy = 92.0% (N=100)
INFO:tensorflow:2019-05-19 15:37:35.129765: Step 3950: Train accuracy = 100.0%
INFO:tensorflow:2019-05-19 15:37:35.129765: Step 3950: Cross entropy = 0.001272
INFO:tensorflow:2019-05-19 15:37:35.223506: Step 3950: Validation accuracy = 95.0% (N=100)
INFO:tensorflow:2019-05-19 15:37:36.145321: Step 3960: Train accuracy = 100.0%
INFO:tensorflow:2019-05-19 15:37:36.145321: Step 3960: Cross entropy = 0.001753
INFO:tensorflow:2019-05-19 15:37:36.239062: Step 3960: Validation accuracy = 92.0% (N=100)
INFO:tensorflow:2019-05-19 15:37:37.198380: Step 3970: Train accuracy = 100.0%
INFO:tensorflow:2019-05-19 15:37:37.198380: Step 3970: Cross entropy = 0.001600
INFO:tensorflow:2019-05-19 15:37:37.307721: Step 3970: Validation accuracy = 94.0% (N=100)
INFO:tensorflow:2019-05-19 15:37:38.229535: Step 3980: Train accuracy = 100.0%
INFO:tensorflow:2019-05-19 15:37:38.229535: Step 3980: Cross entropy = 0.001917
INFO:tensorflow:2019-05-19 15:37:38.338903: Step 3980: Validation accuracy = 96.0% (N=100)
INFO:tensorflow:2019-05-19 15:37:39.291961: Step 3990: Train accuracy = 100.0%
INFO:tensorflow:2019-05-19 15:37:39.291961: Step 3990: Cross entropy = 0.001936
INFO:tensorflow:2019-05-19 15:37:39.395582: Step 3990: Validation accuracy = 93.0% (N=100)
INFO:tensorflow:2019-05-19 15:37:40.176774: Step 3999: Train accuracy = 100.0%
INFO:tensorflow:2019-05-19 15:37:40.176774: Step 3999: Cross entropy = 0.001790
INFO:tensorflow:2019-05-19 15:37:40.254894: Step 3999: Validation accuracy = 96.0% (N=100)
INFO:tensorflow:Final test accuracy = 87.5% (N=32)
INFO:tensorflow:Froze 2 variables.
INFO:tensorflow:Converted 2 variables to const ops.

(tf-gpu) C:\Anaconda3\Book-DL-IoT\chapter4\DL-for-Speech&Speaker\use-case-2new>
```

The following screenshot was generated from the TensorBoard log files. The orange line represents the training and the blue one represents the validation accuracy of the Mobilenet V1 on the `three occupants` dataset:

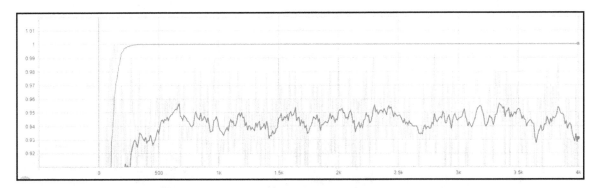

We also tested the Mobilenet V1 on a `five occupants` dataset, and this consistently showed accuracy in the range of 85-94%. Finally, we can export the trained model detail (such as `retrained_mobilenet_graph.pb` and `retrained_labels.txt`) to an IoT device, including a smartphone or Raspberry Pi, and we can test the model on new data from both use cases using the provided `label_image.py` code or something similar.

Summary

Automatic audio/speech/voice recognition is becoming a popular means for people to interact with their devices, including smartphones, wearables, and other smart devices. Machine learning and DL algorithms are essential in audio/speech/voice-based decision making.

In the first part of this chapter, we briefly described different IoT applications and their audio/speech/voice detection-based decision making. We also briefly discussed two potential use cases of IoT where DL algorithms can be useful in speech/command-based decision making. The first use case considered an IoT application to make a home smart using voice-controlled lighting. The second use case also made a home or office smart, where a DL-based IoT solution offered automated access control to the smart home or office. In the second part of the chapter, we briefly discussed the data collection process for the use cases, and discussed the rationale behind selecting a CNN, especially the Mobilenet V1. The rest of the sections of the chapter describe all the necessary components of the DL pipeline for these models and their results.

Many IoT devices and/or users are mobile. Localization of the devices and users is essential for offering them services when they are on the move. GPS can support outdoor localization, but it does not work in indoor environments. Consequently, alternative technologies are necessary for indoor localization. Different indoor technologies, including WiFi-fingerprinting, are available, and generally they work based on a device's communication signal analysis. In the next chapter (`Chapter 5`, *Indoor Localization in IoT*), we will discuss and demonstrate how DL models can be used for indoor localization in IoT applications.

References

- Assistive technology: `http://www.who.int/en/news-room/fact-sheets/detail/assistive-technology`
- *Smart and Robust Speaker Recognition for Context-Aware In-Vehicle Applications*, I Bisio, C Garibotto, A Grattarola, F Lavagetto, and A Sciarrone, in IEEE Transactions on Vehicular Technology, vol. 67, no. 9, pp. 8,808-8,821, September, 2018.
- *Emotion-Aware Connected Healthcare Big Data Towards 5G*, M S Hossain and G Muhammad, in IEEE Internet of Things Journal, vol. 5, no. 4, pp. 2,399-2,406, August, 2018.
- *Machine Learning Paradigms for Speech Recognition*, L Deng, X Li (2013). IEEE Transactions on Audio, Speech, and Language Processing, vol. 2, # 5.
- *On Comparison of Deep Learning Architectures for Distant Speech Recognition*, R Sustika, A R Yuliani, E Zaenudin, and H F Pardede, *2017 Second International Conferences on Information Technology, Information Systems and Electrical Engineering (ICITISEE)*, Yogyakarta, 2017, pp. 17-21.
- *Deep Neural Networks for Acoustic Modeling in Speech Recognition*, G Hinton, L Deng, D Yu, G E Dahl, A R Mohamed, N Jaitly, A Senior, V Vanhoucke, P Nguyen, T N Sainath, and B Kingsbury, IEEE Signal Processing Magazine, vol. 29, # 6, pp. 82–97, 2012.
- *Long Short-Term Memory Recurrent Neural Network Architectures for Large Scale Acoustic Modeling*, H Sak, A Senior, and F Beaufays, in Fifteenth Annual Conference of the International Speech Communication Association, 2014.

- *Phoneme recognition using time delay neural network*, IEEE Transaction on Acoustics, Speech, and Signal Processing, G. H. K. S. K. J. L. Alexander Waibel, Toshiyuki Hanazawa, vol. 37, # 3, 1989.

- *A Time Delay Neural Network Architecture for Efficient Modeling of Long Temporal Contexts*, V Peddinti, D Povey, and S Khudanpur, in Proceedings of Interspeech. ISCA, 2005.

- *Deep Convolutional Neural Network for lvcsr*, B. K. B. R. Tara N Sainath and Abdel Rahman Mohamed, in International Conference on Acoustics, Speech and Signal Processing. IEEE, 2013, pp. 8614–8618.

- *Mel Frequency Cepstral Coefficients for Music Modeling*, Logan, Beth and others, ISMIR,vol. 270, 2000.

- *Launching the Speech Commands Dataset*, Pete Warden: https://ai.googleblog.com/2017/08/launching-speech-commands-dataset.html.

Indoor Localization in IoT

5

Many IoT applications, such as indoor navigation and location-aware marketing by retailers, smart homes, smart campuses, and hospitals, rely on indoor localization. The input data generated from such applications generally comes from numerous sources such as infrared, ultrasound, Wi-Fi, RFID, ultrawideband, Bluetooth, and so on.

The communication fingerprint of those devices and technologies, such as Wi-Fi fingerprinting data, can be analyzed using DL models to predict the location of the device or user in indoor environments. In this chapter, we will discuss how DL techniques can be used for indoor localization in IoT applications in general with a hands-on example. Furthermore, we will discuss some deployment settings for indoor localization services in IoT environments. The following topics will be briefly covered in this chapter:

- Introducing indoor localization in IoT applications
- **Deep learning** (**DL**) for indoor localization in IoT applications
- Example – indoor localization in Wi-Fi fingerprinting
- Different deployment options for DL-based indoor localization

An overview of indoor localization

With the rapid development of mobile internet, **Location-Based Services** (**LBS**) in large public indoor places is becoming increasingly popular. In such an indoor location, the **Received Signal Strength Indicator** (**RSSI**) is often used as an estimated measure of the power level that an IoT device is receiving from **Wireless Access Points** (**WAPs**). However, when the distance from the source is increased, the signal gets weaker and the wireless data rates get slower, leading to a lower overall data throughput.

Techniques for indoor localization

Several indoor localization technologies have been proposed to date based on measuring techniques such as ultrasound, infrared, image, light, magnetic field, and wireless signals. For example, **Bluetooth low energy** (**BLE**)-based indoor localization has been attracting increasing interest because it is low-cost, low-power consumption, and has ubiquitous availability on almost every mobile device. On the other hand, the Wi-Fi localization system is based on the **Channel State Information** (**CSI**) of Wi-Fi signals.

Lately, DL approaches have been proposed in which DL models are used to learn the fingerprint patterns of high-dimensional CSI signals. Although, each Wi-Fi scan contains the signal strength measurements for APs available in its vicinity, only a subset of a total number of networks in the environment are observed.

Also, since those devices are low-end with very small processing power, the unpredictable weakening or strengthening combination used in those approaches affect the multi-path signals, which will break the relationship between the RSSI and the transmission distance, and consequently prove to be less effective. On the other hand, the fingerprinting approach doesn't rely on the recovery of distances but instead uses the measured RSSIs as spatial patterns only. It is thus less vulnerable to the multi-path effect.

Fingerprinting

The fingerprinting approaches used commonly have two phases: an offline phase and an online phase.

One phase uses a fingerprint database to construct position-dependent parameters, which are extracted from measured RSSIs' reference locations, known as **offline phases**. In a localization phase, which is also known as an **online phase**, the mapping of RSSI measurements is done to a reference location using the most relevant RSSI fingerprint from the database, which can be explained as follows:

$$\Omega = \{(\mathbf{f}_1, \mathbf{p}_1), (\mathbf{f}_2, \mathbf{p}_2), \ldots, (\mathbf{f}_N, \mathbf{p}_N)\}$$

In the preceding equation, N is the total number of reference locations in the database, f_i denotes the fingerprint pattern of the ith reference location, and p_i is the spatial coordinates of that reference location. The fingerprint pattern, f, can be raw RSSI values from multiple beacon stations, or any other feature vectors extracted from the RSSIs, which can be expressed as follows:

$$\mathbf{f} = [r_1, r_2, \ldots, r_m]$$

However, the raw RSSI values are used as spatial patterns in existing fingerprinting systems. In the preceding equation, m is the total number of BLE beacon stations or Wi-Fi APs, and r_i represents the measured RSSI value of the ith station.

Now, we roughly know what indoor localization is. In the next section, we'll see how machine learning and DL algorithms can be used to develop such an indoor localization system.

DL-based indoor localization for IoT

Now, if we want to develop a DL application and deploy low-end devices, such IoT devices won't be able to process them. In particular, handling very high-dimensional data would be a bottleneck. So, an outdoor localization problem can be solved with reasonable accuracy using a machine learning algorithm such as **k-nearest neighbors** (**k-NNs**) because the inclusion of GPS sensors in mobile devices means we now have more data at hand.

However, indoor localization is still an open research problem, mainly due to the loss of GPS signals in indoor environments, despite advanced indoor positioning technologies. Fortunately, by using DL techniques, we can solve this problem with reasonable accuracy, especially since using **Autoencoders** (**AEs**) and their representation capabilities can be a pretty good workaround and a viable option. In such a setting, we have two options:

1. Add a fully connected layer and a softmax layer in front of the AE network, which will act as an end-to-end classifier.

2. Use any other classification algorithms, such as logistic regression, k-NN, Random Forest, or a support vector machine for the location estimation (that is, classification), as shown in the following diagram:

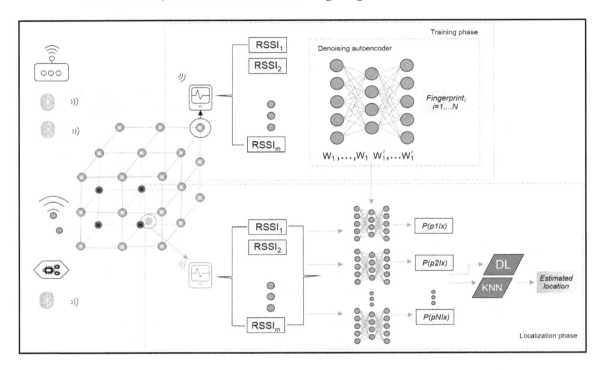

The idea is to use AEs for the representation learning so that the network can learn the features well. Then, the output of the encoder part can be used to initialize the weight of the classifier part. In the following section, we will discuss k-NN and AEs and see how they can be used to solve the indoor localization problem.

K-nearest neighbor (k-NN) classifier

The k-NN algorithm is a non-parametric method that can be trained using the fingerprinting data coming from IoT devices. This tries to classify the collected RSSI values from the gateways to one of the reference points and not to the coordinates. The input consists of the k-closest RSSI values and the output would be a class membership. An input sample is then classified by a plurality vote of its neighbors, with the object being assigned to the class most common among its k-nearest neighbors.

Technically, if the fingerprinting database consists of (X, y)—with X being the RSSI values and y being the set of already known locations—then k-NN first computes the distance $d_i = d(X_i, x)$, where x is the unknown sample. Then, it computes a set, I, containing indices for the k smallest distances from d_i. Then, the majority label for Y_i is returned, where $i \in I$. In other words, using k-NN, the classification is performed by computing the similarity between the observed data and records in the training RSSI samples in the database. Ultimately, the grid cell with the highest occurrence in the first k most similar records is the estimated location, as shown in the following diagram:

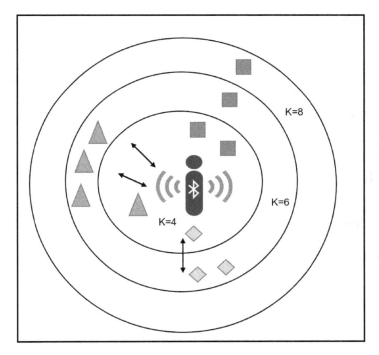

Localization of IoT enabled devices using k-NN algorithm

In the preceding diagram, for k=4, the Wi-Fi packet trace is classified as being in the grid c (green triangles) record, while it is classified as being in grid a (red rectangle) when k=6. So, k-NN can be thought of as a lazy learning approach, where the function is only approximated locally and all computation is deferred until classification occurs. The good thing about the k-NN algorithm is that it is robust against noisy data. In particular, the inverse square of the weighted distance is used as the distance measure. Nevertheless, it performs well if it's already trained on a large amount of training data.

There are possible drawbacks as well. For example, we need to determine the K parameter value, which is the number of nearest neighbors. It performs quite differently based on the distance measure used. The computation cost using the k-NN algorithm is quite high since it is required to compute the distance of each sample in the training data. This becomes even worse in the case of very high-dimensional data. In the next section, we will use k-NN as an end-to-end classifier rather than using a neural network setting to provide a comparative analysis between an AE-based classifier and k-NN classifiers.

AE classifier

As described in `Chapter 2`, *Deep Learning Architectures for IoT*, AEs are special types of neural networks that learn automatically from the input data. AEs consists of two components: an encoder and a decoder. An encoder compresses the input into a latent-space representation. Then, the decoder part, tries to reconstruct the original input data from that representation:

- **Encoder**: Encodes or compresses the input into a latent-space representation using a function known as $h = f(x)$
- **Decoder**: Decodes or reconstructs the input from the latent space representation using a function known as $r = g(h)$

So, an AE can be described by a function of $g(f(x)) = o$, where we want 0 to be as close as the original input of x. AEs are very useful for data denoising and dimensionality reduction for data visualization. AEs can learn data projections, called **representations**, more effectively than PCA. The following diagram shows the architecture of a denoising AE:

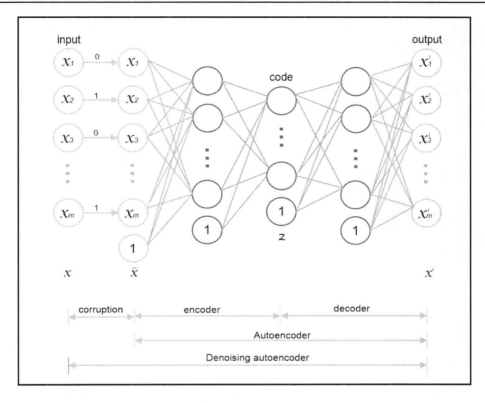

So, once we have a fingerprinting database to hand, AEs can be trained with the raw RSSI measurements and the trained network itself is used as the fingerprint pattern for a specific reference location. Since a deep network can be represented by the weight of each layer, the fingerprint pattern can be expressed as follows:

$$\mathbf{f} = \left[w_1, w_2, \ldots, w_l, w'_1, w'_2, \ldots, w'_l \right]$$

In the preceding equation, l is the number of encoding hidden layers of an AE, and w_i and $w\bar{i}$ represent the weights of the ith encoding hidden layer and its decoding mirror layer, as shown in the following diagram:

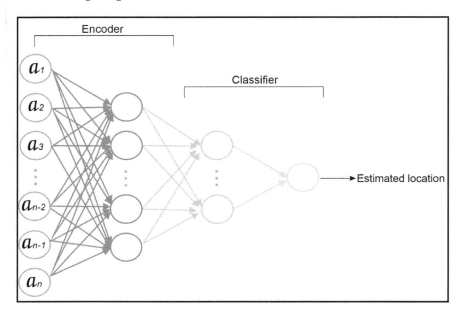

Then, we can use the output of the central hidden layers of the AE as the input to the fully connected softmax layer to predict the location, as shown in the preceding diagram. Now that we know how indoor localization works in a neural network or machine learning setting, we can now start a hands-on example using Wi-Fi fingerprinting.

Example – Indoor localization with Wi-Fi fingerprinting

In this example, we will use a **multi-building, multi-floor indoor localization** database and stacked AEs to localize Wi-Fi fingerprinting. With some minimal effort, this application can be deployed to mobile robots to use Wi-Fi localization subsystems.

Describing the dataset

The `UJIIndoorLoc` dataset is a multi-building, multi-floor indoor localization database designed to test an indoor positioning system relying on Wi-Fi fingerprinting. Automatic user localization consists of estimating the position of the user, such as the latitude, longitude, and altitude, collected from a mobile phone. The `UJIIndoorLoc` database covers three buildings of Universitat Jaume I with 4 or more floors and almost 110,000 square meters, measured in 2013 by means of more than 20 different users and 25 Android devices. The database consists of two CSV files:

- `trainingData.csv`: 19,937 training/reference records
- `validationData.csv`: 1,111 validation/test records

The 529 attributes contain Wi-Fi fingerprints and the coordinates where they were taken. Each Wi-Fi fingerprint can be characterized by the detected WAPs and the corresponding RSSI. The intensity values are represented as negative integer values ranging from 1,04 dBm (extremely poor signal) to 0 dBm. The positive 100 value is used to denote when a WAP was not detected. During the database creation, 520 different WAPs were detected. Thus, the Wi-Fi fingerprint is composed of 520 intensity values. The coordinates' latitude, longitude, floor, and **BuildingID** information are the attributes to be predicted. The following list gives a quick summary of the dataset:

- **Attribute 001 to 520 (that is, WAP001 to WAP520)**: These are the intensity measurement values for the access points in which values are in—104 to 0 and +100. The 100 value signifies that WAP001 was not detected.
- **Attribute 521 (Longitude)**: Negative real values from 7,695.9,387,549,299,299,000 to -7299.786516730871000
- **Attribute 522 (Latitude)**: Positive real values from 4,864,745.7,450,159,714 to 4,865,017.3,646,842,018.
- **Attribute 523 (Floor)**: Altitude in floors inside the building. Integer values from 0 to 4.
- **Attribute 524 (BuildingID)**: ID to identify the building provided as categorical integer values from 0 to 2.
- **Attribute 525 (SpaceID)**: Internal ID number to identify the space, such as the office, the corridor, or the classroom.
- **Attribute 526 (RelativePosition)**: Relative position with respect to the space (1—inside, 2—outside, in front of the door).
- **Attribute 527 (UserID)**: User identifier.
- **Attribute 528 (PhoneID)**: Android device identifier (see the following).
- **Attribute 529 (Timestamp)**: UNIX time when the capture was taken.

Network construction

The AE classifier we will be using will have an AE part consisting of an encoder and a decoder. The following AE architecture is used to determine the floor and building location where the Wi-Fi is located. The input to the AE are signal strengths detected in a scan. Then, one value for each visible network is considered an RSSI record. The output of a decoder is the reconstructed input from the reduced representation, as shown in the following diagram (source: *Low-effort place recognition with Wi-Fi fingerprints using deep learning*, Michał N. et al., arXiv:1611.02049v1):

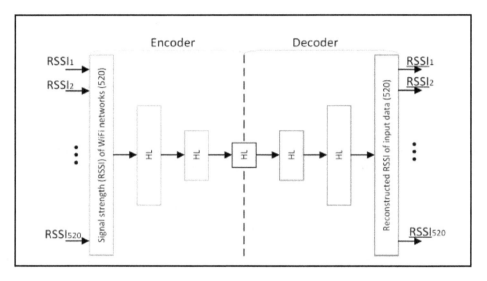

The AE architecture for the feature space representation

The classifier part consists of two hidden layers; depending on the complexity of the problem, the number of neurons needs to be selected. When the unsupervised learning of the weights of AE is finished, the decoder part of the network is disconnected. Then fully-connected layers are typically placed after the output of the encoder by turning the whole network into a classifier. In the following diagram, the pre-trained encoder part is connected to the fully connected softmax layer (source: *Low-effort Place Recognition with Wi-Fi Fingerprints Using Deep Learning*, Michał N. et al., arXiv:1611.02049v1):

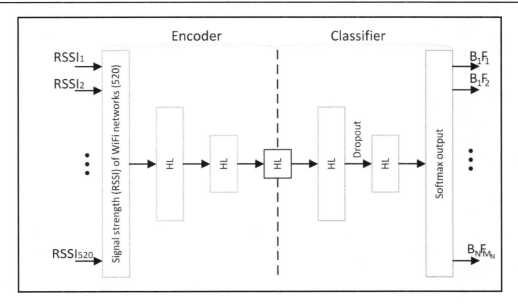

The architecture of an AE classifier for classifying a building and its floor based on Wi-Fi scan input

The final output layer is a softmax layer that outputs the probabilities of the current sample belonging to the analyzed classes. Now, without any further delay, let's start implementing the preceding networks.

Implementation

We will use Keras to wrap up this conceptualization. First, let's import the necessary packages and libraries, as follows:

```
import pandas as pd
import numpy as np
import tensorflow as tf
from sklearn.preprocessing import scale
from keras.models import Sequential
from keras.layers import Input, Dense, Flatten, Dropout, Embedding,
BatchNormalization
from keras.layers.convolutional import Conv1D,MaxPooling1D
from keras.layers import LSTM
from keras.layers.merge import concatenate
from keras.layers import GaussianNoise
from pickle import load
from keras import optimizers
from sklearn.metrics import classification_report
```

```
from sklearn.metrics import confusion_matrix
from sklearn.metrics import precision_recall_curve
from sklearn.metrics import precision_recall_fscore_support
import pandas_profiling
```

Once we have imported all the necessary packages, we can proceed to prepare the training set and test set, which can be used to train and evaluate the model, respectively.

Exploratory analysis

The exploratory analysis of data using the **Python pandas** library provides many powerful features–no doubt. However, using df.describe(), df.dtypes, or using df.isnull().sum() and plotting them separately is always time-consuming. Sometimes, you won't even get the required information in a sophisticated way. In fact, you'll have to write extra lines of code to convert them into a presentable format. However, to make your life easier, you can now start using the pandas_profiling library (see https://github. com/pandas-profiling/pandas-profiling). Just one line of code will give the information you need:

```
pandas_profiling.ProfileReport(df)
```

Surely, it would be worth using pandas_profiling to get a quick understanding of your data. Let's try it out! First, we read the training data by explicitly passing header=0 to be able to replace the existing names:

```
trainDF = pd.read_csv("trainingData.csv",header = 0)
```

To retrieve the list of variables that are rejected due to high correlation, you can use the following command:

```
profile = pandas_profiling.ProfileReport(trainDF)
```

This will produce a report showing information on the dataset:

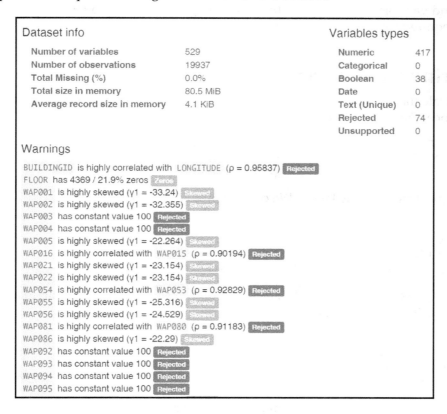

Let's look at the first few lines of the report. As we can see, we don't have any null values and all the variables are numeric, which is great. However, some features are less significant, being highly correlated with other variables (for example, 74 variables were rejected) and some of the variables are very skewed, giving a very wide distribution. Even our training dataset has 637 duplicate rows. Rejected variables would not help the model learn well. Consequently, those can be dropped from the training data (this is optional, though). The list of such rejected variables can be collected using the `get_rejected_variables` method, as follows:

```
rejected_variables = profile.get_rejected_variables(threshold=0.9)
```

If you want to generate a HTML report file, save the profile to an object and use the `to_file` function as follows:

```
profile.to_file(outputfile="Report.html")
```

This will generate an HTML report containing the necessary information. Now that we know the data and variables, let's focus on the feature engineering steps by which we'll prepare the data required for training and testing.

Preparing training and test sets

First, we scale the data to center to the mean. Then, we perform component-wise scaling to unit variance. This will help our model to converge the training more quickly:

```
featureDF = np.asarray(trainDF.iloc[:,0:520]) # First 520 features
featureDF[featureDF == 100] = -110
featureDF = (featureDF - featureDF.mean()) / featureDF.var()
```

Then, we construct the true labels. We convert all the building IDs and building floors to strings:

```
labelDF = np.asarray(trainDF["BUILDINGID"].map(str) +
trainDF["FLOOR"].map(str))
labelDF = np.asarray(pd.get_dummies(labelDF))
```

Then, let's try to create two variables: `train_x` and `train_y`. This will help to avoid confusion during the training evaluation:

```
train_x = featureDF
train_y = labelDF
print(train_x.shape)
print(train_x.shape[1])
```

Now, similar to the training set, we prepare the test set as well:

```
testDF = pd.read_csv("validationData.csv",header = 0)
test_featureDF = np.asarray(testDF.iloc[:,0:520])
test_featureDF[test_featureDF == 100] = -110
test_x = (test_featureDF - test_featureDF.mean()) / test_featureDF.var()
test_labelDF = np.asarray(testDF["BUILDINGID"].map(str) +
testDF["FLOOR"].map(str))
test_y = np.asarray(pd.get_dummies(test_labelDF))
print(test_x.shape)
print(test_y.shape[1])
```

Once we have the training and the test sets ready, we can now proceed with creating an AE.

Creating an AE

Let's create separate encoder and decoder functions since you will be using encoder weights later on for classification purposes. First, we define some parameters, such as the number of epochs and the batch size. Also, we compute the shape of the input data and the number of classes that will be required to construct and train the AE:

```
number_epochs = 100
batch_size = 32
input_size = train_x.shape[1] # 520
num_classes = train_y.shape[1] # 13
```

Then, we create the encoder part of the AE, which has three hidden layers:

```
def encoder():
    model = Sequential()
    model.add(Dense(256, input_dim=input_size, activation='relu',
use_bias=True))
    model.add(Dense(128, activation='relu', use_bias=True))
    model.add(Dense(64, activation='relu', use_bias=True))
    return model
```

Next, we create the decoder part of the AE, which has three hidden layers, followed by the `compile()` method:

```
def decoder(encoder):
    encoder.add(Dense(128, input_dim=64, activation='relu', use_bias=True))
    encoder.add(Dense(256, activation='relu', use_bias=True))
    encoder.add(Dense(input_size, activation='relu', use_bias=True))
    encoder.compile(optimizer='adam', loss='mse')
    return encoder
```

Then, we stack them together to construct an AE:

```
encoderModel = encoder() # Encoder
auto_encoder = decoder(encoderModel) # The autoencoder
auto_encoder.summary()
```

Let's see the structure and a summary of the AE:

```
Layer (type)                    Output Shape              Param #
=================================================================
dense_28 (Dense)                (None, 256)               133376
_____
dense_29 (Dense)                (None, 128)               32896
_____
dense_30 (Dense)                (None, 64)                8256
_____
dense_31 (Dense)                (None, 128)               8320
_____
dense_32 (Dense)                (None, 256)               33024
_____
dense_33 (Dense)                (None, 520)               133640
=================================================================
Total params: 349,512
Trainable params: 349,512
Non-trainable params: 0
```

We can then train the AE with the training data for 100 iterations, where 10% of the training data is to be used for validation:

```
auto_encoder.fit(train_x, train_x, epochs = 100, batch_size = batch_size,
                 validation_split=0.1, verbose = 1)
```

Since we set the `verbose` =1 in the preceding code block, during training, you'll see the following logs:

```
Train on 17943 samples, validate on 1994 samples
Epoch 1/100
17943/17943 [==============================] - 5s 269us/step - loss: 0.0109
- val_loss: 0.0071
Epoch 2/100
17943/17943 [==============================] - 4s 204us/step - loss: 0.0085
- val_loss: 0.0066
Epoch 3/100
17943/17943 [==============================] - 3s 185us/step - loss: 0.0081
- val_loss: 0.0062
Epoch 4/100
17943/17943 [==============================] - 4s 200us/step - loss: 0.0077
- val_loss: 0.0062
Epoch 98/100
17943/17943 [==============================] - 6s 360us/step - loss: 0.0067
- val_loss: 0.0055
.......
```

```
Epoch 99/100
17943/17943 [==============================] - 5s 271us/step - loss: 0.0067
- val_loss: 0.0055
Epoch 100/100
17943/17943 [==============================] - 7s 375us/step - loss: 0.0067
- val_loss: 0.0055
```

Then, we take the output of the encoder network for both the training set and the test set as the latent features:

```
X_train_re = encoderModel.predict(train_x)
X_test_re = encoderModel.predict(test_x)
```

Creating an AE classifier

Next, we will re-train the `auto_encoder` model by making the first three layers trainable as `True` instead of keeping them as `False`:

```
for layer in auto_encoder.layers[0:3]:
    layer.trainable = True
```

Alternatively, we can pop off the first three layers as follows:

```
for i in range(number_of_layers_to_remove):
    auto_encoder.pop()
```

Then, we add fully connected layers in front, with the `BatchNormalization` layer is followed by the first dense layer. Then, we add another dense layer, followed by the `BatchNormalization` and `Dropout` layers. Then, we place another dense layer, followed by a `GaussionNoise` layer and a `Dropout` layer, before we finally have the softmax layer:

```
auto_encoder.add(Dense(128, input_dim=64, activation='relu',
use_bias=True))
auto_encoder.add(BatchNormalization())
auto_encoder.add(Dense(64, activation='relu', kernel_initializer =
'he_normal', use_bias=True))
auto_encoder.add(BatchNormalization())
auto_encoder.add(Dropout(0.2))
auto_encoder.add(Dense(32, activation='relu', kernel_initializer =
'he_normal', use_bias=True))
auto_encoder.add(GaussianNoise(0.1))
auto_encoder.add(Dropout(0.1))
auto_encoder.add(Dense(num_classes, activation = 'softmax', use_bias=True))
```

Finally, we get the full AE classifier:

```
full_model = autoEncoderClassifier(auto_encoder)
```

The full code is given as follows:

```
def autoEncoderClassifier(auto_encoder):
    for layer in auto_encoder.layers[0:3]:
        layer.trainable = True

    auto_encoder.add(Dense(128, input_dim=64, activation='relu',
use_bias=True))
    auto_encoder.add(BatchNormalization())
    auto_encoder.add(Dense(64, activation='relu', kernel_initializer =
'he_normal', use_bias=True))
    auto_encoder.add(BatchNormalization())
    auto_encoder.add(Dropout(0.2))
    auto_encoder.add(Dense(32, activation='relu', kernel_initializer =
'he_normal', use_bias=True))
    auto_encoder.add(GaussianNoise(0.1))
    auto_encoder.add(Dropout(0.1))
    auto_encoder.add(Dense(num_classes, activation = 'softmax',
use_bias=True))
    return auto_encoder

full_model = autoEncoderClassifier(auto_encoder)
```

Then, we compile the model before starting the training:

```
full_model.compile(loss = 'categorical_crossentropy', optimizer =
optimizers.adam(lr = 0.001), metrics = ['accuracy'])
```

Now, we start fine-tuning the network in a supervised way:

```
history = full_model.fit(X_train_re, train_y, epochs = 50, batch_size =
200, validation_split = 0.2, verbose = 1)
```

Since we set `verbose` =1 in the preceding code block, during training, you'll experience the following logs:

```
Train on 15949 samples, validate on 3988 samples
Epoch 1/50
15949/15949 [==============================] - 10s 651us/step - loss:
0.9263 - acc: 0.7086 - val_loss: 1.4313 - val_acc: 0.5747
Epoch 2/50
15949/15949 [==============================] - 5s 289us/step - loss: 0.6103
- acc: 0.7749 - val_loss: 1.2776 - val_acc: 0.5619
Epoch 3/50
```

```
15949/15949 [==============================] - 5s 292us/step - loss: 0.5499
- acc: 0.7942 - val_loss: 1.3871 - val_acc: 0.5364
.......
Epoch 49/50
15949/15949 [==============================] - 5s 342us/step - loss: 1.3861
- acc: 0.4662 - val_loss: 1.8799 - val_acc: 0.2706
Epoch 50/50
15949/15949 [==============================] - 5s 308us/step - loss: 1.3735
- acc: 0.4805 - val_loss: 2.1081 - val_acc: 0.2199
```

Now let's take a look at the training loss versus validation loss, which will help us to understand how the training went. This will also help us to establish whether our neural network has issues such as overfitting and underfitting:

```
import pandas as pd
import numpy as np
import matplotlib.pyplot as plt
%matplotlib inline

plt.plot(history.history['acc'])
plt.plot(history.history['val_acc'])
plt.ylabel('Accuracy')
plt.xlabel('Epochs')
plt.legend(['Training loss', 'Validation loss'], loc='upper left')
plt.show()
```

The preceding code block will plot the training loss and validation losses:

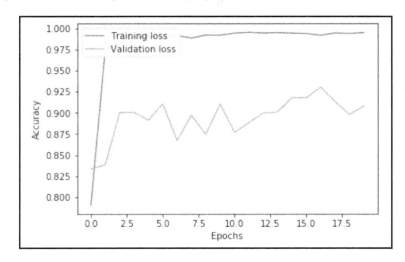

As seen in the preceding graph, the training losses across epochs are higher than the validation loss, which is a sign of overfitting. We don't have enough training samples to train the neural network well. Some samples were even repeated in the dataset, which literally turned out to be trivial and redundant in the network. This was probably the reason adding the **Dropout** and **Gaussian** noise layers didn't help much. Anyway, we can also save the trained model for future reuse, which we'll discuss in the next section.

Saving the trained model

Now that we have the AE classifier fully trained, we can save it so that we can restore it from disk later on:

```
import os
from pickle import load
from keras.models import load_model
os.environ["PATH"] += os.pathsep + 'C:/Program Files
(x86)/Graphviz2.38/bin/'
from keras.utils.vis_utils import plot_model

plot_model(full_model, show_shapes=True, to_file='Localization.png')
# save the model
full_model.save('model.h5')
# load the model
model = load_model('model.h5')
```

In the next section, we will evaluate the trained model on the test set, which we will discuss in the next subsection.

Evaluating the model

Now that our model is fully trained, we can evaluate its performance on unseen data:

```
results = full_model.evaluate(X_test_re, test_y)
print('Test accuracy: ', results[1])
```

The preceding lines of code will show the accuracy score, something like this:

```
1111/1111 [==============================] - 0s 142us/step
Test accuracy: 0.8874887488748875
```

Then, let's compute the performance metrics:

```
predicted_classes = full_model.predict(test_x)
pred_y = np.argmax(np.round(predicted_classes),axis=1)
y = np.argmax(np.round(test_y),axis=1)
p, r, f1, s = precision_recall_fscore_support(y, pred_y,
average='weighted')
print("Precision: " + str(p*100) + "%")
print("Recall: " + str(r*100) + "%")
print("F1-score: " + str(f1*100) + "%")
```

The preceding code block will show the following output, giving an F1-score of 88%, approximately:

```
Precision: 90.29611866225324%
Recall: 88.11881188118812%
F1-score: 88.17976604784566%
```

Additionally, we can print the classification report to know the class-specific localization as well:

```
print(classification_report(y, pred_y))
```

The preceding line of code will produce the following output:

	precision	recall	f1-score	support
0	0.87	0.95	0.91	78
1	0.95	0.98	0.96	208
2	0.93	0.95	0.94	165
3	0.99	0.89	0.94	85
4	0.78	0.70	0.74	30
5	0.94	0.67	0.78	143
6	0.57	0.94	0.71	87
7	1.00	0.55	0.71	47
8	0.95	0.83	0.89	24
9	0.96	0.97	0.96	111
10	0.96	0.87	0.91	54
11	0.75	0.95	0.84	40
12	0.89	0.79	0.84	39
avg / total	0.90	0.88	0.88	1111

Additionally, we will plot the confusion matrix:

```
print(confusion_matrix(y, pred_y))
```

The preceding line of code will produce the following confusion matrix:

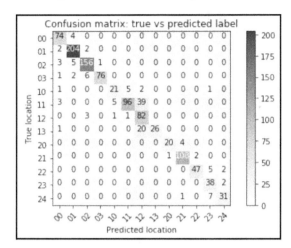

As seen in the preceding confusion matrix, our AE classifier was mostly confused for class 11 and predicted as many as 39 samples to be classified in grid 12. However, we have still managed to get very good accuracy. Possible suggestions for improvements could be as follows:

- Training the network after removing the rejected variables
- Training the network on more epochs
- Performing hyperparameter tuning using grid search and cross-validation
- Adding more layers to the network

Once you find the optimized model trained on more data, giving stable, improved performance, it can be deployed in on IoT enabled device. We will discuss some possible deployment options in the next section.

Deployment techniques

As we argued earlier, each Wi-Fi scan contains the signal strength measurements for APs available in its vicinity, but only a subset of the total number of networks in the environment are observed. Many IoT devices, such as a mobile phone or a Raspberry Pi, are low-end with very little processing power. So, deploying such a DL model would be a challenging task.

Many solution providers and technology companies provide smart positioning services commercially. Using Wi-Fi fingerprinting from indoor and outdoor location data, the accurate tracking of devices is now possible. In most of these companies, the RSSI fingerprint positioning is used as the core technology. In such a setting, signals or messages that bear different sensitivity levels across RSSI values (which is of course subject to the proximity) can be picked up by gateways. Then, if there are n gateways in a network, the RSSI values acquired from a particular indoor or outdoor location will form the RSSI fingerprint having n entries at that location, which is as follows:

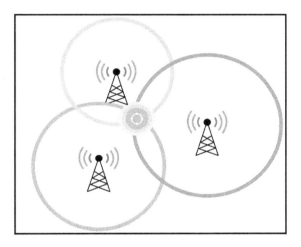

The preceding diagram corresponds to the following equation:

$$F_{RSSI} = (RSSI_1, RSSI_2, RSSI_3, \ldots . RSSI_n)$$

However, in cases with a large number of gateways (> 4), the fingerprint could be distinctly unique within a certain range. One deployment technique could be using the trained model serving at the backend and serving it as an Android or iOS mobile application. The application then monitors the signals from the IoT devices already deployed in the indoor location, inserts them as RSSI values in the SQLite database and, based on the RSSI values, prepares the test set and sends a query to the pre-trained model to get the location.

The following diagram shows a schematic architecture outlining all the steps required for such a deployment:

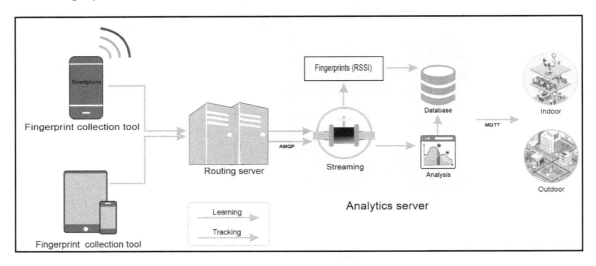

In such a case, the trained model will serve as the transfer learning. Nevertheless, the trained model can be served as a web application using Flask or the DJango Python framework. Then, the RSSI values and signals from the IoT devices can be stored in a database to enrich the historical data. The location can subsequently be tracked using an Android or iOS application.

Summary

In this chapter, we have discussed how indoor localization works for IoT enabled devices. In particular, we have seen how DL techniques can be used for indoor localization in IoT applications employing that data in general with a hands-on example. Furthermore, we have looked at some deployment settings of indoor localization services in IoT environments.

In Chapter 6, *Physiological and Psychological State Detection in IoT*, we will discuss DL-based human physiological and psychological state detection techniques for IoT applications in general. Considering a real-world scenario, we will look at two IoT applications based on physiological and psychological state detection.

6
Physiological and Psychological State Detection in IoT

Human physiological and psychological states can provide very useful information about a person's activity and emotions. This information can be used in many application domains, including smart homes, smart cars, entertainment, education, rehabilitation and health support, sports, and industrial manufacturing, to improve existing services and/or offer new services. Many IoT applications incorporate sensors and processors for human pose estimation or activity and emotion recognition. However, the detection of activities or emotions based on the sensor data is a challenging task. In recent years, DL-based approaches have become a popular and effective way to address this challenge.

This chapter presents DL-based human physiological and psychological state detection techniques for IoT applications in general. The first part of this chapter will briefly describe different IoT applications and their physiological and psychological state detection-based decision making. In addition, it will briefly discuss two IoT applications and their physiological and psychological state detection-based implementations in a real-world scenario. In the second part of the chapter, we will present the DL-based implementations of the two IoT applications. In this chapter, we will cover the following topics:

- IoT-based human physiological and psychological state detection
- Use case one: IoT-based remote progress monitoring of physiotherapy
- Implementation of IoT-based remote progress monitoring of physiotherapy
- Use case two: the smart classroom
- Implementation of the smart classroom
- Deep learning for human activity and emotion detection in IoT
- LSTM and CNNs and transfer learning for HAR/FER in IoT applications

- Data collection
- Data preprocessing
- Model training
- Evaluation of the models

IoT-based human physiological and psychological state detection

In recent years, human physiological and psychological state detection have been used in many application domains to improve existing services and/or offer new services. IoT, combined with DL techniques, can be used in applications to detect human physiological and psychological states. The following diagram highlights a few key applications of these detection approaches:

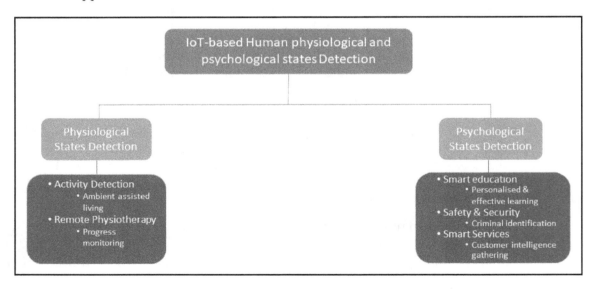

Now, we will learn in detail about the two state detection variants:

- **Physiological state detection**: Physiological state or activity detection are useful tools in many applications, including assisted living for vulnerable people, such as the elderly, and in remote physical therapy/rehabilitation systems. In assisted living for elderly people, falls among older people are detrimental to the health of the victim because of the associated risk of physical injury. A fall can also have financial consequences, due to the medical costs and need for hospitalization. Moreover, falls can also reduce the person's life expectancy, especially in the case of a **long-lie**. It is also worth noting that the medical expenses linked with falls are extremely high. For example, the yearly cost of falls in the US alone is expected to reach US $67 billion by 2020. In this context, automated and remote fall detection using DL-supported IoT applications can address the challenge, thus improving the quality of life for elderly people and minimizing the associated costs. Another key area of human activity detection applications is the remote physical therapy monitoring system. This is the first use case for this chapter, and we will present an overview of it in the next section.

- **Psychological state detection:** Facial expressions are good reflections of human psychological states, and they are important factors in human communication that help us to understand the intentions of humans. Generally, we can infer the emotional states of other people, such as joy, sadness, and anger, by analyzing their facial expressions and vocal tone. Forms of non-verbal communication make up two-thirds of all human interactions. Facial expressions, in their imparted emotional meaning, are one of the main non-verbal interpersonal communication channels. Hence, facial expression-based emotion detection can be useful in understanding people's behavior. It can, therefore, help to improve existing services and/or new services, including personalized customer services. IoT applications, such as smart healthcare, smart education, and security and safety, can improve their services through DL-based emotion detection or sentiment analysis. For example, in a smart classroom, a teacher can analyze the students' sentiment in real time or quasi real time to offer personalized and/or group-orientated teaching. This will improve their learning experience.

Use case one – remote progress monitoring of physiotherapy

Physical therapy is a big part of healthcare. There is a huge gap between the demand for physical therapy and our ability to deliver that therapy. Most countries in the world are still greatly dependent on the one-to-one patient-therapist interaction (which is the gold standard), but it is not a scalable solution and not cost-effective for either patients or healthcare providers. In addition, most existing therapies and their updates rely on average data instead of an individual's unique data, and sometimes this data is qualitative (for example, *Yes, I did what you told me to do*) rather than quantitative. This is a challenge regarding effective therapy. Finally, many people—especially elderly people—are living with **multiple chronic conditions** (**MCC**), and these conditions are generally treated separately. This can result in suboptimal care or even cases where these conditions can conflict with each other. For example, in the case of a patient with diabetes and back pain: a diabetic carer may recommend walking, whereas a back pain carer may forbid it. In this context, IoT is already changing healthcare. It can address most of these challenges with the support of machine learning/deep learning and data analysis tools, and offer effective physiotherapy by providing real-time or quasi real-time information.

Implementation of use case one

Progress monitoring is a key challenge in traditional therapy. An IoT-based therapy can solve the progress monitoring issue. The following diagram briefly presents how the IoT-based remote physiotherapy monitoring system will work:

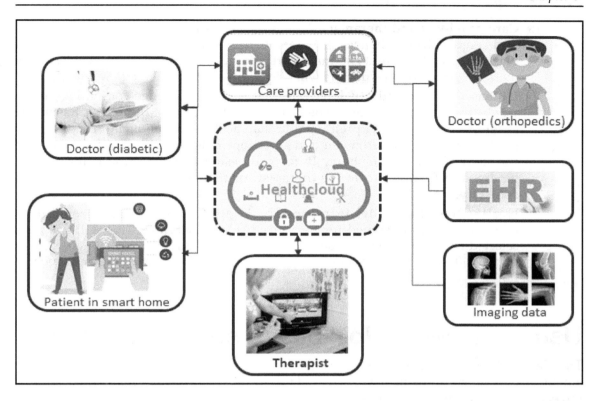

One of the key components of this application is the activity monitoring of the subject (patient) that will help the therapist remotely observe how the patient is complying with the suggested therapy, and whether they are making progress. As shown in the preceding diagram, the IoT-based remote physiotherapy monitoring system consists of four main elements:

- **Sensors and patient-side computing platform**: For this use case, we are considering two sensors: an accelerometer and a gyroscope. Both of them measure three-dimensional readings linked with the subject's activities. For these sensors, we can use dedicated sensors or a smartphone's sensors (these sensors are embedded within most smartphones). For the client-side computing platform, we can consider Raspberry Pi for the dedicated sensors and the smartphone (if we are using the smartphone sensors). The sensors need to be properly placed in order to measure signals correctly. The sensors can be used for continuous or event-wise (such as during exercise) monitoring of the subject's activities.

- **Care providers and therapists**: Care providers, such as hospitals with doctors and medical/healthcare databases, are connected through a cloud platform/HealthCloud. The main care provider for the therapy use case is a therapist, and hospitals/doctors will offer support to the therapist when required.
- **DL-based human activity detection**: In this phase, the edge-computing device will be installed with an app. The installed app on the smartphone or Raspberry Pi will be loaded with a pretrained human activity detection and classification model. Once the accelerometer and gyroscope detect any signal, they send it to the smartphone or Raspberry Pi for processing and detection using the DL model, and finally inform the therapist for their feedback or intervention if necessary.
- **HealthCloud for model learning**: The HealthCloud is a cloud computing platform mainly designed for healthcare-related services. This will train the selected DL model in human activity detection and classification using reference datasets. This learned model will be preinstalled in the smartphone or Raspberry Pi.

Use case two — IoT-based smart classroom

The higher education dropout rate is increasing worldwide. For example, dropout rates among UK university students have increased for the third consecutive year. Three of the top eight reasons for these dropouts are:

- Lack of quality time with teachers and counselors
- Demotivating school environment
- Lack of student support

One of the key challenges in addressing these issues is knowing the students (such as knowing whether a student is following a topic or not) and delivering lectures/tutorials and other support accordingly. One potential approach is to know the emotions of the students, which is challenging in a large classroom, computer lab, or in e-learning environments. The use of technologies (including IoT with the support of DL models) can help to recognize emotion using facial expression and/or speech. The second use case of this chapter aims at increasing student performance in the classroom by detecting emotions and managing the lecture/lab accordingly.

Implementation of use case two

The following diagram shows a simplified implementation of an IoT-based smart classroom application:

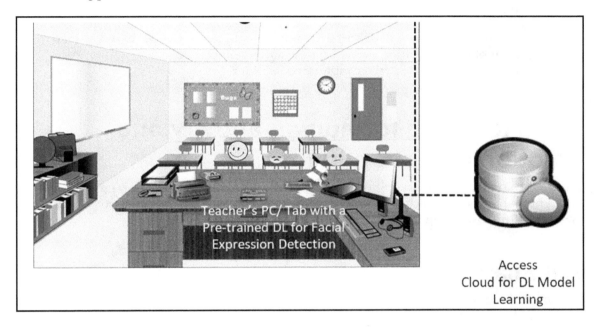

The facial-expression-based emotion analysis implementation consists of three main elements:

- **Sensors and computing platform:** For this use case, we need at least one CCTV camera that can cover the classroom and be connected to the computing platform wirelessly or via a concealed cable in the walls. The lecturer's computer in the classroom can work as the computing platform. The computer will continuously process the video signals and convert them into images for the image-based facial expression analysis.

- **Facial expression-based emotion detection**: The lecturer's computer will be installed with an app. The installed app will be loaded with a pretrained facial expression-based detection and classification model. Once the DL model receives the facial images of the students, it identifies their emotions (such as happy/unhappy/confused) regarding a lecture and notifies the lecturer to take the necessary action.

- **Desktop or server for model learning:** The lecturer's computer will be connected to a university server or cloud computing platform, and this will train/retrain the model for facial expression-based emotion recognition and classification using reference datasets. This learned model will be preinstalled in the lecturer's PC in the classroom.

All of the following sections will describe the implementation of the DL-based human activity and emotion recognition needed for the aforementioned use cases. All of the necessary codes are available in the chapter's code folder.

Deep learning for human activity and emotion detection in IoT

It is important to understand the working principle of an accelerometer- and gyroscope-based human activity detection system, and of a facial expression-based emotion detection system, before discussing the useful deep learning models.

Automatic human activity recognition system

Automatic **human activity recognition (HAR)** systems detect human activity, based on raw accelerometer and gyroscope signals. The following diagram shows a schematic of a DL-based HAR that consists of three different phases. They are as follows:

- IoT deployment or instrumentation of the subject or person
- Feature extraction and model development
- Activity classification/identification

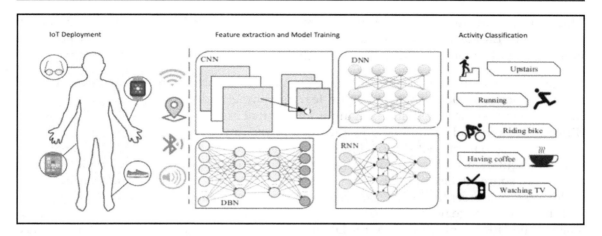

Generally, classical HAR approaches mainly rely on heuristic hand-crafted feature extraction methods, which is a complex process and not well suited for resource-constrained IoT devices. More recent DL-based HAR approaches perform the feature extraction automatically, and they can work well on resource-constrained IoT devices. Most HAR approaches consider six different activities, including walking, running, sitting, standing, climbing upstairs, and coming downstairs. These activities exhibit differences in accelerometer and gyroscope signals, and a classifier exploits the differences to identify the current activity—which could form a part of physiotherapy (such as running).

Automated human emotion detection system

Automated **human emotion recognition** (**HER**) can be done by using either one of the following signals/inputs from the subject (human) or a combination thereof:

- Facial expression
- Speech/audio
- Text

This chapter considers the **facial expression recognition** (**FER**)-based HER. A DL-based automated FER consists of three main steps: preprocessing, deep feature learning, and classification. The following diagram highlights these main steps in an FER-based HER.

Image processing for facial expression analysis requires preprocessing, since the different types of emotions (such as anger, disgust, fear, happiness, sadness, surprise, and neutral) have subtle differences. Variations in input images that are irrelevant to FER, including different backgrounds, illuminations, and head poses, can be removed through preprocessing to improve the model prediction/classification accuracy. Face alignment, data augmentation, and image normalization are a few of the key preprocessing techniques. Most open source datasets for FER are not sufficient to generalize the FER approach. Data augmentation is essential in order to improve an existing dataset in terms of FER. Face alignment and image normalization are useful for improving individual images. The final stage of the FER DL pipeline is for the DL algorithm to learn and classify the features, hence emotions. Most image recognition DL algorithms, including CNN and RNN, are suitable for the final stage:

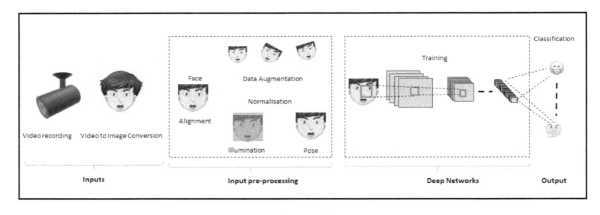

Deep learning models for HAR and emotion detection

Generally, human activity recognition systems use accelerometer and gyroscope signals, which are time series data. Sometimes, the recognition process uses a combination of time series and spatial data. In this context, **Recurrent Neural Network** (**RNN**) and LSTM are potential candidates for the former type of signals because of their capability to incorporate temporal features of input during evolution. On the other hand, CNNs are good for spatial aspects of accelerometer and gyroscope signals. Hence, a combination or hybrid of CNNs and LSTMs/RNNs is ideal for the former type of signals. We will use an LSTM model for the HAR use case as it can address the temporal aspects of human activities.

Unlike HAR systems, FER-based human emotion detection systems generally rely on facial expressions images, which rely on the local or spatial correlations between the pixel values of the images. Any DL model that works well for image recognition is fine for an FER task and, equally, for emotion detection. A number of deep learning algorithms or models have been used for image recognition, and the **deep belief network** (**DBN**) and CNNs are the top two candidates. In this chapter, we are considering CNNs because of their performance in image recognition.

LSTM, CNNs, and transfer learning for HAR/FER in IoT applications

LSTM is the widely used DL model for HAR—including in IoT-based HAR—because its memory capacity can deal better with time series data (such as HAR data) than other models, including CNN. The LSTM implementation of HAR can support transfer learning and is suitable for resource-constrained IoT devices. Generally, FER relies on image processing, and the CNN is the best model for image processing. Therefore, we implement use case two (FER) using a CNN model. In `Chapter 3`, *Image Recognition in IoT*, we presented an overview of two popular implementations of the CNN (such as incentive V3 and Mobilenets) and their corresponding transfer learning. In the following paragraphs, we briefly present an overview of the baseline LSTM.

LSTM is an extension of RNNs. Many variants of LSTM are proposed, and they follow the baseline LSTM. The following is a schematic diagram of the baseline LSTM:

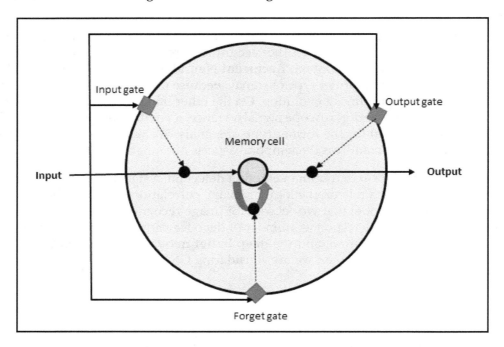

As shown in the preceding diagram, LSTM mainly consists of two components. They have a memory cell or neuron, and each cell or neuron has a multiplicative forget gate, read gate, and write gate. These gates control the access to memory cells/neurons and prevent them from being disturbed by irrelevant inputs. These gates are controlled through 0/1 or off/on. For example, if the forget gate is on/1, the neuron/cell writes its data to itself, and if the gate is off/0, the neuron forgets its last content. Other gates are controlled in a similar fashion.

Unlike RNNs, LSTMs use forget gates to actively control the cell/neuron states and ensure they do not degrade. Importantly, LSTM models perform better than RNN models in the case of data that has a long dependency in time. Many IoT applications, such as human activity recognition and disaster prediction based on environmental monitoring, exhibit this long-time dependency.

As the FER considered for use case two is based on image processing, CNNs are the best choice. CNN has different implementations, including a simple CNN, two versions of Mobilenets, and Incentive3. Use case two will explore a simple CNN and Mobilenet V1 for the FER part of the implementation.

Data collection

Data collection for HAR and/FER is a challenging task for many reasons, including privacy. As a result, open source quality datasets are limited in number. For the HAR implementation in use case one, we are using a very popular and open source **Wireless Sensor Data Mining** (**WISDM**) lab dataset . The dataset consists of 54,901 samples collected from 36 different subjects. For privacy reasons, usernames are masked with ID numbers from 1-36. The data was collected for six different activities undertaken by the subjects: standing, sitting, jogging, walking, going downstairs, and climbing upstairs. The dataset contains three-axis accelerometer data with more than 200 time steps for each sample. The following screenshot is a sample of the dataset:

```
columns = ['user','activity','timestamp', 'x-axis', 'y-axis', 'z-axis']
df = pd.read_csv('data/WISDM_ar_v1.1_raw.txt', header = None, names = columns)
df = df.dropna()

df.head()
```

	user	activity	timestamp	x-axis	y-axis	z-axis
0	33	Jogging	49105962326000	-0.694638	12.680544	0.503953
1	33	Jogging	49106062271000	5.012288	11.264028	0.953424
2	33	Jogging	49106112167000	4.903325	10.882658	-0.081722
3	33	Jogging	49106222305000	-0.612916	18.496431	3.023717
4	33	Jogging	49106332290000	-1.184970	12.108489	7.205164

For the FER-based emotion detection in use case two, we used two different datasets. The first one is the popular and open source FER2013 dataset. This dataset contains 48 x 48 pixel grayscale images of human faces. These images are preprocessed and ready to be used directly for training and validation. The images can be classified into seven categories (*0=Angry, 1=Disgust, 2=Fear, 3=Happy, 4=Sad, 5=Surprise,* and *6=Neutral*). The dataset in CSV format contains information about pixel values of the face images rather than the images. The following screenshot shows a few values of the dataset:

emotion	pixels	Usage
0	70 80 82 72 58 58 60 63 54 58 60 48 89 115 121 119 115 110 98 91 84 84 90 99 110 126 143 153 158 171 1	Training
0	151 150 147 155 148 133 111 140 170 174 182 154 153 164 173 178 185 185 189 187 186 193 194 185 183	Training
2	231 212 156 164 174 138 161 173 182 200 106 38 39 74 138 161 164 179 190 201 210 216 220 224 222 21!	Training
4	24 32 36 30 32 23 19 20 30 41 21 22 32 34 21 19 43 52 13 26 40 59 65 12 20 63 99 98 98 111 75 62 41 73 1	Training
6	4 0 0 0 0 0 0 0 0 0 0 0 3 15 23 28 48 50 58 84 115 127 137 142 151 156 155 149 153 152 157 160 162 159 1	Training
2	55 55 55 55 55 54 60 68 54 85 151 163 170 179 181 185 188 188 191 196 189 194 198 197 195 194 190 19!	Training
4	20 17 19 21 25 38 42 42 46 54 56 62 63 66 82 108 118 130 139 134 132 126 113 97 126 148 157 161 155 1!	Training
3	77 78 79 79 78 75 60 55 47 48 58 73 77 79 57 50 37 44 56 70 80 82 87 91 86 80 73 66 54 57 68 69 68 68 49	Training
3	85 84 90 121 101 102 133 153 153 169 177 189 195 199 205 207 209 216 221 225 221 220 218 222 223 21'	Training
2	255 254 255 254 254 179 122 107 95 124 149 150 169 178 179 179 181 181 184 190 191 191 193 190 190	Training
0	30 24 21 23 25 25 49 67 84 103 120 125 130 139 140 139 148 171 178 175 176 174 180 180 178 178 182 1!	Training
6	39 75 78 58 58 45 49 48 103 156 81 45 41 38 49 56 60 49 32 31 28 52 83 81 78 75 62 31 18 19 19 20 17 20	Training
6	219 213 206 202 209 217 216 215 219 218 223 230 227 227 233 235 234 236 237 238 234 226 219 212 208	Training
6	148 144 130 129 119 122 129 131 139 153 140 128 139 144 146 143 132 133 134 130 140 142 150 152 150	Training
3	4 2 13 41 56 62 67 87 95 62 65 70 80 107 127 149 153 150 165 168 177 187 176 167 152 128 130 149 149	Training
5	107 107 109 109 109 109 110 101 123 140 144 144 149 153 160 161 161 167 168 169 172 172 173 175 176	Training

The split ratio between the training and the validation dataset is *80:20*.

We also prepared a dataset through Google search, particularly for Mobilenet V1. The dataset is not a big one, as it consists of five classes of emotions, and each of those consists of more than 100 images. These images are not preprocessed. The following diagram shows a folder view of the prepared dataset:

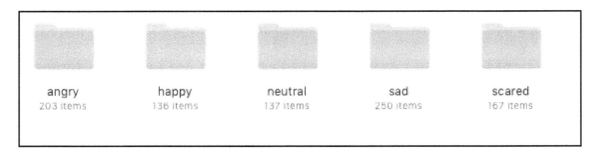

angry	happy	neutral	sad	scared
203 items	136 items	137 items	250 items	167 items

For data collection (each class of the dataset), we can follow a four step process:

1. **Search:** Use any browser (we used Chrome), go to Google, and search the appropriate word combination for the class/emotion (such as *angry human*) in Google images.

2. **Image URL gatherings:** This step utilizes a few lines of JavaScript code to gather the image URLs. The gathered URLs can be used in Python to download the images. To do that, select the JavaScript console (assuming you will use the Chrome web browser, but you can use Firefox as well) by clicking the **View** | **Developer** | **JavaScript** console (in macOS) and customize and control **Google Chrome** | **More tools** | **Developer tools** (Windows OS). Once you have selected the JavaScript console, this will enable you to execute JavaScript in a REPL-like manner. Now, do the following in order:

   1. Scroll down the page until you have found all images relevant to your query. From there, you need to grab the URLs for the images.

      Switch back to the JavaScript console and then copy and paste the following JavaScript snippet into the console:

      ```
      // Get the jquery into the JavaScript console
      var script = document.createElement('script');
      script.src =
      "https://ajax.googleapis.com/ajax/libs/jquery/2.2.0/jq
      uery.min.js";
      document.getElementsByTagName('head')[0].appendChild(s
      cript)
      ```

   2. The preceding code snippet will pull down the jQuery JavaScript library, and now you can use a CSS selector to grab a list of URLs using the following snippet:

      ```
      // Grab the chosen URLs
      var urls = $('.rg_di .rg_meta').map(function() { return
      JSON.parse($(this).text()).ou; });
      ```

   3. Finally, write the URLs to a file (one per line) using the following snippet:

      ```
      // write the URls to file (one per line)
      var textToSave = urls.toArray().join('\n');
      var hiddenElement = document.createElement('a');
      hiddenElement.href = 'data:attachment/text,' +
      encodeURI(textToSave);
      ```

```
hiddenElement.target = '_blank';
hiddenElement.download = 'emotion_images_urls.txt';
hiddenElement.click();
```

Once you execute the preceding code snippet, you will have a file named `emotion_images_urls.txt` in your default download directory.

3. **Downloading the images**: Now, you are ready to download the images running `download_images.py` (available in the code folder of the chapter) on the previously downloaded `emotion_images_urls.txt`:

```
python download_images.py emotion_images_urls.txt
```

4. **Exploration**: Once we have downloaded the images, we need to explore the images in order to delete the irrelevant ones. We can do this through a bit of manual inspection. After that, we need to resize and crop match our requirements.

Data exploration

In this section, we will examine in more detail the datasets that we will be using:

- **HAR dataset**: The dataset is a text file that consists of the different subjects accelerations for each of the six activities. We can do a data distribution check for the dataset as it is not easy to perceive the data distribution by looking at the text file only. The following graph summarizes the breakdown for the training set:

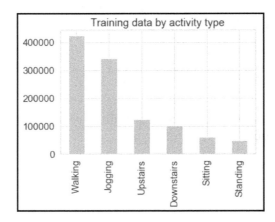

As we can see from the preceding graph, the training dataset consists of more walking and jogging data than the other four activities. This is good for the DL model, since walking and jogging are moving activities, where the range of acceleration data could be wide. To visualize this, we have explored activity-wise acceleration measurements/data for 200 time steps for each activity. The following screenshot represents 200 time step acceleration measurements for sitting:

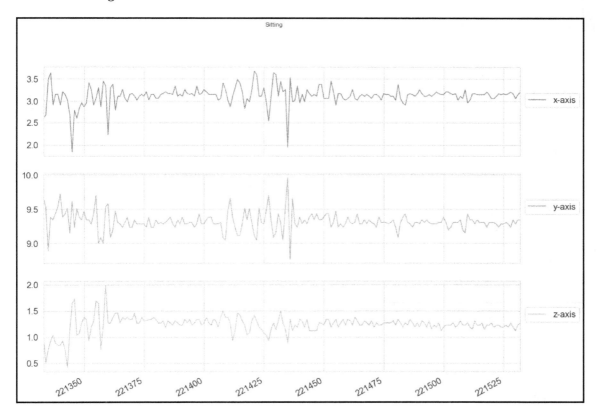

The following screenshot represents 200 time step acceleration measurements for standing:

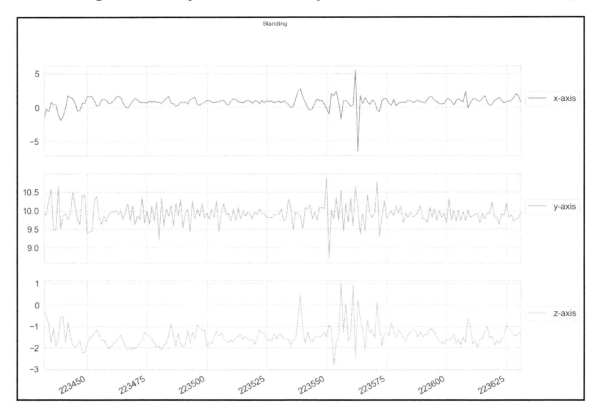

The following screenshot represents 200 time step acceleration measurements for walking:

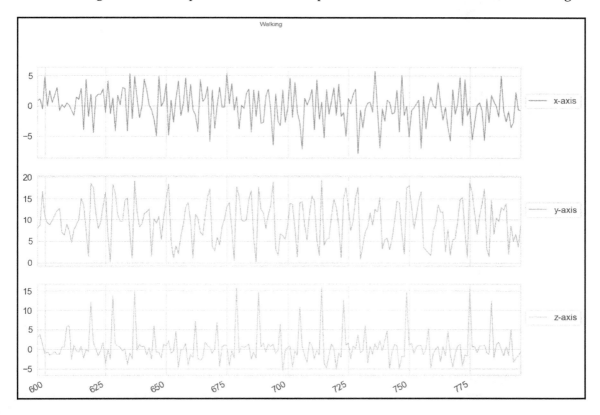

The following screenshot represents 200 time step acceleration measurements for jogging:

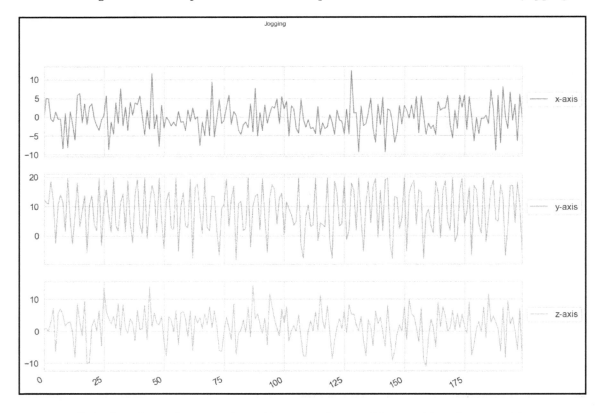

It is clear from the preceding diagrams that walking and jogging activities are busier than the other activities as they reflect the user's movements.

- **FER dataset**: We need to convert the FER2013 dataset pixel values of the face images into actual images to explore them. We can use the following code to convert the pixel values to images:

```
import os
import csv
import argparse
import numpy as np
import scipy.misc
parser = argparse.ArgumentParser()
parser.add_argument('-f', '--file', required=True, help="path of
the csv file")
parser.add_argument('-o', '--output', required=True, help="path of
the output directory")
args = parser.parse_args()
w, h = 48, 48
image = np.zeros((h, w), dtype=np.uint8)
id = 1
with open(args.file) as csvfile:
    datareader = csv.reader(csvfile, delimiter =',')
    next(datareader,None)
    for row in datareader:
        emotion = row[0]
        pixels = row[1].split()
        usage = row[2]
        pixels_array = np.asarray(pixels, dtype=np.int)
        image = pixels_array.reshape(w, h)
        stacked_image = np.dstack((image,) * 3)
        image_folder = os.path.join(args.output, usage)
        if not os.path.exists(image_folder):
            os.makedirs(image_folder)
        image_file =  os.path.join(image_folder , emotion +'_'+
str(id) +'.jpg')
        scipy.misc.imsave(image_file, stacked_image)
        id+=1
        if id % 100 == 0:
            print('Processed {} images'.format(id))
print("Finished conversion to {} images".format(id))
```

We can execute the previous code using the following code:

```
python imager_converter.py
```

Once we have the diagram, we can run the following code for image exploration:

```
python image_explorer.py
```

This will produce a figure similar to the following image:

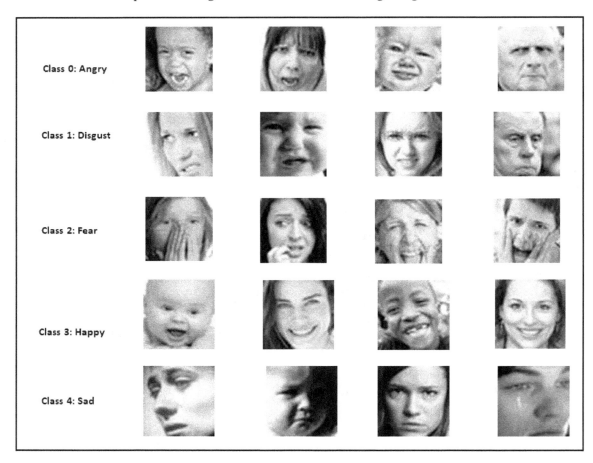

As we can see in the preceding image, the FER dataset is preprocessed well. On the other hand, the second dataset (we named it FER2019) is not preprocessed, including the image sizes, as can be seen in the following image:

Class 0: Angry

Class 1: happy

Class 2 neutral

Class 3: sad

Class 4: scared

Data preprocessing

Data preprocessing is an essential step for a deep learning pipeline. The HAR and FER2013 datasets are preprocessed well. However, the downloaded image files for the second dataset of use case two are not preprocessed. As shown in the preceding image, the images are not uniform in size or pixels and the dataset is not large in size; hence, they require data augmentation. Popular augmentation techniques are flip, rotation, scale, crop, translation, and Gaussian noise. Many tools are available for each of these activities. You can use the tools or write their own script to do the data augmentation. A useful tool is **Augmentor**, a Python library for machine learning. We can install the tool in our Python and use it for augmentation. The following code (`data_augmentation.py`) is a simple data augmentation process that executes flipping, rotation, cropping, and resizing of the input images:

```
# Import the module
import Augmentor
da = Augmentor.Pipeline("data_augmentation_test")
# Define the augmentation
```

```
da.rotate90(probability=0.5)
da.rotate270(probability=0.5)
da.flip_left_right(probability=0.8)
da.flip_top_bottom(probability=0.3)
da.crop_random(probability=1, percentage_area=0.5)
da.resize(probability=1.0, width=120, height=120)
# Do the augmentation operation: sampling
da.sample(25)
```

The following image presents two original images and their augmented samples (3 out of 25 samples):

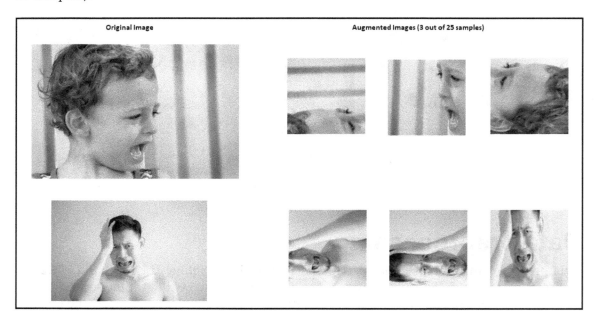

As shown in the preceding image, the augmented images are uniform in size, flipped, and rotated.

The following are two key issues to be noted during the training image set preparation:

- **Data size**: We need to collect at least 100 images for each class to train a model that works well. The more we can gather, the better the likely accuracy of the trained model. However, one-shot learning (an object categorization technique) can work using fewer than 100 training samples. We also made sure that the images are a good representation of what our application will actually face in real implementation.
- **Data heterogeneity**: Data collected for training should be heterogeneous. For example, images for FER should be from a diverse range of skin tones or different views of the same expressions.

Model training

As we mentioned earlier, we are using LSTM for use case one and two implementations of CNN (simple CNN and Mobilenet V1) for use case two. All of these DL implementations support transfer learning for both use cases that do not require training from scratch.

Use case one

We consider a stacked LSTM, which is a popular DL model for sequence prediction, including time series problems. A stacked LSTM architecture consists of two or more LSTM layers. We implemented the HAR for use case one, using a two-layered stacked LSTM architecture. The following diagram presents a two-layered LSTM, where the first layer provides a sequence of outputs instead of a single value output to the second LSTM layer:

We can train and test the model by running the `LSTM -HAR.py` code, available in the `use-case-1` folder (after making the necessary changes to your setup, such as the `data` directory):

```
python LSTM-HAR.py
```

Use case two

We used two different architectures of CNN for the FER-based emotion detection in the smart classroom. The first one is a simple CNN architecture. To train the model on the FER2013 dataset, we need to run `CNN-FER2013.py`, which is available in the chapter's `use-case-2` code folder, or use the notebook. To run in all default settings of `CNN-FER2013.py` (after making any necessary changes to your setup, such as the `data` directory), we need to run the following in the Command Prompt:

```
python CNN-FER2013.py
```

The training and testing of the model on the FER2103 dataset could take a few hours. The following diagram, generated from the TensorBoard log files, presents the network used for use case two:

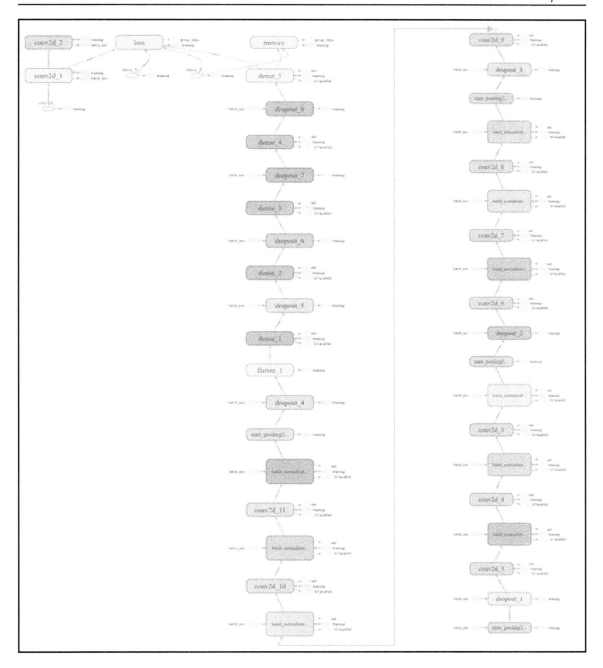

We can retrain Mobilenet V1 on FER2019 by running the following code:

```
python retrain.py \

--output_graph=trained_model_mobilenetv1/retrained_graph.pb \
--output_labels=trained_model_mobilenetv1/retrained_labels.txt    \
--architecture =mobilenet_1.0_224 \
--image_dir= your dataset directory
```

Once we run the preceding commands, they will generate the retrain models (`retrained_graph.pb`) and label text (`retrained_labels.txt`) in the given directory. This will also store the model's summary information in a directory. The summary information (the `--summaries_dir` argument with `retrain_logs` as the default value) can be used by the TensorBoard to visualize different aspects of the models, including the networks and their performance graphs. If we type the following command into the Terminal or command window, it will run the TensorBoard:

```
tensorboard --logdir retrain_logs
```

Once the TensorBoard is running, navigate your web browser to `localhost:6006` to view the TensorBoard and the network of the corresponding model. The following diagram presents a network for the Mobilenet V1 architecture used in the implementation:

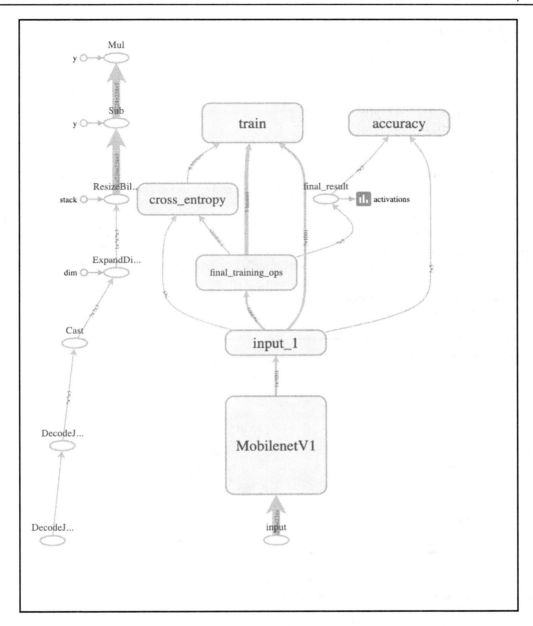

Model evaluation

We can evaluate the models in three different aspects:

- Learning/(re)training time
- Storage requirement
- Performance (accuracy)

In terms of training time, in a desktop (Intel Xenon CPU E5-1650 v3@3.5 GHz and 32 GB RAM) with GPU support, LSTM on the HAR dataset, CNN on FER2013, and Mobilenet V1 on the FER2019 dataset, it took less than an hour to train/retrain the model.

The storage requirement of a model is an essential consideration in resource-constrained IoT devices. The following diagram presents the storage requirements for the three models we tested for the two use cases. As shown in the diagram, the simple CNN takes up only 2.6 MB, smaller than one sixth of the Mobilenet V1 (17.1 MB). Also, the LSTM for the HAR took up 1.6 MB (not in the diagram) of storage. In terms of storage requirements, all the models are fine to be deployed in many resource-constrained IoT devices, including Raspberry Pi or smartphones:

Finally, we have evaluated the performance of the models. Two levels of performance evaluation can be executed for the use cases:

- Dataset-wide evaluation or testing has been done during the retraining phase in the desktop PC platform/server side.
- Individual activity signals for human activity and facial images for emotion detection were tested or evaluated in the Raspberry Pi 3 environment.

Model performance (use case one)

The following graph presents the progressive training and test accuracy of the LSTM model against the HAR dataset. As we can see from the graph, training accuracy is close to 1.0, or 100%, and test accuracy is above .90, or 90%. With this test accuracy, we believe that the LSTM model can detect human activities in most cases, including whether the subject is doing the assigned physiotherapy activities:

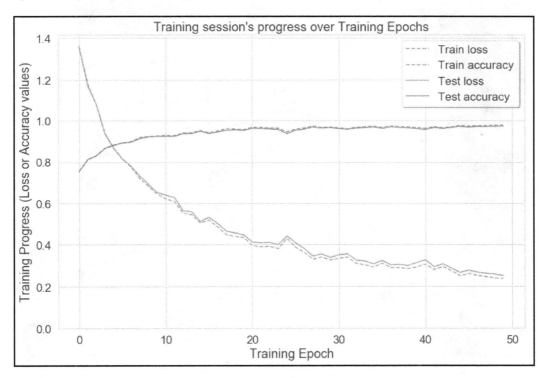

The following diagram is a confusion matrix of the model against the HAR test dataset. As seen in the diagram, the model gets confused between **Downstairs** and **Upstairs**, and **Sitting** and **Standing** activities, as they have very limited or zero mobility, which means there is no significant acceleration to differentiate them:

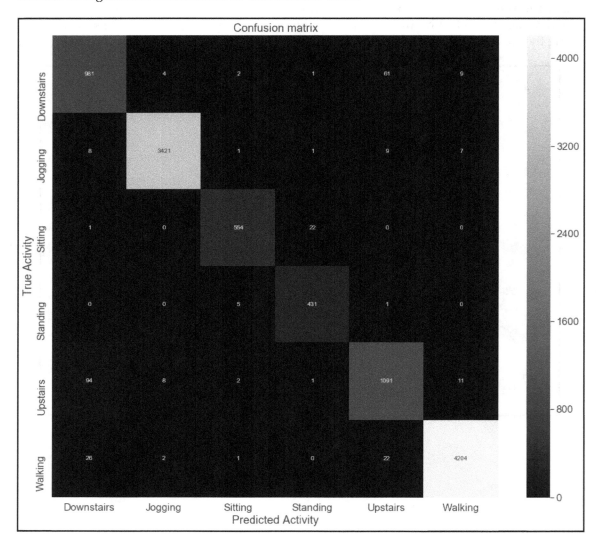

Model performance (use case two)

The following screenshot shows the training and validation performance of the simple CNN model on the FER2013 dataset. The accuracy of this dataset is not great (training–.83, and validation–.63), but the test or validation accuracy should be able to detect the distinctive and necessary emotions (such as happy, sad, and confused) for the smart classroom:

The following diagram is a confusion matrix of the model against the FER2013 test dataset. As expected, the model is showing confusion for all the expressions (such as 156 angry expressions being detected as sad expressions). This is one of the applications of deep learning where further research is needed to improve performance:

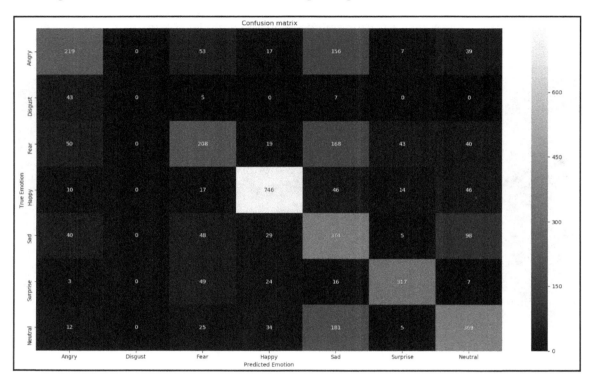

For use case two, we have tested Mobilenet V1. The following diagrams shows the overall performance of model Mobilenet V1 on the FER2019 dataset. As we can see from the figure, this is showing better training accuracy, but no improvement in validation and test accuracy. One potential reason for this could be the size and quality of the data, since, after data augmentation, every sample may not contain a facial expression image. Further preprocessing that includes manual inspection may improve data quality and the model's performance:

```
INFO:tensorflow:2019-04-12 22:01:57.172090: Step 3950: Validation accuracy = 56.0% (N=10(
INFO:tensorflow:2019-04-12 22:01:57.717492: Step 3960: Train accuracy = 100.0%
INFO:tensorflow:2019-04-12 22:01:57.717706: Step 3960: Cross entropy = 0.025000
INFO:tensorflow:2019-04-12 22:01:57.771880: Step 3960: Validation accuracy = 56.0% (N=10(
INFO:tensorflow:2019-04-12 22:01:58.327694: Step 3970: Train accuracy = 100.0%
INFO:tensorflow:2019-04-12 22:01:58.327912: Step 3970: Cross entropy = 0.019784
INFO:tensorflow:2019-04-12 22:01:58.382137: Step 3970: Validation accuracy = 51.0% (N=10(
INFO:tensorflow:2019-04-12 22:01:58.960856: Step 3980: Train accuracy = 100.0%
INFO:tensorflow:2019-04-12 22:01:58.961076: Step 3980: Cross entropy = 0.019178
INFO:tensorflow:2019-04-12 22:01:59.013968: Step 3980: Validation accuracy = 54.0% (N=10(
INFO:tensorflow:2019-04-12 22:01:59.570253: Step 3990: Train accuracy = 100.0%
INFO:tensorflow:2019-04-12 22:01:59.570446: Step 3990: Cross entropy = 0.024673
INFO:tensorflow:2019-04-12 22:01:59.623518: Step 3990: Validation accuracy = 62.0% (N=10(
INFO:tensorflow:2019-04-12 22:02:00.125422: Step 3999: Train accuracy = 100.0%
INFO:tensorflow:2019-04-12 22:02:00.125639: Step 3999: Cross entropy = 0.019731
INFO:tensorflow:2019-04-12 22:02:00.180063: Step 3999: Validation accuracy = 64.0% (N=10(
INFO:tensorflow:Final test accuracy = 48.4% (N=95)
WARNING:tensorflow:From retrain.py:838: convert_variables_to_constants (from tensorflow.
Instructions for updating:
Use tf.compat.v1.graph_util.convert_variables_to_constants
WARNING:tensorflow:From /Users/raz/anaconda3/lib/python3.7/site-packages/tensorflow/pyth(
ted and will be removed in a future version.
Instructions for updating:
Use tf.compat.v1.graph_util.extract_sub_graph
INFO:tensorflow:Froze 2 variables.
INFO:tensorflow:Converted 2 variables to const ops.
```

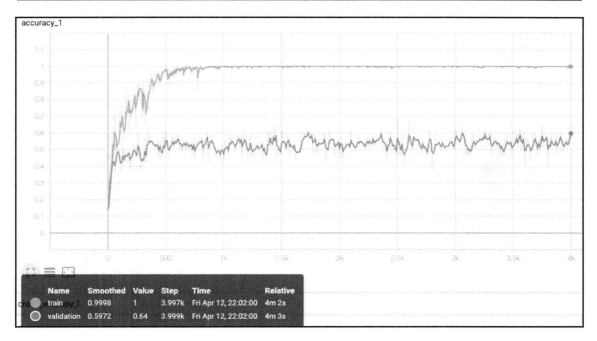

In order to test the model on an individual image, and transfer the learning of the model, we need to do the following:

- Export the trained model (such as `fer2013_trained.hdf5`) and the `label_image.py` file (image classifier) into a Raspberry Pi (installed with TensorFlow)/smartphone.
- Run the image classifier (do not forget to update the `test_image` path) using the following command:

```
python label_image.py
```

This will produce the test result for your test image.

Summary

Automatic human physiological and psychological state detection is becoming a popular means by which people can learn a person's physical and mental state to interact and react accordingly. There are many applications within smart education, healthcare, and entertainment where these state detection techniques can be useful. Machine learning and DL algorithms are essential for these detection techniques. In the first part of this chapter, we briefly described different IoT applications using human physiological and psychological state detection. We also briefly discussed two potential use cases of IoT where DL algorithms can be useful in human physiological and psychological state detection. The first use case considers an IoT-based remote physiotherapy progress monitoring system. The second use case is an IoT-based smart classroom application that uses facial expressions of the students to know their feedback. In the second part of the chapter, we briefly discussed the data collection process for the use cases, and we discussed the rationale behind selecting LSTM for the HAR and CNNs for the FER. The remainder of the chapter described all of the necessary components of the DL pipeline for these models and their results.

One of the key challenges in IoT applications is security. Many IoT applications, such as driverless cars, connected healthcare, and smart grid, are mission-critical applications. Security is an essential element for these and many other IoT applications. In the next chapter, we will discuss security in IoT applications, and show how deep learning can be used for IoT security solutions.

References

- K. Rapp, C. Becker, I.D. Cameron, H.H. König, and G. Büchele, *Epidemiology of falls in residential aged care: analysis of more than 70,000 falls from residents of Bavarian nursing homes*, J. Am. Med. Dir. Assoc. 13 (2) (2012) 187.e1–187.e6.

- Centers for disease control and prevention. *Cost of Falls Among Older Adults*, 2014. http://www.cdc.gov/homeandrecreationalsafety/falls/fallcost.html (accessed 14.04.19).

- M. S. Hossain and G. Muhammad, *Emotion-Aware Connected Healthcare Big Data Towards 5G*, in IEEE Internet of Things Journal, vol. 5, no. 4, pp. 2399-2406, Aug. 2018.

- M. A. Razzaque, Muta Tah Hira, and Mukta Dira. 2017. *QoS in Body Area Networks: A Survey. ACM Trans.* Sen. Netw. 13, 3, Article 25 (August 2017), 46 pages.

- Nigel Bosch, Sidney K. D'Mello, Ryan S. Baker, Jaclyn Ocumpaugh, Valerie Shute, Matthew Ventura, Lubin Wang, and Weinan Zhao. 2016. Detecting student emotions in computer-enabled classrooms. In *Proceedings of the Twenty-Fifth International Joint Conference on Artificial Intelligence*(IJCAI'16), Gerhard Brewka (Ed.). AAAI Press 4125-4129.

- Isabel Sagenmüller, *Student retention: 8 reasons people drop out of higher education*, https://www.u-planner.com/en-us/blog/student-retention-8-reasons-people-drop-out-of-higher-education.

- Nikki Bardsley, *Drop-out rates among university students increases for third consecutive year*, https://www.fenews.co.uk/featured-article/24449-drop-out-rates-among-university-students-increases-for-third-consecutive-year.

- S. Hochreiter and J. Schmidhuber, *Long Short-Term Memory*, neural computation, vol. 9, no. 8, pp. 1735–1780, 1997.

- http://www.cis.fordham.edu/wisdm/dataset.php.

- I. Goodfellow, D. Erhan, PL Carrier, A. Courville, M. Mirza, B. Hamner, W. Cukierski, Y. Tang, DH Lee, Y. Zhou, C. Ramaiah, F. Feng, R. Li, X. Wang, D. Athanasakis, J. Shawe-Taylor, M. Milakov, J. Park, R. Ionescu, M. Popescu, C. Grozea, J. Bergstra, J. Xie, L. Romaszko, B. Xu, Z. Chuang, and Y. Bengio., *Challenges in Representation Learning: A report on three machine learning contests.* arXiv 2013.

IoT Security

7

The use of IoT is growing at a dangerously fast pace, and both researchers and industries have estimated that, the number of active wirelessly connected devices will exceed 20 billion. This exponential growth of IoT devices is increasing the risks to our lives and property, as well as to the entire IT industry. To have more connected devices means more attack vectors, and more opportunities for hackers to exploit. In this context, secure IoT is not only essential for its applications, but also for the rest of the IT industry.

In IoT security solutions, networks and devices can be viewed as either signature-based or behavior-based. Behavior-based solutions, such as anomaly detection, are preferable in IoT as preparing and maintaining signatures of dynamic and unknown IoT attacks is very difficult. Similarly to human behavior analysis, **deep learning (DL)/machine learning (ML)** models can be used in IoT for data exploration, and for learning normal and abnormal behavior (security perspective) of IoT devices and networks, in various IoT application environments.

This chapter presents behavioral data analysis of DL-based networks and devices, and security incident detection techniques for IoT applications in general. In the first part of this chapter, we will briefly describe different IoT security attacks and their potential detection techniques, including DL/ML-based methods. In addition, we will briefly discuss two IoT use cases where security attacks—such as **Denial of Service (DoS)** and **Distributed DoS (DDoS)** attacks—can be detected intelligently and automatically through DL-based anomaly detection. In the second part of the chapter, we will present hands-on DL-based security incident detection implementations. In this chapter, we will cover the following topics:

- IoT security attacks and potential detection approaches
- Use case one—intelligent host intrusion detection in IoT
- Implementation of intelligent host intrusion detection in IoT

- Use case two—intelligent network intrusion detection in IoT
- Implementation of intelligent network intrusion detection in IoT
- DL for IoT security incident detection
- **Deep neural networks (DNN)**, **autoencoder**, and **long short-term memory (LSTM)** in IoT security incident detection
- Data collection
- Data preprocessing
- Models training
- Evaluation of the models

Security attacks in IoT and detections

According to statistics, there will be more than 26 billion connected IoT devices worldwide. These devices, which include smart TVs, tablets, smartphones, notebooks, wearables, sensors, thermostats, and others, will make our lives more efficient, more energy saving, more comfortable, and less costly. However, these can only be realized when the security of these applications are maintained as, in many cases, these devices are dealing with mission-critical applications.

The reality is that IoT security is currently the number-one challenge faced by IoT industries. Without proper security solutions in place, data traversing the public internet, especially wirelessly connected devices, is vulnerable to hackers. In this context, the entire IoT pipeline or pathway needs to be secure. In other words, IoT needs **end-to-end (E2E)** security, where data must be secured from the time it leaves the end device or appliance, throughout its journey to and from the cloud, until it reaches the end user's mobile app or browser-based application. In addition, once it has been processed and a decision has been made on this in the user device/app, it has to follow a secure backward path for actuating or carrying the control instructions to the device. The following diagram presents an E2E (three-layered) view of an IoT solution, and the security requirements of the main three layers:

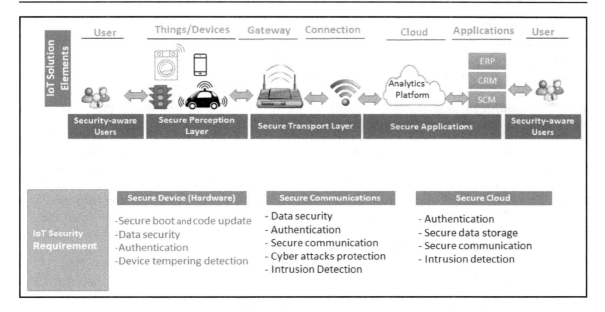

The following diagram presents a summary of the main attacks in IoT in a three-layered perspective:

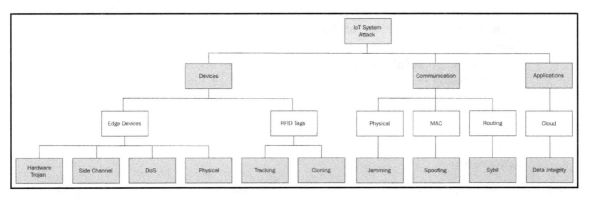

Designing and developing IoT security solutions is a very challenging task. For example, such devices are generally termed "embedded" devices; these have a fixed function designed specifically to perform a specialized task. They are resource-constrained, in terms of operating system, processing power, and memory. Traditional and PC security solutions are not suitable, as they will not even run on most embedded devices. Importantly, there are a large number of devices with vulnerabilities to be exploited by attackers. For example, in a smart home, we have more IoT/smart devices than our PC/laptops.

Very soon, our homes will be equipped with ample connected devices that could compete with the number of connections in a mid-sized company. In this context, managing updates, passwords, and settings for these connected devices alone, without the support of an IT security team or any expensive and enterprise level security tools, will be nightmare. Automated approaches based on **artificial intelligence** (**AI**)—especially DL/ML—can reactively and/or proactively find the security issues and help us to manage them. AI-based solutions can take two different forms:

- **Network-based solution**: A network-based solution aims to secure IoT devices of an IoT application by making a protective shield around the network of the application. This approach maintains a whitelist of devices that are allowed to access an IoT application network to prevent intruders from getting into the network. However, the IoT devices need to access to and be accessed from the outside world, such as from the cloud and smartphone applications. A DL/ML engine can monitor incoming and outgoing traffic to the IoT devices, and create a profile that defines the normal behavior of the IoT application. The DL/ML engine will detect any incoming threat by comparing it with established normal behavior. Unlike enterprise networks, AI-based threat detection is easier in IoT as, generally, the functionality of an IoT device is very limited, and it is not easy to disguise the IoT devices in malicious requests. In addition, it is easier to define a finite set of rules to determine normal and anomalous behavior for IoT devices. For example, a smart bulb communicating with the smart fridge in a smart home is not a normal behavior, and it is easy to detect as the bulb is for lighting and does not need to communicate with the fridge to produce light.
- **Device-based solutions**: Generally, IoT devices are resource-constrained in terms of processing power and storage capacity. Hence, signature-based security solutions are not suitable for IoT devices as they require huge databases of threat and malware signature storage. Like network-based solutions, DL/ML-supported automated behavior-based solutions are better alternatives as they are less resource-hungry. In addition, they can run without bogging down small processors.

Although, many people prefer network-based solutions over device-based ones, our recommendation would be to opt for both as they will offer stronger protection for your IoT devices as well as for the rest of the world.

Anomaly detection and IoT security

Network- and device-level behavioral anomaly detection is an important means of detecting potential security incidents, including DoS or DDoS, or any general intrusions. Anomaly detection mechanisms can be divided into many subclasses:

- **Statistical methods**: These methods use past behaviors to approximate a model of the correct behavior of a sensor or thing. If the things or networks observe a new behavior, it is compared to the model and, if statistically incompatible, is marked as an anomaly.
- **Probabilistic methods**: These methods center around the definition of a probabilistic model (parametric or nonparametric). If any the probability of an incident within a device or network falls below a predefined threshold, then it is labelled as an anomalous event.
- **Proximity-based methods**: These methods are based on the distances between normal and anomalous behavior. Clustering methods also fall into this class.
- **Prediction-based methods**: These methods use past network/device behavioral data to train a model that can predict the behavior of any incoming or outgoing traffic and identify anomalies. This is the method we will be using in our two use cases. The first is anomaly detection for host level or device level intrusion detection, and the second is network level intrusion detection.

DoS and DDoS intrusion incidents are common in IoT applications. IoT devices could be the target for these attacks and/or IoT devices can be exploited by attackers to generate flooding traffic to initiate and run DDoS attacks. These attacks can be launched in different layers of an IoT protocol stack, including the network, transport, and application layers. Generally, the detection of DDoS attacks launched at the application layer is very challenging, as the request packets look similar to the normal request packets. As a consequence of this attack, we may observe explicit behaviors in terms of resource exhaustion, such as network bandwidth, CPU processing, and memory. For instance, a swarm of IoT devices hijacked by Mirai malware generated about 1 Tbps of DDoS traffic to a French web host in September 2016[3]. In this context, it is essential to detect host/IoT device level as well as IoT network level intrusions so that IoT applications become available for their intended use and/or they do not become the means for making a DDoS attack on others. In the following sections, we present one use case on IoT device-level intrusion detection, and another on IoT network level intrusion detection.

Use case one: intelligent host intrusion detection in IoT

Very often, resource-constrained IoT devices become the target for DoS or DDoS attacks by intruders that can make the IoT application unavailable to the consumers. For example, consider an IoT-based remote patient-monitoring system. If the sensor's reading of the patient at a critical time, such as during a heart attack, are not available to their doctors or hospital, the patient may lose their life. In this context, devices or host level intrusion detection is essential for most IoT applications. In use case one, we will consider IoT device or host level intrusion detection.

It is essential to select a good feature or set of features to determine anomalies in IoT devices and networks (such as DoS and DDoS) using predictive methods, including DL. Often, we need time series data for real-time or online anomaly detection, and if we can exploit any data source that is already in this form, we do not need additional feature engineering. CPU utilization data of IoT devices do not need further engineering for host/device level anomaly detection.

Implementation of use case one

We are considering an IoT-based, remote patient-monitoring application for the implementation of intelligent host-level intrusion detection. Monitoring of physiotherapy is a challenging task. An IoT-based therapy can solve the progress-monitoring issue. The following diagram briefly presents how the IoT-based remote-patient monitoring system and its device-level intrusion detection will work:

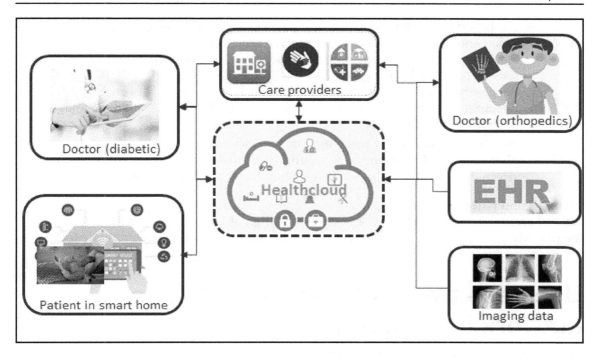

As shown in the preceding diagram, an IoT-based remote patient-monitoring system consists of three main elements:

- **Sensors and patient-side computing platform**: A patient will be attached to multiple sensors, including an electrocardiograph, blood pressure sensor, accelerometer, and a gyroscope. These sensors will be collecting physiological and activity-related information and sending it to care providers for necessary and real-time feedback. However, the data from these sensors or things can be unavailable because of DoS or DDoS attack. An intruder can launch a DoS attack by flooding these sensors with excessive requests in an attempt to overload it, preventing legitimate requests from being fulfilled. Similarly, the attacker can launch a DDoS attack by flooding these sensors from many different distributed sources. A Raspberry Pi 3 connected with the home network can work as the patient-side computing platform and as the sensor-level intrusion detector.

- **DL-based intrusion detection**: The Raspberry Pi 3 will be preinstalled with a DL-based anomaly detector that will analyze sensors and its CPU utilization to detect any potential intrusion into the sensors and computing platform. If the sensors come without any MCU, we will consider intrusion detection for the Raspberry Pi 3. The detector will continuously monitor CPU-utilization of the Raspberry Pi 3, and if an anomaly is found it will be reported to the management team for countermeasure.
- **Healthcloud for model learning**: The healthcloud is a cloud computing platform, mainly designed for healthcare-related services. This will train the selected DL model for anomaly detection using a reference dataset.

In the second part of the chapter (that is, the sections starting from *DL for IoT security incident detection*), we will describe the implementation of DL-based anomaly detection in the preceding use case. All the necessary codes are available in the chapter's code folder.

Use case two: traffic-based intelligent network intrusion detection in IoT

Generally, host intrusion (including device level intrusion) exploits outside world communications, and most of the time a successful host intrusion comes with the success of a network intrusion. For example, in botnets, remote command-and-control servers communicate with the compromised machines to give instructions on operations to execute. More importantly, a large number of insecure IoT devices has resulted in a surge of IoT botnet attacks in worldwide IT infrastructure. The Dyn **domain name system** (**DNS**) attack in October 2016 is an example of this, wherein the Mirai botnet commanded 100,000 IoT devices to launch the DDoS attack. This incident impacted many popular websites, including GitHub, Amazon, Netflix, Twitter, CNN, and PayPal. In this context, detection of network-level intrusion in IoT is not only necessary for IoT applications, but also for the rest of the IT industry.

Generally, a network intrusion detector identifies intruders by inspecting traffic that passes between the hosts in the network. Like host intrusion detection, network intrusion detection can be signature-based or anomaly detection-based. In the signature-based approach, all incoming traffic will be compared with a list of known signatures of malicious traffic, and the in the anomaly detection approach, it compares the incoming traffic with previously established normal behavior. Considering the resource-intensive aspect of the former approach, we will consider anomaly detection-based **intrusion detection system** (**IDS**).

Implementation of use case two

Unlike traditional networks, IDS in IoT needs to be lightweight, distributed to different layers, and long-lasting. The first condition is obvious for resource-constrained IoT devices. The solution needs to be distributed over many layers to optimize the effectiveness of the detection process. Importantly, the solution needs to be usable for long-lasting IoT devices. For example, a smart fridge could be in a house for more than 10 years, and finding a security solution that can withstand that length of time is a difficult task.

The following diagram presents an IoT infrastructure, including a multilayered network IDS, which can address the first two requirements of the IDS in an IoT. For example, an IoT deployment consists of different components that are distributed and resource constrained. A system-wide holistic IDS may not work well in terms of a real-time response. In this context, each layer in a multilayered IDS will work on identifying the layer-specific anomalies and the corresponding intruders in real time or quasi real time:

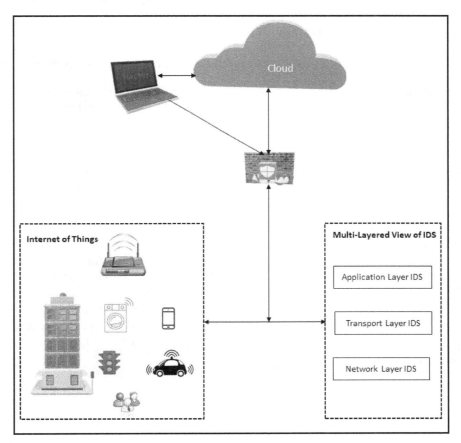

The multilayered network IDS of an IoT (especially in a smart home application) consists of the following three main elements:

- **Sensors/things and an edge computing platform**: Smart-home devices, such as smart TVs, smart fridges, thermostats, smart bulbs, and home physical security cameras, are the sensors or 'things' of the use case. These devices are connected to the internet via a home router/gateway. In this use case, we are considering a network-based security solution rather than a device-based solution. We are also assuming that the home router will work as the edge computing device and allow us to install the multilayered IDS.
- **DL-based intrusion detection**: The home router/gateway will be preinstalled with three (one for each layer) DL-based anomaly detectors that will analyze the traffics/packets coming from the home's connected things. Each of the detectors will analyze and compare with that layer's normal traffic to find any anomaly or intrusion that, if detected, will be reported to the home owner and/or automatically set up countermeasure.
- **Model learning platform**: A home desktop or cloud platform will be needed to learn and update the DL model for the anomaly detectors. This will train the selected DL model/models for anomaly detection using three reference datasets.

All of the following sections will describe the implementation of the DL-based network-level and node-level anomaly detection of the above use cases. All of the necessary code is available in the chapter's code folder.

DL for IoT security incident detection

Traditional security solutions (such as encryption, authentication, access control, and network security) are ineffective for IoT devices. In recent years, DL/ML-based solutions have become very popular alternatives to traditional solutions. DL/ML-based solutions can monitor IoT devices and their networks intelligently and detect various new or zero-day attacks. Importantly, DL/ML can detect and/or predict various devices and network level security incidents through anomaly detection. By gathering, processing, and analyzing data about various normal and abnormal activities of devices/things and their networks, these DL/ML methods can identify various security incidents, including IoT device and network level intrusions. In the following sections, we briefly present a few DL models that are useful in IoT device and network level IDS.

DNN, autoencoder, and LSTM in IoT security incidents detection

A number of DL models, including simple DNNs, autoencoders, and recurrent neural networks (RNNs)[6], are already being used for IoT security enhancement. These approaches can be supervised or unsupervised. In this chapter, we will use both supervised and unsupervised approaches. For the first use case, we will use the LSTM-based supervised approach for device-level intrusion detection. In use case two, we will use DNNs and autoencoders for supervised and unsupervised network-level intrusion detection, respectively. We are using LSTM for the first use case, as device-level intrusion detection is based on time series CPU utilization data and LSTM works well with temporal data. On the other hand, an autoencoder is a lightweight model and is well suited for resource-constrained IoT devices. We have already presented a brief overview of LSTM in the previous chapter and so, in the following diagram, we briefly present an overview of autoencoders as a review of the model.

As the name suggests, autoencoders encode and decode algorithms. The following diagram presents a simple architecture of an autoencoder model:

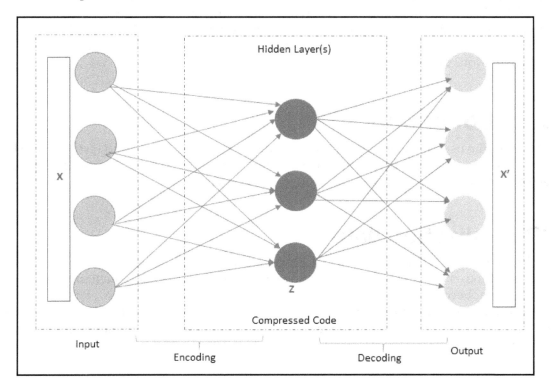

As shown in the preceding diagram, autoencoders consist of an input layer and an output layer that are connected through one or more hidden layers [7]. As autoencoders reproduce the inputs, they have the same number of input and output neurons. Generally, an autoencoder consists of two components: an encoder and a decoder. The encoder is connected with the input layer and, once it receives the input (X), it transforms it to a new and compressed representation (Z). The compressed code is also known as the code or latent variable (Z). In the output layer, the decoder receives the generated code or compressed code, and transforms it to a reconstruction of the original input. The aim of the training procedure in autoencoders is to minimize reconstruction errors in the output layer.

Autoencoders are good for diagnosis and fault detection because of their input reconstruction at the output layer. Importantly, this special feature of autoencoders is really useful in IoT, including **industrial IoT (IIoT)**, for fault diagnosis in hardware devices and machines, and for anomaly detection in operation/data gathering/performance. The anomaly detection capability of autoencoders motivates us to use the model in the network intrusion detection use case. Also, autoencoders are easily transferred between various IoT devices and the network once they are available in the cloud or server. Various types of autoencoders are available, including denoising, contractive, stacked, sparse, and variational autoencoders. In the use case, we will use a simple autoencoder architecture with a standalone DL model for intrusion detection, but autoencoders can be integrated with other DL models, including **convolutional neural networks (CNNs)** and LSTMs. In the following sections, starting with data collection, we will discuss DL-based implementations of the aforementioned use cases.

Data collection

For both of the use cases, we can generate our own datasets and train and test the models on them. In the following paragraphs, we briefly present how we can create a dataset for device-level host intrusion detection through a DoS attack.

CPU utilisation data

For the DoS attack, we need an attack machine and a target machine. We are using a Kali Linux machine as the attacker and a Windows machine as the target (which can be home gateway/Raspberry Pi 3/sensors). In Kali Linux, a DoS attack can be achieved in multiple ways. One way is to use the `hping3`. `hping3` command as a network tool to send custom TCP/IP packets, and allowing for the testing of firewalls, port scanning, address spoofing, and more.

This can be used to perform a DoS attack by sending multiple requests in quick succession, taking up an IoT server's/sensor's resources and making it slower or unable to respond. The following screenshot shows CPU utilization of the target Windows server before sending the hping3 command or launching the DoS attack:

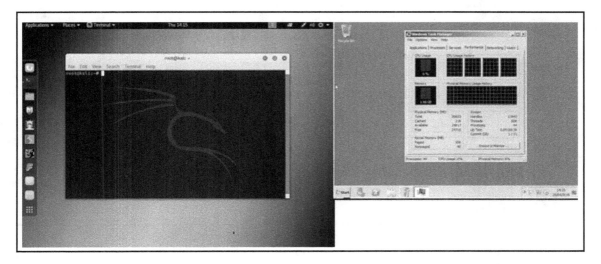

The following command is an example of a DoS attack using Kali Linux's hping3 tool.

```
hping3 -c 10000 -d 120 -S -w 64 -p 21 --flood --rand-source example.com
```

The following list is the syntax description of the preceding command:

- hping3: The name of the binary application
- -c 100000: The amount of packets
- -d 120: The sizing of each packet
- -S: SYN packets only
- -w 64: TCP window size
- -p 21: The destination port
- --flood: Means sending packets as fast as possible, without taking care to show incoming replies
- --rand-source: Using random source IP addresses; you can also use -a or -spoof to hide hostnames
- example.com: The website or destination IP address or the target machine's IP address

The following screenshot presents CPU utilization of the windows server after the DoS attack. We can clearly see that the CPU utilization of the attacked machine has increased by 30%:

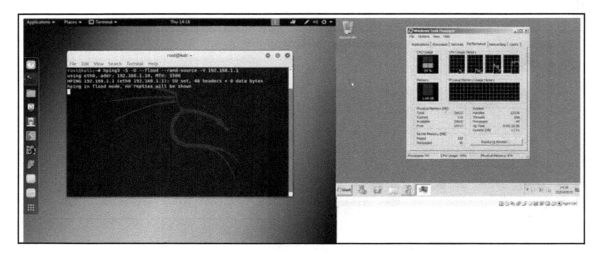

We can run different `hping3` sessions to different target machines, and save CPU utilization data. In Windows, a process monitor can be used to save the data. For use case one, we are using CPU utilization data for an LSTM-based intrusion detection algorithm.

KDD cup 1999 IDS dataset

Traffic-based intelligent network intrusion detection in IoT, we can use the Wireshark network monitoring tool to record and save network traffic against different attacks related to network intrusion, and create our own dataset. In addition, we can use an existing open source dataset. We are using the the KDD cup 1999 IDS dataset. This dataset is well suited for use case two as it is on the network-level intrusions. In the following paragraphs, we will briefly present an overview of the dataset. Please see reference for further detail.

The KDD cup 1999 datasets were generated by the **Defense Advanced Research Projects Agency (DARPA)** on a simulated air force model. The datasets were collected using two different sessions:

- Training data was collected for 7 weeks
- Testing data was collected for 2 weeks

The complete dataset includes 39 network level attack types and 200 instances of background traffic. The network traffic dataset is either classified as one of the attack types or as 'normal'. There are three versions of the KDD cup 1999 IDS datasets—a full KDD dataset, corrected KDD dataset, and 10% KDD dataset. The 10% KDD dataset is the most frequently used of the three datasets, and we are using this for use case two. In use case two, we will use an autoencoder for the clustering of normal and attack or intrusion traffic. Also, we will test a DNN for the classification of normal and attack traffic.

Data exploration

In the following paragraphs, we will explore the two datasets used for the two use cases (the CPU utilization dataset for IoT device level, and the KDD cup 1999 IDS dataset for network-level intrusion detection).

- **CPU utilization dataset**: The dataset is a CSV file consisting of dates and times with the corresponding CPU utilization rates (%). The dataset consists of 700 utilization values recorded every minute. The following screenshot presents a snapshot of the dataset:

time	cpu utilisation (%)
05/04/2019 19:42	44.8
05/04/2019 19:43	44
05/04/2019 19:44	43.6
05/04/2019 19:45	43.2
05/04/2019 19:46	44
05/04/2019 19:47	43.2
05/04/2019 19:48	45.2
05/04/2019 19:49	44.8
05/04/2019 19:50	43.6
05/04/2019 19:51	42.4
05/04/2019 19:52	41.6
05/04/2019 19:53	41.2
05/04/2019 19:54	40.4
05/04/2019 19:55	40
05/04/2019 19:56	39.6
05/04/2019 19:57	39.2
05/04/2019 19:58	38.8
05/04/2019 19:59	38
05/04/2019 20:00	37.2
05/04/2019 20:01	36.8
05/04/2019 20:02	36
05/04/2019 20:03	35.2
05/04/2019 20:04	35.2
05/04/2019 20:05	34.8
05/04/2019 20:06	34
05/04/2019 20:07	35.6
05/04/2019 20:08	34.4

- **KDD cup 1999 IDS dataset**: The following screenshot shows a snapshot of the KDD cup 1999 IDS dataset. It is clear from the screenshot that the dataset is not ready to be used in the model. The dataset has protocol types, categorical values, and data values are not normalized. Also, we need to split the data into three sets in order to implement a three-layered, network-level IDS implementation.

The following screenshot presents a network traffic pattern of normal communication:

```
0,tcp,http,SF,181,5450,0,0,0,0,0,1,0,0,0,0,0,0,0,0,0,0,8,8,0.00,0.00,0.00,0.00,1.00,0.00,0.00,9,9,1.00,0.00,0.11,0.00,0.00,0.00,0.00,0.00,normal.
0,tcp,http,SF,239,486,0,0,0,0,0,1,0,0,0,0,0,0,0,0,0,0,8,8,0.00,0.00,0.00,0.00,1.00,0.00,0.00,19,19,1.00,0.00,0.05,0.00,0.00,0.00,0.00,0.00,normal.
0,tcp,http,SF,235,1337,0,0,0,0,0,1,0,0,0,0,0,0,0,0,0,0,8,8,0.00,0.00,0.00,0.00,1.00,0.00,0.00,29,29,1.00,0.00,0.03,0.00,0.00,0.00,0.00,0.00,normal.
0,tcp,http,SF,219,1337,0,0,0,0,0,1,0,0,0,0,0,0,0,0,0,0,6,6,0.00,0.00,0.00,0.00,1.00,0.00,0.00,39,39,1.00,0.00,0.03,0.00,0.00,0.00,0.00,0.00,normal.
0,tcp,http,SF,217,2032,0,0,0,0,0,1,0,0,0,0,0,0,0,0,0,0,6,6,0.00,0.00,0.00,0.00,1.00,0.00,0.00,49,49,1.00,0.00,0.02,0.00,0.00,0.00,0.00,0.00,normal.
0,tcp,http,SF,217,2032,0,0,0,0,0,1,0,0,0,0,0,0,0,0,0,0,6,6,0.00,0.00,0.00,0.00,1.00,0.00,0.00,59,59,1.00,0.00,0.02,0.00,0.00,0.00,0.00,0.00,normal.
0,tcp,http,SF,212,1940,0,0,0,0,0,1,0,0,0,0,0,0,0,0,0,0,1,2,0.00,0.00,0.00,0.00,1.00,0.00,1.00,1,69,1.00,0.00,1.00,0.04,0.00,0.00,0.00,0.00,normal.
0,tcp,http,SF,159,4087,0,0,0,0,0,1,0,0,0,0,0,0,0,0,0,0,5,5,0.00,0.00,0.00,0.00,1.00,0.00,0.00,11,79,1.00,0.00,0.09,0.04,0.00,0.00,0.00,0.00,normal.
0,tcp,http,SF,210,151,0,0,0,0,0,1,0,0,0,0,0,0,0,0,0,0,8,8,0.00,0.00,0.00,0.00,1.00,0.00,0.00,8,89,1.00,0.00,0.12,0.04,0.00,0.00,0.00,0.00,normal.
0,tcp,http,SF,212,786,0,0,0,1,0,1,0,0,0,0,0,0,0,0,0,0,8,8,0.00,0.00,0.00,0.00,1.00,0.00,0.00,8,99,1.00,0.00,0.12,0.05,0.00,0.00,0.00,0.00,normal.
0,tcp,http,SF,210,624,0,0,0,0,0,1,0,0,0,0,0,0,0,0,0,0,18,18,0.00,0.00,0.00,0.00,1.00,0.00,0.00,18,109,1.00,0.00,0.06,0.05,0.00,0.00,0.00,0.00,normal.
0,tcp,http,SF,177,1985,0,0,0,0,0,1,0,0,0,0,0,0,0,0,0,0,1,1,0.00,0.00,0.00,0.00,1.00,0.00,0.00,28,119,1.00,0.00,0.04,0.04,0.00,0.00,0.00,0.00,normal.
0,tcp,http,SF,222,773,0,0,0,0,0,1,0,0,0,0,0,0,0,0,0,0,11,11,0.00,0.00,0.00,0.00,1.00,0.00,0.00,38,129,1.00,0.00,0.03,0.04,0.00,0.00,0.00,0.00,normal.
0,tcp,http,SF,256,1169,0,0,0,0,0,1,0,0,0,0,0,0,0,0,0,0,4,4,0.00,0.00,0.00,0.00,1.00,0.00,0.00,4,139,1.00,0.00,0.25,0.04,0.00,0.00,0.00,0.00,normal.
0,tcp,http,SF,241,259,0,0,0,0,0,1,0,0,0,0,0,0,0,0,0,0,1,1,0.00,0.00,0.00,0.00,1.00,0.00,0.00,14,149,1.00,0.00,0.07,0.04,0.00,0.00,0.00,0.00,normal.
```

The following screenshot presents a network traffic pattern of abnormal or attack (such as those by smurf-it, a network-level distributed DoS attack) communication:

```
0,icmp,ecr_i,SF,1032,0,0,0,0,0,0,0,0,0,0,0,0,0,0,0,0,511,511,0.00,0.00,0.00,0.00,1.00,0.00,0.00,255,255,1.00,0.00,1.00,0.00,0.00,0.00,0.00,0.00,smurf.
0,icmp,ecr_i,SF,1032,0,0,0,0,0,0,0,0,0,0,0,0,0,0,0,0,511,511,0.00,0.00,0.00,0.00,1.00,0.00,0.00,255,255,1.00,0.00,1.00,0.00,0.00,0.00,0.00,0.00,smurf.
0,icmp,ecr_i,SF,1032,0,0,0,0,0,0,0,0,0,0,0,0,0,0,0,0,511,511,0.00,0.00,0.00,0.00,1.00,0.00,0.00,255,255,1.00,0.00,1.00,0.00,0.00,0.00,0.00,0.00,smurf.
0,icmp,ecr_i,SF,1032,0,0,0,0,0,0,0,0,0,0,0,0,0,0,0,0,511,511,0.00,0.00,0.00,0.00,1.00,0.00,0.00,255,255,1.00,0.00,1.00,0.00,0.00,0.00,0.00,0.00,smurf.
0,icmp,ecr_i,SF,1032,0,0,0,0,0,0,0,0,0,0,0,0,0,0,0,0,511,511,0.00,0.00,0.00,0.00,1.00,0.00,0.00,255,255,1.00,0.00,1.00,0.00,0.00,0.00,0.00,0.00,smurf.
0,icmp,ecr_i,SF,1032,0,0,0,0,0,0,0,0,0,0,0,0,0,0,0,0,511,511,0.00,0.00,0.00,0.00,1.00,0.00,0.00,255,255,1.00,0.00,1.00,0.00,0.00,0.00,0.00,0.00,smurf.
0,icmp,ecr_i,SF,1032,0,0,0,0,0,0,0,0,0,0,0,0,0,0,0,0,511,511,0.00,0.00,0.00,0.00,1.00,0.00,0.00,255,255,1.00,0.00,1.00,0.00,0.00,0.00,0.00,0.00,smurf.
0,icmp,ecr_i,SF,1032,0,0,0,0,0,0,0,0,0,0,0,0,0,0,0,0,511,511,0.00,0.00,0.00,0.00,1.00,0.00,0.00,255,255,1.00,0.00,1.00,0.00,0.00,0.00,0.00,0.00,smurf.
0,icmp,ecr_i,SF,1032,0,0,0,0,0,0,0,0,0,0,0,0,0,0,0,0,511,511,0.00,0.00,0.00,0.00,1.00,0.00,0.00,255,255,1.00,0.00,1.00,0.00,0.00,0.00,0.00,0.00,smurf.
0,icmp,ecr_i,SF,1032,0,0,0,0,0,0,0,0,0,0,0,0,0,0,0,0,511,511,0.00,0.00,0.00,0.00,1.00,0.00,0.00,255,255,1.00,0.00,1.00,0.00,0.00,0.00,0.00,0.00,smurf.
0,icmp,ecr_i,SF,1032,0,0,0,0,0,0,0,0,0,0,0,0,0,0,0,0,511,511,0.00,0.00,0.00,0.00,1.00,0.00,0.00,255,255,1.00,0.00,1.00,0.00,0.00,0.00,0.00,0.00,smurf.
0,icmp,ecr_i,SF,1032,0,0,0,0,0,0,0,0,0,0,0,0,0,0,0,0,511,511,0.00,0.00,0.00,0.00,1.00,0.00,0.00,255,255,1.00,0.00,1.00,0.00,0.00,0.00,0.00,0.00,smurf.
0,icmp,ecr_i,SF,1032,0,0,0,0,0,0,0,0,0,0,0,0,0,0,0,0,511,511,0.00,0.00,0.00,0.00,1.00,0.00,0.00,255,255,1.00,0.00,1.00,0.00,0.00,0.00,0.00,0.00,smurf.
0,icmp,ecr_i,SF,1032,0,0,0,0,0,0,0,0,0,0,0,0,0,0,0,0,511,511,0.00,0.00,0.00,0.00,1.00,0.00,0.00,255,255,1.00,0.00,1.00,0.00,0.00,0.00,0.00,0.00,smurf.
0,icmp,ecr_i,SF,1032,0,0,0,0,0,0,0,0,0,0,0,0,0,0,0,0,511,511,0.00,0.00,0.00,0.00,1.00,0.00,0.00,255,255,1.00,0.00,1.00,0.00,0.00,0.00,0.00,0.00,smurf.
```

Data preprocessing

Data preprocessing is an essential step for a DL pipeline. The CPU utilization dataset is ready to be used in the training, but the KDD cup 1999 IDS dataset needs multilevel preprocessing that includes the following three steps:

1. Splitting the data into three different protocol sets (application, transport, and network)
2. Duplicate data removal, categorical data conversion, and normalization
3. Feature selection (optional)

Using the following lines of code is a potential way of splitting the dataset into three datasets, namely `Final_App_Layer`, `Final_Transport_Layer`, and `Final_Network_Layer`:

```python
#Importing all the required Libraries
import pandas as pd
IDSdata = pd.read_csv("kddcup.data_10_percent.csv",header = None,engine =
'python',sep=",")

# Add column header
IDSdata.columns =
["duration","protocol_type","service","flag","src_bytes","dst_bytes","land"
,"wrong_fragement","urgent",
"hot","num_failed_logins","logged_in","num_compressed","root_shell","su_att
empted","num_root","num_file_creations",
"num_shells","num_access_files","num_outbound_cmds","is_hot_login","is_gues
t_login","count","srv_count","serror_rate","srv_serror_rate","rerror_rate",
"srv_rerror_rate","same_srv_rate","diff_srv_rate","srv_diff_host_rate","dst
_host_count","dst_host_srv_count","dst_host_same_srv_rate","dst_host_diff_s
rv_rate","dst_host_same_src_port_rate","dst_host_srv_diff_host_rate","dst_h
ost_serror_rate","dst_host_srv_serror_rate","dst_host_rerror_rate","dst_hos
t_srv_rerror_rate","labels"]

# Explore the Application Layer IDS Data
ApplicationLayer =
IDSdata[(IDSdata['labels'].isin(['normal.','smurf.','back.','satan.','pod.'
,'guess_passwd.','buffer_overflow.','warezmaster.','imap.','loadmodule.','f
tp_write.','multihop.','perl.']))]
print (ApplicationLayer['labels'].value_counts())

# Save a Applayer data only into a text file
ApplicationLayer.to_csv('Final_App_Layer.txt',header = None,index = False)

# Explore the Transport Layer IDS Data
TransportLayer =
IDSdata[(IDSdata['labels'].isin(['normal.','neptune.','portsweep.','teardro
p.','buffer_overflow.','land.','nmap.']))]
print (TransportLayer['labels'].value_counts())
TransportLayer.to_csv('Final_Transport_Layer.txt',header = None,index =
False)

# Explore the Network Layer IDS Data
NetworkLayer =
IDSdata[(IDSdata['labels'].isin(['normal.','smurf.','ipsweep.','pod.','buff
er_overflow.']))]
print (NetworkLayer['labels'].value_counts())
NetworkLayer.to_csv('Final_Network_Layer.txt',header = None,index = False)
```

Once the datasets are ready, we remove the duplicate data entries and normalize the values of the remaining entries. The following lines of code or function can be used for duplicate removal and normalization:

```python
def DataPreprocessing(IDSdataframe):
 # Duplicate entry removal
    recordcount = len(IDSdataframe)
    print ("Original number of records in the training dataset before
removing duplicates is: " , recordcount)
    IDSdataframe.drop_duplicates(subset=None, inplace=True)  # Python
command to drop duplicates
    newrecordcount = len(IDSdataframe)
    print ("Number of records in the training dataset after removing the
duplicates is :", newrecordcount,"\n")

    #Dropping the labels to a different dataset which is used to train the
recurrent neural network classifier
    df_X = IDSdataframe.drop(IDSdataframe.columns[41],axis=1,inplace =
False)
    df_Y = IDSdataframe.drop(IDSdataframe.columns[0:41],axis=1, inplace =
False)

    # Categorial data to numerical data conversion
    df_X[df_X.columns[1:4]] =
df_X[df_X.columns[1:4]].stack().rank(method='dense').unstack()
    # Coding the normal as " 1 0" and attack as "0 1"
    df_Y[df_Y[41]!='normal.'] = 0
    df_Y[df_Y[41]=='normal.'] = 1

    #converting input data into float
    df_X = df_X.loc[:,df_X.columns[0:41]].astype(float)

    # Normal is "1 0" and the attack is "0 1"
    df_Y.columns = ["y1"]
    df_Y.loc[:,('y2')] = df_Y['y1'] ==0
    df_Y.loc[:,('y2')] = df_Y['y2'].astype(int)
    return df_X,df_Y
```

The final preprocessing of the datasets is the optimal set of features selection for the classifier. This is an optional process, but is useful for resource-constrained IoT devices, as this will minimize the size of the input layer or neurons of the network. The following lines of code or functions exploiting random forest can be used to do this preprocessing:

```
def FeatureSelection(myinputX, myinputY):
    labels = np.array(myinputY).astype(int)
    inputX = np.array(myinputX)

    #Random Forest Model
    model = RandomForestClassifier(random_state = 0)
    model.fit(inputX,labels)
    importances = model.feature_importances

    #Plotting the Features agains their importance scores
    indices = np.argsort(importances)[::-1]
    std = np.std([tree.feature_importances_ for tree in model.estimators_],
axis=0)
    plt.figure(figsize = (10,5))
    plt.title("Feature importances (y-axis) vs Features IDs(x-axis)")
    plt.bar(range(inputX.shape[1]), importances[indices],
        color="g", yerr=std[indices], align="center")
    plt.xticks(range(inputX.shape[1]), indices)
    plt.xlim([-1, inputX.shape[1]])
    plt.show()
    # Selecting top featueres which have higher importance values
    newX = myinputX.iloc[:,model.feature_importances_.argsort()[::-1][:10]]

    # Converting the dataframe into tensors
    myX = newX.as_matrix()
    myY = labels
    return myX,myY
```

The following two graphs highlight the 41 features of the application-layer and network-layer datasets, respectively. Features are ordered according to their importance, and it is clear from the graphs that different sets of features are important for different layer dataset. We tested the DL models with 8-12 and 41 features:

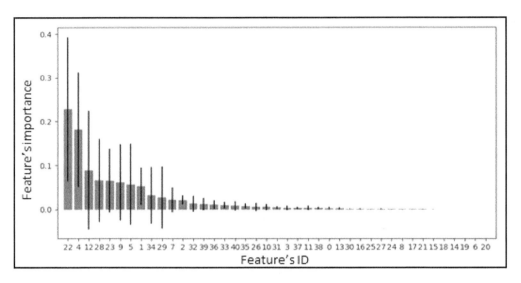

The following graphs highlight the 41 features of the network-layer datasets:

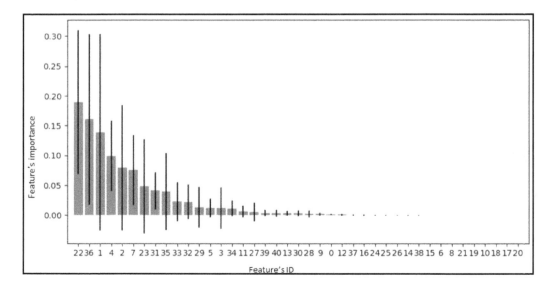

Model training

As we mentioned earlier in the chapter, we are using LSTM for use case one, an autoencoder for the multilayer IDS dataset, and DNN for the overall IDS dataset. In the following subsections, we will present the DL model-training process for the two use cases.

Use case one

We considered a three-LSTMs-layered network architecture for the CPU utilization based host/device-level intrusion detection. The following diagram presents the LSTM architecture we used:

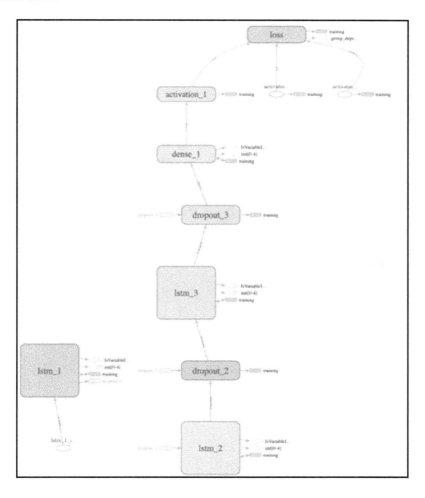

We can train and test the model by running the `lstm_anomaly_detection.py` file (available in the chapter's code folder) as follows:

```
python lstm_anomaly_detection.py
```

Use case two

We used an autoencoder for the multilayered IDS implementation using the KDD cup 1999 IDS dataset, and we have trained and tested the autoencoder on the three datasets. To train the model on each layer's dataset, we need to run the `IDS_AutoEncoder_KDD.py` file (available in the chapter's code folder) on the dataset as follows:

```
python IDS_AutoEncoder_KDD.py
```

We also trained and tested a DNN model on the overall KDD cup 1999 IDS dataset. To do so, we need to run the `DNN-KDD-Overall.py` file (available in the chapter's code folder) as follows:

```
python DNN-KDD-Overall.py
```

For all of the models, we have saved the best possible model to import and use in IoT devices. Also, we have saved models' logs using TensorBoard to visualize different aspects of the models, including the networks, and their performance graphs. We can generate the performance graphs and networks by running following command:

```
tensorboard --logdir logs
```

Once TensorBoard is running, navigate your web browser to `localhost:6006` to view the TensorBoard and view the network of the corresponding model. The following diagram is the architecture for the autoencoder used in the multilayered IDS for IoT:

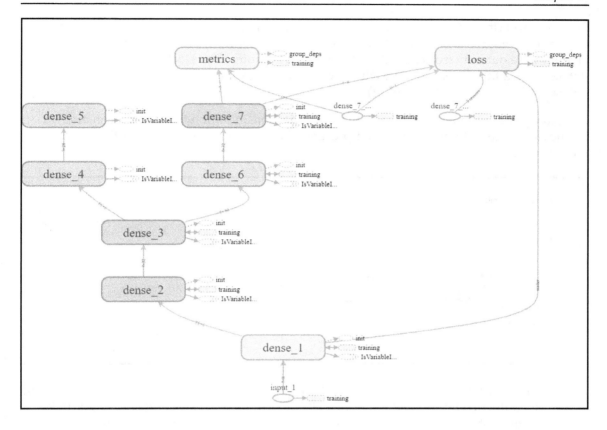

Model evaluation

We can evaluate three different aspects of the models:

- Learning/(re)training time
- Storage requirement
- Performance (accuracy)

On a desktop (Intel Xenon CPU E5-1650 v3@3.5GHz and 32 GB RAM) with GPU support, the training of LSTM on the CPU-utilization dataset and the autoencoder on the KDD layered wise dataset (reduced dataset) took a few minutes. The DNN model on the overall dataset took a little over an hour, which was expected as it has been trained on a larger dataset (KDD's overall 10% dataset).

The storage requirement of a model is an essential consideration in resource-constrained IoT devices. The following screenshot presents the storage requirements for the three models we tested for the two use cases:

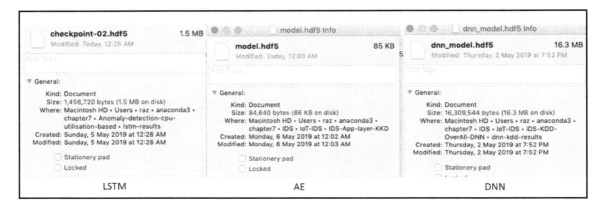

As shown in the screenshot, autoencoders took storage in the range of KB. The final version of a stored autoencoder model took only 85 KB, LSTM took 1.5 MB, and DNN took 16.3 MB. In terms of storage requirements, all the models are fine to be deployed in many resource-constrained IoT devices, including the Raspberry Pi and smartphones. Also, it is clear from the screenshot that an autoencoder is a very lightweight model, because of the optimal feature selection process, among other reasons.

Finally, we have evaluated the performance of the models. In both of the use cases, dataset-wide evaluation or testing has been done during the training phase in the PC platform/server side. We can also test them on the Raspberry Pi 3 or any IoT edge-computing devices as the models are saved and importable.

Model performance (use case one)

The following graph shows the validation result of the LSTM used on the CPU utilization dataset:

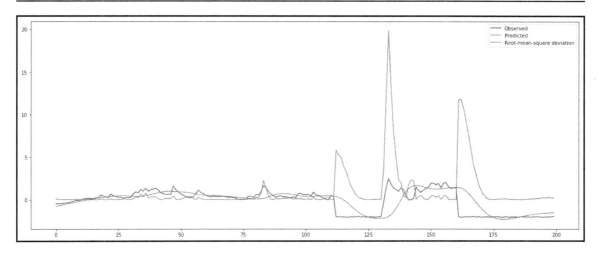

As we can see in the graph, the prediction follows the nonanomalous or 'normal' CPU utilization data series closely, and this is a hint that it is working fine. Importantly, when it finds the anomalous observations, the difference between the observed and predicted CPU utilization values (normalized) are significantly different to the normal behavior. This is an indication that there might be a DoS or DDoS attack to the IoT device. The error differences are plotted as a root mean squared (RMS) value, one of the most popular metrics of this kind.

Model performance (use case two)

We have tested the autoencoder model on the three datasets for three different layer's IDS. The following screenshot presents the evaluation result snapshot for the application layer's IDS:

```
8000/8000 [==============================] - 1s 119us/step - loss: 6.1625e-04 - acc: 0.9849 - val_loss: 0.0043 - val_acc: 0.9910
Epoch 92/100
8000/8000 [==============================] - 1s 94us/step - loss: 6.0790e-04 - acc: 0.9863 - val_loss: 0.0043 - val_acc: 0.9925
Epoch 93/100
8000/8000 [==============================] - 1s 73us/step - loss: 6.1403e-04 - acc: 0.9846 - val_loss: 0.0043 - val_acc: 0.9925
Epoch 94/100
8000/8000 [==============================] - 1s 107us/step - loss: 6.0658e-04 - acc: 0.9856 - val_loss: 0.0042 - val_acc: 0.9925
Epoch 95/100
8000/8000 [==============================] - 1s 80us/step - loss: 6.0448e-04 - acc: 0.9851 - val_loss: 0.0043 - val_acc: 0.9795
Epoch 96/100
8000/8000 [==============================] - 1s 121us/step - loss: 6.2155e-04 - acc: 0.9840 - val_loss: 0.0043 - val_acc: 0.9925
Epoch 97/100
8000/8000 [==============================] - 1s 111us/step - loss: 5.7116e-04 - acc: 0.9848 - val_loss: 0.0036 - val_acc: 0.9900
Epoch 98/100
8000/8000 [==============================] - 1s 88us/step - loss: 5.2258e-04 - acc: 0.9830 - val_loss: 0.0038 - val_acc: 0.9920
Epoch 99/100
8000/8000 [==============================] - 1s 84us/step - loss: 5.0029e-04 - acc: 0.9824 - val_loss: 0.0032 - val_acc: 0.9925
Epoch 100/100
8000/8000 [==============================] - 1s 78us/step - loss: 5.0952e-04 - acc: 0.9850 - val_loss: 0.0033 - val_acc: 0.9920
```

As we can see from the screenshot, training accuracy and validation and test accuracy are well above 90% when we used the first 12 most important features for the training. The performance could be different if we used a different feature set.

The following graph presents epoch-wise training accuracy of the preceding model on the application layer IDS dataset:

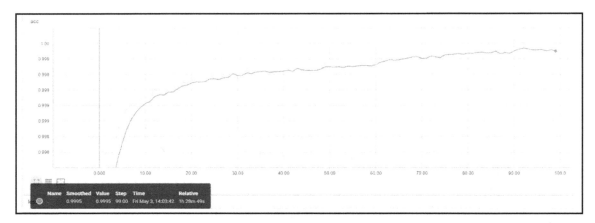

We obtained some interesting evaluation results for the network and transport layers IDS model training. If we use the first 12 most important features, the validation accuracy is in the range of 50%, and if we change the feature set to be in between 8 and 10, the accuracy moves into the range of 80–90%. The following two screenshots present a snapshot of the evaluation on the network layer IDS experimentation:

```
Epoch 88/100
8000/8000 [==============================] - 1s 107us/step - loss: 2.1088e-04 - acc: 0.9899 - val_loss: 0.0059 - val_acc: 0.9270
Epoch 89/100
8000/8000 [==============================] - 1s 110us/step - loss: 2.0525e-04 - acc: 0.9881 - val_loss: 0.0059 - val_acc: 0.9070
Epoch 90/100
8000/8000 [==============================] - 1s 119us/step - loss: 2.6043e-04 - acc: 0.9841 - val_loss: 0.0058 - val_acc: 0.9160
Epoch 91/100
8000/8000 [==============================] - 1s 97us/step - loss: 1.9234e-04 - acc: 0.9901 - val_loss: 0.0059 - val_acc: 0.9070
Epoch 92/100
8000/8000 [==============================] - 1s 95us/step - loss: 1.7994e-04 - acc: 0.9918 - val_loss: 0.0054 - val_acc: 0.9210
Epoch 93/100
8000/8000 [==============================] - 1s 109us/step - loss: 1.9276e-04 - acc: 0.9889 - val_loss: 0.0055 - val_acc: 0.9445
Epoch 94/100
8000/8000 [==============================] - 1s 79us/step - loss: 2.1188e-04 - acc: 0.9884 - val_loss: 0.0059 - val_acc: 0.9005
Epoch 95/100
8000/8000 [==============================] - 1s 82us/step - loss: 1.7335e-04 - acc: 0.9913 - val_loss: 0.0057 - val_acc: 0.9180
Epoch 96/100
8000/8000 [==============================] - 1s 79us/step - loss: 1.9446e-04 - acc: 0.9890 - val_loss: 0.0060 - val_acc: 0.8909
Epoch 97/100
8000/8000 [==============================] - 1s 80us/step - loss: 1.8210e-04 - acc: 0.9881 - val_loss: 0.0052 - val_acc: 0.9340
Epoch 98/100
8000/8000 [==============================] - 1s 108us/step - loss: 2.1122e-04 - acc: 0.9864 - val_loss: 0.0056 - val_acc: 0.9230
Epoch 99/100
8000/8000 [==============================] - 1s 101us/step - loss: 2.0366e-04 - acc: 0.9889 - val_loss: 0.0053 - val_acc: 0.9325
Epoch 100/100
8000/8000 [==============================] - 1s 71us/step - loss: 1.7829e-04 - acc: 0.9895 - val_loss: 0.0055 - val_acc: 0.9195

(tf-gpu) C:\Anaconda3\Book-DL-IoT\chapter7\IoT-IDS\IDS-Network-layer-KDD>_
```

Interestingly, as we can see from the second screenshot, the accuracy is in the range of 50% up to 50 epochs, and then it jumps into the range of 90%. The final accuracy, or the accuracy of the saved model, is in the range 91–98%. So, they are sufficient for detecting network and transport layer anomalies.

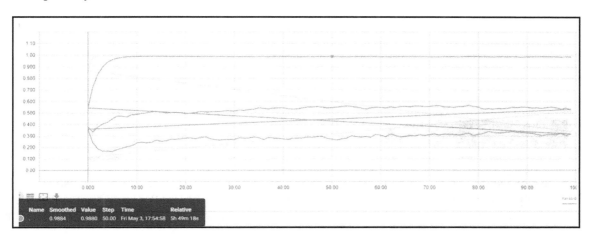

The following screenshot shows the training performance of the DNN model on the overall KDD dataset:

```
Epoch 00093: loss did not improve from 0.00189
Epoch 94/100
494021/494021 [==============================] - 50s 101us/step - loss: 0.0022 - acc: 0.9995

Epoch 00094: loss did not improve from 0.00189
Epoch 95/100
494021/494021 [==============================] - 53s 108us/step - loss: 0.0025 - acc: 0.9995

Epoch 00095: loss did not improve from 0.00189
Epoch 96/100
494021/494021 [==============================] - 51s 104us/step - loss: 0.0022 - acc: 0.9995

Epoch 00096: loss did not improve from 0.00189
Epoch 97/100
494021/494021 [==============================] - 55s 111us/step - loss: 0.0022 - acc: 0.9995

Epoch 00097: loss did not improve from 0.00189
Epoch 98/100
494021/494021 [==============================] - 50s 101us/step - loss: 0.0023 - acc: 0.9995

Epoch 00098: loss did not improve from 0.00189
Epoch 99/100
494021/494021 [==============================] - 52s 104us/step - loss: 0.0023 - acc: 0.9995

Epoch 00099: loss did not improve from 0.00189
Epoch 100/100
494021/494021 [==============================] - 51s 103us/step - loss: 0.0028 - acc: 0.9995

Epoch 00100: loss did not improve from 0.00189

(tf-gpu) C:\Anaconda3\Book-DL-IoT\chapter7\IoT-IDS\IDS-KDD-OverAll-DNN>
```

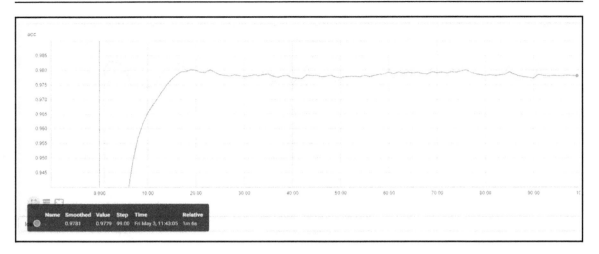

As we can see from the preceding figures, test accuracy is close to 1 or 100%. We also separately tested the saved model and test accuracy was well above 0.90 or 90%. Hence, the DNN is also good enough to detect network-level intrusions in IoT networks.

Summary

Security is the single most important issue in IoT realization. Traditional PC/desktop security solutions, especially signature-based solutions, are not effective in IoT applications. Behavior-based solutions, such as anomaly detection, are preferable in IoT. DL/ML models are very useful tools in IoT for data analysis and also for security incident detection. In this chapter, we presented DL-based network and device behavioral data analysis, and security incident detection techniques for IoT applications in general. In the first part of this chapter, we briefly described various IoT security attacks and their potential detection techniques, including DL/ML based techniques. We considered two different levels of intrusion detection in IoT applications. The first use case is on device-level or host-level intrusion detection, and the second use case is on network-level intrusion detection. In the second part of the chapter, we presented the DL-based anomaly or incident detection part of the use cases' implementations. As found in the evaluations, the chosen DL models are good enough to detect device- and network-level intrusions in IoT applications.

IoT will be used in various applications, such as infrastructure and industry, to monitor their health conditions. One of the potential applications of health monitoring is predictive maintenance of the monitored subject (such as a motor) to avoid service disruption or any other incidents.

In the next chapter, we will briefly introduce the importance of IoT-based predictive maintenance and its implementation using DL models.

References

- *Internet of Things (IoT) connected devices installed base worldwide from 2015 to 2025 (in billions)*, at `https://www.statista.com/statistics/471264/iot-number-of-connected-devices-worldwide/`.

- *Real-Time Detection of Application-Layer DDoS Attack Using Time Series Analysis*, T. Ni, X. Gu, H. Wang, and Y. Li, Journal of Control Science and Engineering, vol. 2013, pp. 1–6, 2013.

- *DDoS in the IoT: Mirai and Other Botnets*, C. Kolias, G. Kambourakis, A. Stavrou, and J. Voas, IEEE Computer, vol. 50, no. 7, pp. 80–84, 2017.

- 2016 Dyn cyberattack, at `https://en.wikipedia.org/wiki/2016_Dyn_cyberattack`.

- *A Big Network Traffic Data Fusion Approach Based on Fisher and Deep Auto-Encoder*, Tao X., Kong D., Wei Y., and Wang Y. (2016), Information, 7(2), 20.

- *An Effective Intrusion Detection Classifier Using Long Short-Term Memory with Gradient Descent Optimization*, Kim J., and Kim H. (2017, February), In Platform Technology and Service (PlatCon), 2017 International Conference on (pp. 1-6), IEEE.

- Pierre Baldi, *Autoencoders, Unsupervised Learning and Deep Architectures*, Isabelle Guyon, Gideon Dror, Vincent Lemaire, Graham Taylor, and Daniel Silver (Eds.), In Proceedings of the 2011 International Conference on Unsupervised and Transfer Learning workshop—Volume 27 (UTLW'11), Vol. 27, JMLR.org 37-50, 2011.

- KDD Cup 1999 Data, at `http://kdd.ics.uci.edu/databases/kddcup99/kddcup99.html`.

Section 3: Advanced Aspects and Analytics in IoT

3

In this section we will learn how to develop a DL solution for the predictive maintenance of IoT using the Turbofan Engine Degradation Simulation dataset. Moving on, in this section, we will examine how we can use DL-based IoT solutions in the field of healthcare and discuss two use cases in detail, looking at where healthcare services can be improved and/or automatized using DL-supported IoT solutions. Then, we will look at different challenges faced by existing DL techniques in IoT, especially in resource-constrained and embedded IoT devices, and introduce ourselves to a few future solution directions in order to address the remaining issues.

This section consists of the following chapters:

- Chapter 8, *Predictive Maintenance for IoT*
- Chapter 9, *Deep Learning in Healthcare IoT*
- Chapter 10, *What's Next: Wrapping Up and Future Directions*

Predictive Maintenance for IoT 8

In **Internet of Things** (**IoT**) devices, streaming data is generated for one event at a time. DL-based approaches can examine this data in order to diagnose the problem across the fleet in real time, and the future health of individual units can be predicted in order to enable on-demand maintenance. This strategy is known as **predictive** (or **condition-based**) **maintenance**. This approach is now emerging as one of the most promising and lucrative industrial applications of the IoT.

Considering these motivations, in this chapter, we will look at how to develop a DL solution for predictive maintenance for IoT using the **Turbofan Engine Degradation Simulation** dataset. The idea behind predictive maintenance is to determine whether the failure patterns of various types can be predictable. Furthermore, we will discuss how to collect data from IoT-enabled devices for the predictive maintenance. In a nutshell, the following topics will be covered in this chapter:

- Predictive maintenance for IoT
- Developing a predictive maintenance application
- Preparing the data
- Training ML baselines
- Training the LSTM model
- Evaluating the model
- FAQs

Predictive maintenance for IoT

With advances in real-time data capture and streaming architecture, it is now possible to have real-time data monitoring, where an organization can gain real-time insight into individual components and all processes. Monitoring still requires active involvement and quick responses—for example, an oil well sensor that is indicating increased temperature or volume or a network traffic for bot-net activity or insider threats.

Let's consider a real-world example called **equipment failures in industrial engineering,** which is always considered a costly issue. Conducting preventative maintenance at regular intervals has always been the conventional strategy. Consequently, the schedules tend to be very unadventurous, which is often based on operator experience. This manual intervention has several downsides. Firstly, it tends to increase maintenance costs. Secondly, it's impossible to adapt such a setting to a highly complex or changing industrial scenario.

Collecting IoT data in an industrial setting

According to **RT Insights**, a single jet engine could cost $16 million, and on a transatlantic flight it can consume 36,000 gallons of fuel. Today's airline fuel prices come to around $54,000 per trip, or more than $5,000 an hour. The majority of jet engines are gas turbine engines in which the thermal energy is converted into kinetic energy by expanding through nozzles, then into rotational mechanical energy in a spinning rotor. Such engines produce huge amounts of IoT data. Let's try to perceive how predictive maintenance with ML could help us to reduce the maintenance costs.

The first step is to collect the sensor data representing healthy and faulty operations under different operating conditions, for example, temperature, flow, and pressure. In a real-life scenario, those might be deployed in different environments and locations (suppose you are in Siberia at an operating temperature of -20 degree Celsius with high fluid viscosity, and another one in a Middle Eastern country with a temperature of 45 degree Celsius with high fluid viscosity).

Even though both of them are supposed to work normally, one of the engines might fail sooner because of different operating conditions. Unfortunately, without having enough data, there's no further way to investigate the root cause of the failure. Once such a jet turbine engine is deployed, sensor data can be collected using streaming technologies in the following settings:

- Real sensor data from normal system operations
- Real sensor data from a system operating in a faulty condition
- Real sensor data from system failures (*run-to-failure* data)

However, if we don't have many such engines deployed, we won't have much data, which would represent both healthy and faulty conditions and operations. There are two workarounds to overcome this data scarcity:

- Using historical data from similar/ the same engine, which might resemble the currently-deployed engines.
- Secondly, we can build a mathematical model of the engines and estimate their parameters from the available sensor data. Based on the statistical distribution and operating conditions, we can then generate failure data.

If we go with the second option, after generating the sensor data, we can combine them with the real sensor data to generate large-scale sensor data for the developing predictive maintenance model, as shown in the following diagram:

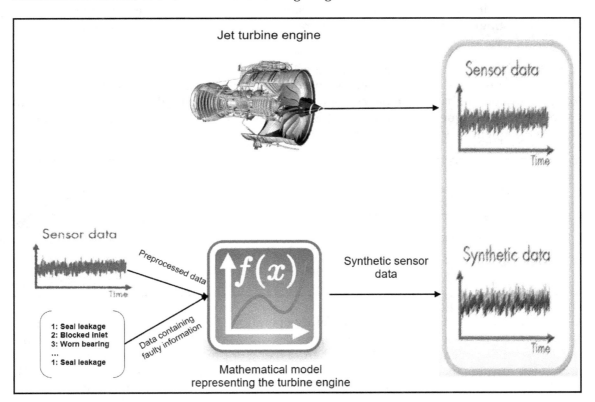

ML techniques for predictive maintenance

Deep learning (DL) techniques can be applied to process the massive amount of IoT data and can be an appealing emerging alternative to classical machine learning algorithms. The idea is that when equipment is given with sensors and networked, a huge amount of sensor data is produced. In a more complex industrial setting, data from the sensor channels is quite noisy and fluctuates over time, but some of the data does not seem to change at all. This is more-or-less true for every industrial setting because the data produced in an IoT setting is a multivariate series of sensor measurements each with its own amount of noise containing many missing or uninformative values.

A key step in predictive maintenance application development is identifying the **Condition Indicators** (**CIs**) and features from the collected sensor data, inspecting the behavior changes of CIs in a predictable way as the system degrades. Usually, CIs contain features that help distinguish normal and faulty operations and predict **Remaining Useful Life** (**RUL**).

The RUL of an engine or machine is the expected life or usage time remaining before the engine requires repair or replacement. Consequently, predicting RUL from sensor data is key in many predictive-maintenance applications. In the following diagram, we can see that the peaks in the frequency data shifts to the left as the turbine engine degrades. Therefore, the peak frequency can serve as condition indicators:

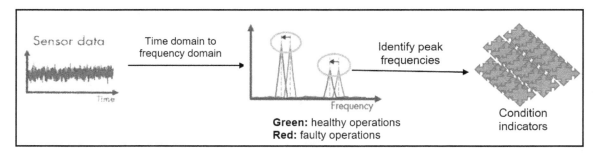

CIs can help us understand healthy and faulty operation in the turbine engine. However, they don't tell us what parts need to be repaired or how much time remains until the failure occurs. We either identify the fault types before fixing or predict the RUL before the scheduled maintenance. For the former option, use the extracted CIs features to train an ML or DL model and identify the fault types, such as seal leakage, blocked inlet, or worn bearing, as shown in the following diagram:

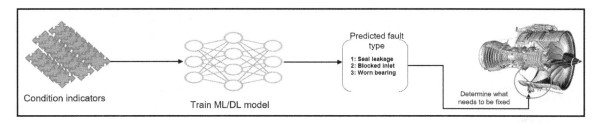

For the latter strategy, we can also train the ML/DL model to predict the trend that the pumps will continue to transition between these two states (current condition and the failure). A DL model can capture the relationships between CI features, and the degradation path of the turbine engine will help us to predict how much time we have until the next failure or when we should schedule maintenance, as depicted in the following diagram:

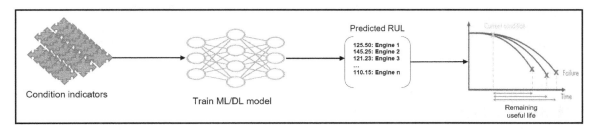

Finally, a stable model can be deployed in an industrial setting. The preceding steps can be summarized in the following diagram:

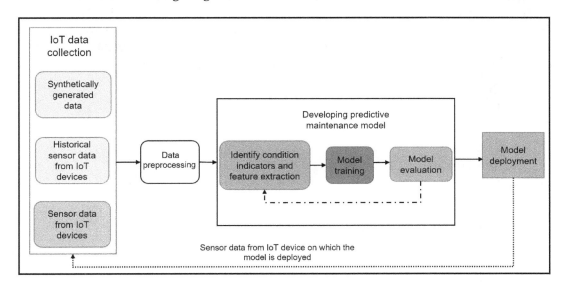

Unfortunately, due to the lack of sensor data for predicting fault types, in the next section, we will see a hands-on example on predicting RUL using both ML and DL techniques.

Example – PM for an aircraft gas turbine engine

To give a real-life glimpse into predictive maintenance, we will use the open source **Turbofan Engine Degradation Simulation** dataset, which was released in 2008 by the **Prognostics Center of Excellence** at NASA's Ames research centre. The dataset can be downloaded from `https://ti.arc.nasa.gov/c/6/`. We're thankful to the authors of the following research for providing this dataset:

 Turbofan Engine Degradation Simulation Data Set, A Saxena and K Goebel (2008), NASA Ames Prognostics Data Repository (`https://ti.arc.nasa.gov/tech/dash/groups/pcoe/prognostic-data-repository/`), NASA Ames Research Center, Moffett Field, CA.

Describing the dataset

The dataset consists of sensor readings from a fleet of simulated aircraft gas turbine engines operating conditions as a multiple multivariate time series. The dataset consists of separate training and test sets. The testset is similar to the training set, except that each engine's measurements are truncated some (unknown) amount of time before it fails. The data is provided as a ZIP-compressed text file with 26 columns of numbers. Each row represents a snapshot of data taken during a single operational cycle and each column represents a different variable. The columns correspond to the following attributes:

- Unit number
- Time, in cycles
- Operational setting 1
- Operational setting 2
- Operational setting 3
- Sensor measurement 1
- Sensor measurement 2
- Sensor measurement 26

In addition, the dataset has a vector of true RUL values for the data, which will be used as the ground truths for training the models.

Exploratory analysis

To give an idea of the sensor readings in areas such as the physical state of the engine (for example, with regard to the temperature of a component, the fan speed of the turbine, and so on) we decided to extract the first unit from the first dataset for all the sensors on a single engine. For this, we have written a script (see make_dataset.py) that gets all of the data files from the input directory. Then it parses a set of raw data files into a single DataFrame object and returns an aggregated representation of all files with the appropriate column names:

```python
data_sets = []
    for data_file in glob(file_pattern):
        if label_data:
            # read in contents as a DataFrame
            subset_df = pd.read_csv(data_file, header=None)
            # need to create a unit_id column explicitly
            unit_id = range(1, subset_df.shape[0] + 1)
            subset_df.insert(0, 'unit_id', unit_id)
        else:
            # read in contents as a DataFrame
            subset_df = pd.read_csv(data_file, sep=' ', header=None,
usecols=range(26))
            # extract the id of the dataset from the name and add as a column
            dataset_id = basename(data_file).split("_")[1][:5]
            subset_df.insert(0, 'dataset_id', dataset_id)
            # add to list
            data_sets.append(subset_df)
        # combine dataframes
        df = pd.concat(data_sets)
        df.columns = columns
        # return the result

        return df
```

To use this script, first copy all the files in the data/raw/ directory, and then execute the following command:

```
$python3 make_dataset.py data/raw/ /data/processed/
```

This command will generate three files—train.csv, test.csv, and RUL.csv—for the training set, testset, and labels, respectively. Now that our dataset is ready for exploratory analysis, we can now read each CSV file as a pandas DataFrame:

```
# load the processed data in CSV format
train_df = pd.read_csv('train.csv')
test_df = pd.read_csv('test.csv')
rul_df = pd.read_csv('RUL.csv')

# for convenience, identify the sensor and operational setting columns
sensor_columns = [col for col in train_df.columns if
col.startswith("sensor")]
setting_columns = [col for col in train_df.columns if
col.startswith("setting")]
```

Then, extract the first unit from the first dataset:

```
slice = train_df[(train_df.dataset_id == 'FD001') & (train_df.unit_id ==
1)]
```

Then, we plot its sensor traces over time on a $7 * 3 = 21$ plots grid to see all sensor channels. We have to plot the channel corresponding to this position:

```
fig, axes = plt.subplots(7, 3, figsize=(15, 10), sharex=True)

for index, ax in enumerate(axes.ravel()):
    sensor_col = sensor_columns[index]
    slice.plot(x='cycle', y=sensor_col, ax=ax, color='blue');
    # label formatting
    if index % 3 == 0:
        ax.set_ylabel("Sensor reading", size=10);
    else:
        ax.set_ylabel("");
    ax.set_xlabel("Time (cycle)");
    ax.set_title(sensor_col.title(), size=14);
    ax.legend_.remove();

# plot formatting
fig.suptitle("Sensor reading : unit 1, dataset 1", size=20, y=1.025)
fig.tight_layout();
```

As seen in the following diagram, data from the sensor channels is quite noisy and fluctuates over time, while other data does not seem to change at all. Each sensor's life cycle is different in terms of the starting and ending value on the x axis:

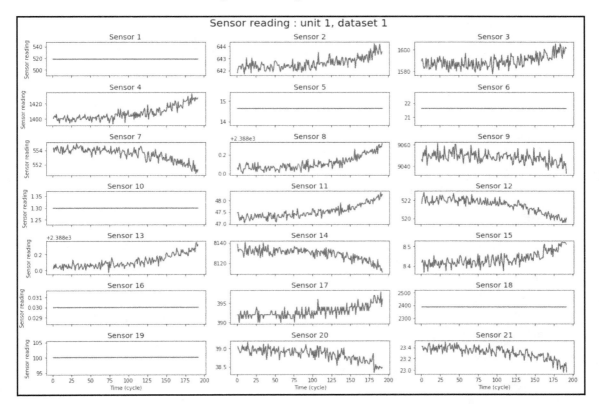

We can see that each engine has a slightly different lifetime and failure pattern. Next, we can visualize the data from all the sensor channels against time for a random sample of 10 engines from the training set:

```
# randomly select 10 units from dataset 1 to plot
all_units = train_df[train_df['dataset_id'] == 'FD001']['unit_id'].unique()
units_to_plot = np.random.choice(all_units, size=10, replace=False)

# get the data for these units
plot_data = train_df[(train_df['dataset_id'] == 'FD001') &
                     (train_df['unit_id'].isin(units_to_plot))].copy()

# plot their sensor traces (overlaid)
fig, axes = plt.subplots(7, 3, figsize=(15, 10), sharex=True)

for index, ax in enumerate(axes.ravel()):
    sensor_col = sensor_columns[index]

    for unit_id, group in plot_data.groupby('unit_id'):
        # plot the raw sensor trace
        (group.plot(x='cycle', y=sensor_col, alpha=0.45, ax=ax,
color='gray', legend=False));
        # overlay the 10-cycle rolling mean sensor trace for visual clarity
        (group.rolling(window=10, on='cycle')
            .mean()
            .plot(x='cycle', y=sensor_col, alpha=.75, ax=ax,
color='black', legend=False));
    # label formatting
    if index % 3 == 0:
        ax.set_ylabel("Sensor Value", size=10);
    else:
        ax.set_ylabel("");
    ax.set_title(sensor_col.title());
    ax.set_xlabel("Time (Cycles)");

# plot formatting
fig.suptitle("All Sensor Traces: Dataset 1 (Random Sample of 10 Units)",
size=20, y=1.025);
fig.tight_layout();
```

The preceding code segment shows the following graph of random samples of 10 units from the sensor reading from dataset 1:

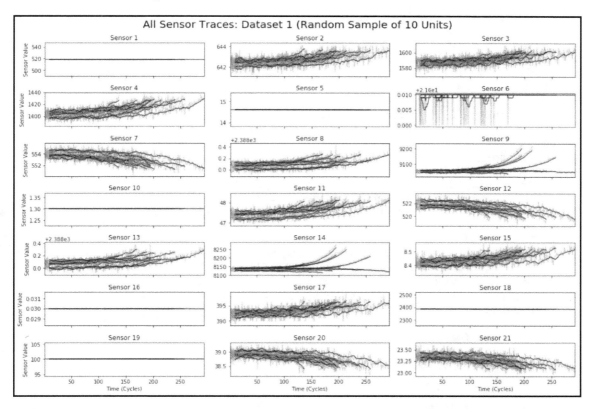

From the preceding graph, we can inspect that an engine's progress with respect to time is not quite aligned with the others. This is an impedance that does not allow us to compare the fifth cycle of one engine to the fifth cycle of another, for example.

Inspecting failure modes

Since it is already known when each engine in the training set will fail, we can compute a **time before failure** value at each time step, which can be defined as follows:

Time before failure (TBF) = engine elapsed life at failure time (EEL) - total operating lifetime (TOL)

This number can be considered as the countdown to failure for each engine, which allows us to align different engines' data to a common end:

```
# generate the lifetimes series
lifetimes = train_df.groupby(['dataset_id', 'unit_id'])['cycle'].max()

# apply the above function to the data we're plotting
plot_data['ctf'] = plot_data.apply(lambda r: cycles_until_failure(r,
lifetimes), axis=1)

# plot the sensor traces (overlaid)
fig, axes = plt.subplots(7, 3, figsize=(15, 10), sharex=True)
for index, ax in enumerate(axes.ravel()):
    sensor_col = sensor_columns[index]
    # use the same subset of data as above
    for unit_id, group in plot_data.groupby('unit_id'):
        # plot the raw sensor trace, using ctf on the time axis
        (group.plot(x='ctf', y=sensor_col, alpha=0.45, ax=ax, color='gray',
legend=False));

        # overlay the 10-cycle rolling mean sensor trace for visual clarity
        (group.rolling(window=10, on='ctf')
            .mean()
            .plot(x='ctf', y=sensor_col, alpha=.75, ax=ax, color='black',
legend=False));

    # label formatting
    if index % 3 == 0:
        ax.set_ylabel("Sensor Value", size=10);
    else:
        ax.set_ylabel("");
    ax.set_title(sensor_col.title());
    ax.set_xlabel("Time Before Failure (Cycles)");

    # add a vertical red line to signal common time of failure
    ax.axvline(x=0, color='r', linewidth=3);

    # extend the x-axis to compensate
    ax.set_xlim([None, 10]);
fig.suptitle("All Sensor Traces: Dataset 1 (Random Sample of 10 Units)",
size=20, y=1.025);
fig.tight_layout();
```

The following shows the sensor channels in the same engines. The only difference is that the previous graph is plotted against the time before failure, where each engine ends at the same instant (*t=0*). It also gives us a common pattern across different engines, which shows that some sensor readings consistently rise or fall right before a failure, while others—for example, sensor 14—exhibit different failure behaviors:

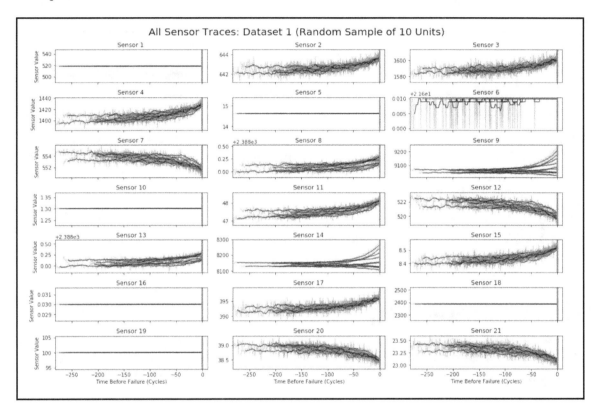

This pattern is very common in many predictive maintenance problems: failure is often a confluence of different processes, and as a result, things in the real world are likely to exhibit multiple failure modes. Due to this unpredictable pattern of data, predicting the RUL is very challenging.

Prediction challenges

As shown in the following diagram, after observing the engine's sensor measurements and operating conditions for a certain amount of time (133 cycles in the diagram), the challenge is to predict the amount of time (in other words, the RUL) that the engine will continue to function before it fails:

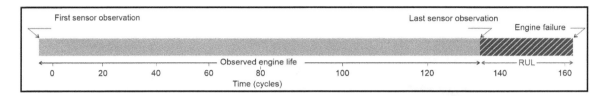

However, making an incorrect prediction for an ML/DL model is basically underestimating the true RUL of a particular engine. This can bring the turbine engine to maintenance too early, when it could have operated for a bit longer without any issues arising. So, what would happen if our model were to overestimate the true RUL instead? In that case, we might allow a degrading aircraft to keep flying, and risk catastrophic engine failure. Clearly, the costs of these two outcomes would not be the same. Considering these challenges, in the next section, we will focus on using DL-based techniques for predicting RUL.

DL for predicting RLU

As we have discussed, we are trying to calculate the amount of time before an engine needs maintenance. What makes this dataset special is that the engines run all the way until failure, giving us the precise RLU information for every engine at every point in time.

Calculating cut-off times

Let's consider the FD004 dataset, that contains as much as 249 engines (engine_no) monitored over time (time_in_cycles). Each engine has operational_settings and sensor_measurements recorded for each cycle:

```
data_path = 'train_FD004.txt'
data = utils.load_data(data_path)
```

To train a model that will predict RUL, we can simulate real predictions by choosing a random point in the life of the engine and only using the data from before that point. We can create features with that restriction easily by using cut-off times:

```
def make_cutoff_times(data):
    gb = data.groupby(['unit_id'])
    labels = []
    for engine_no_df in gb:
        instances = engine_no_df[1].shape[0]
        label = [instances - i - 1 for i in range(instances)]
        labels += label
    return new_labels(data, labels)
```

The preceding function generates the cut-off times by sampling for both `cutoff_time` and `label`, which can be called as follows:

```
cutoff_times = utils.make_cutoff_times(data)
cutoff_times.head()
```

The preceding lines of code show the following RUL and cut-off time for five engines only:

index	engine_no	cutoff_time	RUL
1	1	2000-01-01 12:00:00	119
2	2	2000-01-03 00:10:00	189
3	3	2000-01-05 09:50:00	22
4	4	2000-01-06 06:00:00	90
5	5	2000-01-07 02:30:00	236

Deep feature synthesis

Then, we generate the features using **Deep Feature Synthesis (DFS)**. For this, we need to establish an entity set structure for our data. We can create an engines entity by normalizing the `engine_no` column in the raw data:

```
def make_entityset(data):
    es = ft.EntitySet('Dataset')
    es.entity_from_dataframe(dataframe=data,
                            entity_id='recordings',
                            index='index',
                            time_index='time')
```

```
    es.normalize_entity(base_entity_id='recordings',
                        new_entity_id='engines',
                        index='engine_no')
    es.normalize_entity(base_entity_id='recordings',
                        new_entity_id='cycles',
                        index='time_in_cycles')
    return es
es = make_entityset(data)
```

The preceding code block will generate the following statistics of the entity set:

```
Entityset: Dataset
  Entities:
    recordings [Rows: 20631, Columns: 28]
    engines [Rows: 100, Columns: 2]
    cycles [Rows: 362, Columns: 2]
  Relationships:
    recordings.engine_no -> engines.engine_no
    recordings.time_in_cycles -> cycles.time_in_cycles
```

The `ft.dfs` function takes an entity set and stacks primitives such as max, min, and last exhaustively across entities:

```
fm, features = ft.dfs(entityset=es,
                      target_entity='engines',
                      agg_primitives=['last', 'max', 'min'],
                      trans_primitives=[],
                      cutoff_time=cutoff_times,
                      max_depth=3,
                      verbose=True)
fm.to_csv('FM.csv')
```

ML baselines

Now that we have generated the features, we can start training a first ML model called `RandomForestRegressor`. Then, we will gradually move to using DL using **Long Short-Term Memory (LSTM)** network. **Random forest (RF)** is an ensemble technique that builds several decision trees and integrates them together to get a more accurate and stable prediction. In general, a deeper tree signifies more complex decision rules and a better-fitted model for example the following image shows Decision tree for university admission data:

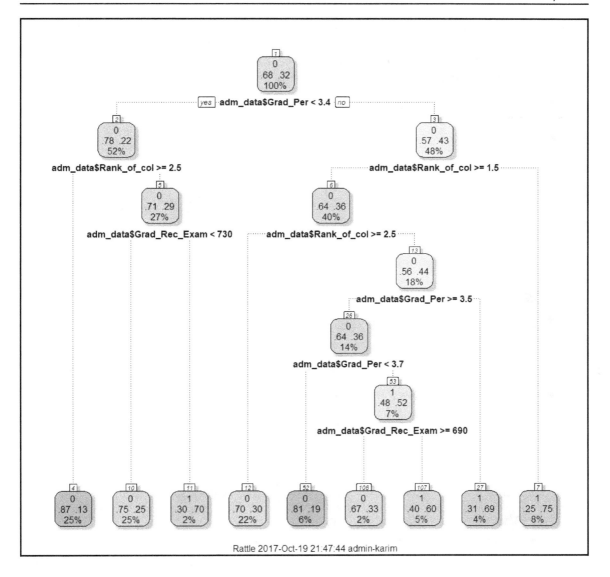

Rattle 2017-Oct-19 21:47:44 admin-karim

Consequently, the deeper the tree, the more complex the decision rules and the better fitted the model is. This is a direct consequence of Random Forest. In other words, the final prediction based on the majority vote from a panel of independent juries is always better and more reliable than the best jury. The following diagram shows random forest and its assembling technique:

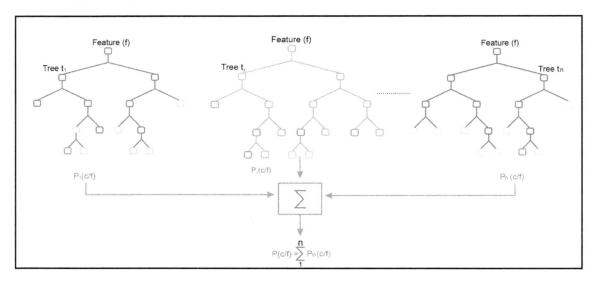

So, let's get started by preparing the separate training set and test set:

```
fm = pd.read_csv('FM.csv', index_col='engine_no')
X = fm.copy().fillna(0)
y = X.pop('RUL')
X_train, X_test, y_train, y_test = train_test_split(X, y)
```

Then, using the training set, we will check the following baselines:

- Always predict the median value of y_train.
- Always predict the RUL as if every engine has the median lifespan in X_train.

We will check those predictions by finding the mean of the absolute value of the errors called the **Mean Absolute Error (MAE)** using RandomForestRegressor from scikit-learn:

```
from sklearn.model_selection import train_test_split
from sklearn.metrics import mean_absolute_error

yhat_median_predict = [np.median(y_train) for _ in y_test]
print('Baseline by median label: MAE = {:.2f}'.format(
    mean_absolute_error(yhat_median_predict, y_test)))
```

```
# Collect sensor readings from the sensor in training set
recordings_from_train =
es['recordings'].df[es['recordings'].df['engine_no'].isin(y_train.index)]
median_life =
np.median(recordings_from_train.groupby(['engine_no']).apply(lambda df:
df.shape[0]))

# Collect sensor readings from the sensor in training set
recordings_from_test =
es['recordings'].df[es['recordings'].df['engine_no'].isin(y_test.index)]
life_in_test = recordings_from_test.groupby(['engine_no']).apply(lambda df:
df.shape[0])-y_test

# Compute mean absolute error as the baseline by meadian of the RUL
yhat_median_predict2 = (median_life - life_in_test).apply(lambda row:
max(row, 0))
print('Baseline by median life: MAE = {:.2f}'.format(
    mean_absolute_error(yhat_median_predict2, y_test)))
```

The preceding code block should produce the following output showing the baseline MAE values:

```
Baseline by median label: MAE = 66.72
Baseline by median life: MAE = 59.96
```

Making predictions

Now we can use our created features to fit RandomForestRegressor to our data and see whether we can improve on the previous scores:

```
rf = RandomForestRegressor() # first we instantiate RandomForestRegressor
from scikit-learn
rf.fit(X_train, y_train) # train the regressor model with traing set
preds = rf.predict(X_test) # making predictin on unseen observation
scores = mean_absolute_error(preds, y_test) # Computing MAE

print('Mean Abs Error: {:.2f}'.format(scores))
high_imp_feats = utils.feature_importances(X, reg, feats=10) # Printing
feature importance
```

The preceding code block should produce the following output showing the baseline MAE values and statistics about the engine recording cycles:

```
Mean Abs Error: 31.04
 1: LAST(recordings.cycles.LAST(recordings.sensor_measurement_4)) [0.395]
 2: LAST(recordings.sensor_measurement_4) [0.192]
```

```
3: MAX(recordings.sensor_measurement_4) [0.064]
4: LAST(recordings.cycles.MIN(recordings.sensor_measurement_11)) [0.037]
5: LAST(recordings.cycles.MAX(recordings.sensor_measurement_12)) [0.029]
6: LAST(recordings.sensor_measurement_15) [0.020]
7: LAST(recordings.cycles.MAX(recordings.sensor_measurement_11)) [0.020]
8: LAST(recordings.cycles.LAST(recordings.sensor_measurement_15)) [0.018]
9: MAX(recordings.cycles.MAX(recordings.sensor_measurement_20)) [0.016]
10: LAST(recordings.time_in_cycles) [0.014]
```

Then, we have to prepare both the features and label, which we can do using the following code:

```
data2 = utils.load_data('test_FD001.txt')
es2 = make_entityset(data2)
fm2 = ft.calculate_feature_matrix(entityset=es2, features=features,
verbose=True)
fm2.head()
```

The loaded data should have 41,214 recordings from 249 engines in which 21 sensor measurements are used under three operational settings. Then, we have to prepare both the features and labels using the loaded data, which we can do using the following code:

```
X = fm2.copy().fillna(0)
y = pd.read_csv('RUL_FD004.txt', sep=' ', header=-1, names=['RUL'],
index_col=False)

preds2 = rf.predict(X)
print('Mean Abs Error: {:.2f}'.format(mean_absolute_error(preds2, y)))

yhat_median_predict = [np.median(y_train) for _ in preds2]
print('Baseline by median label: MAE = {:.2f}'.format(
    mean_absolute_error(yhat_median_predict, y)))

yhat_median_predict2 = (median_life -
es2['recordings'].df.groupby(['engine_no']).apply(lambda df:
df.shape[0])).apply(lambda row: max(row, 0))

print('Baseline by median life: MAE = {:.2f}'.format(
    mean_absolute_error(yhat_median_predict2 y)))
```

The preceding code block should produce the following output showing the prediced MAE and baseline MEA values:

```
Mean Abs Error: 40.33
Baseline by median label: Mean Abs Error = 52.08
Baseline by median life: Mean Abs Error = 49.55
```

As seen, the predicted MAE value is lower than both baseline MAE values. Next, we try to improve the MAE even more using the LSTM network.

Improving MAE with LSTM

We will use the Keras-based LSTM network to predict RUL. However, for this, we first need to convert the data so that the LSTM model, which expects data in three-dimensional format, can consume it:

```
#Prepare data for Keras based LSTM model
def prepareData(X, y):
    X_train, X_test, y_train, y_test = train_test_split(X, y)
    X_train = X_train.as_matrix(columns=None)
    X_test = X_test.as_matrix(columns=None)
    y_train = y_train.as_matrix(columns=None)
    y_test = y_test.as_matrix(columns=None)
    y_train = y_train.reshape((y_train.shape[0], 1))
    y_test = y_test.reshape((y_test.shape[0], 1))
    X_train = np.reshape(X_train, (X_train.shape[0], 1, X_train.shape[1]))
    X_test = np.reshape(X_test, (X_test.shape[0], 1, X_test.shape[1]))
    return X_train, X_test, y_train, y_test
```

Now that we have the data appropriate for the LSTM model, we can construct the LSTM network. For this, we have a fancy LSTM network that has only an LSTM layer followed by a dense layer, before we apply a dropout layer for better regularization. Then, we have another dense layer, before we project the output from this dense layer through to the activation layer using the linear activation function so that it outputs real-value outputs. We then use the SGD version, called RMSProp, which tries to optimize the **Mean Square Error (MSE)**:

```
#Create LSTM model
from keras.models import Sequential
from keras.layers.core import Dense, Activation
from keras.layers.recurrent import LSTM
from keras.layers import Dropout
from keras.layers import GaussianNoise

def createLSTMModel(X_train, hidden_neurons):
    model = Sequential()
    model.add(LSTM(hidden_neurons, input_shape=(X_train.shape[1],
X_train.shape[2])))
    model.add(Dense(hidden_neurons))
    model.add(Dropout(0.7))
    model.add(Dense(1))
    model.add(Activation("linear"))
```

```
model.compile(loss="mean_squared_error", optimizer="rmsprop")
return model
```

Then, we train the LSTM model with the training set:

```
X_train, X_test, y_train, y_test = prepareData(X, y)
hidden_neurons = 128
model = createLSTMModel(X_train, hidden_neurons)
history = model.fit(X_train, y_train, batch_size=32, nb_epoch=5000,
validation_split=0.20)
```

The preceding lines of code should produce some logs, which give us an idea of whether the training and the validation losses are getting reduced across iterations:

```
Train on 60 samples, validate on 15 samples
Epoch 1/5000
60/60 [==============================] - ETA: 0s - loss: 7996.37 - 1s
11ms/step - loss: 7795.0232 - val_loss: 8052.6118
Epoch 2/5000
60/60 [==============================] - ETA: 0s - loss: 6937.66 - 0s
301us/step - loss: 7466.3648 - val_loss: 7833.4321
...
60/60 [==============================] - ETA: 0s - loss: 1754.92 - 0s
259us/step - loss: 1822.5668 - val_loss: 1420.7977
Epoch 4976/5000
60/60 [==============================] - ETA: 0s - loss: 1862.04
```

Now that the training has been finished, we can plot the training and validation loss:

```
# plot history
plt.plot(history.history['loss'], label='Training')
plt.plot(history.history['val_loss'], label='Validation')
plt.legend()
plt.show()
```

The preceding code block should produce the following graph, in which we can see that the validation loss drops below the training loss:

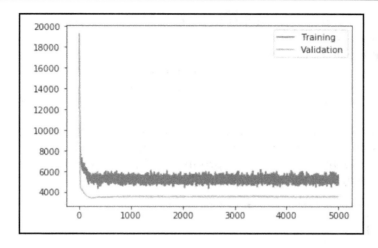

The model may be overfitting the training data. Measuring and plotting MAE during training may shed more light on this. Let's take a look at the MAE on the testset:

```
predicted = model.predict(X_test)
rmse = np.sqrt(((predicted - y_test) ** 2).mean(axis=0))
print('Mean Abs Error: {:.2f}'.format(mean_absolute_error(predicted,
y_test)))
```

We should get an MAE of 38.32, which means the MAE error has been reduced a bit (whereas RF gave an MAE of 40.33), which is, however, still not convincing. There could be several reasons behind such a high MAE. For example, we do not have sufficient training data. Secondly, we used an inefficient method for generating the entity set. For the first problem, we can use all the dataset to train the model. However, we can also use other regularization techniques, such as a Gaussian Noise layer, by specifying the noise threshold:

```
def createLSTMModel(X_train, hidden_neurons):
    model = Sequential()
    model.add(LSTM(hidden_neurons, input_shape=(X_train.shape[1],
X_train.shape[2])))
    model.add(GaussianNoise(0.2))
    model.add(Dense(hidden_neurons))
    model.add(Dropout(0.7))
    model.add(Dense(1))
    model.add(GaussianNoise(0.5))
    model.add(Activation("linear"))
    model.compile(loss="mean_squared_error", optimizer="rmsprop")
    return model
```

The Gaussian noise layer can be used as an input layer to add noise directly to input variables. This is the traditional use of noise as a regularization method in neural networks, which states that the noise can be added before or after the use of the activation function. It may make more sense to add this before activation, but, nevertheless, both options are possible. In our case, we added a Gaussian noise layer with a dropout of 0.2 after the LSTM layer and before the dense layer.

Then, we have another Gaussian noise layer that adds noise to the linear output of a dense layer before a rectified linear activation function. Then, training the LSTM model with the same data with noise introduced should produce a slightly lower MAE value of around 35.25. We can even inspect the plot showing the training and validation loss:

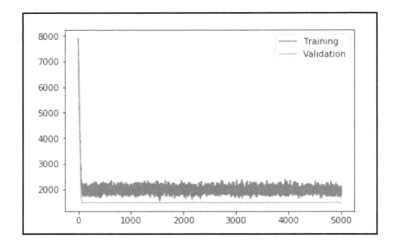

The preceding diagram shows that the training loss and test loss are more or less the same, which indicates a better regularization of the model. Hence, the model performed better on the testset as well. However, the MAE can still be reduced using better quality features, perhaps. Let's explore this with a better feature generation technique.

Unsupervised deep feature synthesis

We will see how the entity set structures can contribute to improve the predictive accuracy. We will build custom primitives using time-series functions from the `tsfresh` library. Before that, we will make cut-off times by selecting a random one from the life of each engine. We are going to make five sets of cut-off times to use for cross-validation:

```
from tqdm import tqdm
splits = 10
```

```
cutoff_time_list = []
for i in tqdm(range(splits)):
    cutoff_time_list.append(utils.make_cutoff_times(data))
cutoff_time_list[0].head()
```

The preceding code block should show the cut-off time and the RUL values for five engines, as shown here:

index	engine_no	cutoff_time	RUL
1	1	2000-01-03 00:20:00	30
2	2	2000-01-04 07:20:00	143
3	3	2000-01-06 14:30:00	119
4	4	2000-01-07 15:30:00	243
5	5	2000-01-09 15:50:00	146

Then, we will use an unsupervised way of generating the entity set. As we can see, the values of operational settings 1—3 are continuous, but they create an implicit relation between different engines. Consequently, if two engines have a similar operational setting, the sensor measurements give a similar value. The idea is to apply the clustering technique through k-means to those settings. Then, we create a new entity from clusters with similar values:

```
from sklearn.cluster import KMeans
nclusters = 50
def make_entityset(data, nclusters, kmeans=None):
    X = data[['operational_setting_1', 'operational_setting_2',
'operational_setting_3']]
    if kmeans:
        kmeans=kmeans
    else:
        kmeans = KMeans(n_clusters=nclusters).fit(X)
    data['settings_clusters'] = kmeans.predict(X)
        es = ft.EntitySet('Dataset')
    es.entity_from_dataframe(dataframe=data,
                            entity_id='recordings',
                            index='index',
                            time_index='time')
    es.normalize_entity(base_entity_id='recordings',
                        new_entity_id='engines',
                        index='engine_no')
    es.normalize_entity(base_entity_id='recordings',
```

```
                            new_entity_id='settings_clusters',
                            index='settings_clusters')
        return es, kmeans
    es, kmeans = make_entityset(data, nclusters)
```

The preceding code segment generates an entity set showing the following relations:

```
Entityset: Dataset
  Entities:
    settings_clusters [Rows: 50, Columns: 2]
    recordings [Rows: 61249, Columns: 29]
    engines [Rows: 249, Columns: 2]
  Relationships:
    recordings.engine_no -> engines.engine_no
    recordings.settings_clusters -> settings_clusters.settings_clusters
```

In addition to changing our entity set structure, we are also going to use the complexity time-series primitive from the `tsfresh` package. Any function that takes in a pandas series and outputs a float can be converted into an aggregation primitive using the `make_agg_primitive` function, as shown here:

```
from featuretools.primitives import make_agg_primitive
import featuretools.variable_types as vtypes
from tsfresh.feature_extraction.feature_calculators import (number_peaks,
mean_abs_change,
                                                            cid_ce,
last_location_of_maximum, length)
Complexity = make_agg_primitive(lambda x: cid_ce(x, False),
                                input_types=[vtypes.Numeric],
                                return_type=vtypes.Numeric,
                                name="complexity")
fm, features = ft.dfs(entityset=es,
                      target_entity='engines',
                      agg_primitives=['last', 'max', Complexity],
                      trans_primitives=[],
                      chunk_size=.26,
                      cutoff_time=cutoff_time_list[0],
                      max_depth=3,
                      verbose=True)
fm.to_csv('Advanced_FM.csv')
fm.head()
```

Using this approach, we managed to generate 12 more features (previously, we had 290). Then, we built four more feature matrices with the same feature set but different cut-off times. This lets us test the pipeline multiple times before using it on test data:

```
fm_list = [fm]
for i in tqdm(range(1, splits)):
```

```
    fm = ft.calculate_feature_matrix(entityset=make_entityset(data,
nclusters, kmeans=kmeans)[0],
        features=features, chunk_size=.26,
cutoff_time=cutoff_time_list[i])
    fm_list.append(fm)
```

Then, using the recursive feature elimination, we again model RF regressors so that the model picks only important features, so it makes better predictions:

```
from sklearn.ensemble import RandomForestRegressor
from sklearn.model_selection import train_test_split
from sklearn.metrics import mean_absolute_error
from sklearn.feature_selection import RFE

def pipeline_for_test(fm_list, hyperparams={'n_estimators':100,
'max_feats':50, 'nfeats':50}, do_selection=False):
    scores = []
    regs = []
    selectors = []
    for fm in fm_list:
        X = fm.copy().fillna(0)
        y = X.pop('RUL')
        reg =
RandomForestRegressor(n_estimators=int(hyperparams['n_estimators']),
            max_features=min(int(hyperparams['max_feats']),
int(hyperparams['nfeats'])))
        X_train, X_test, y_train, y_test = train_test_split(X, y)

        if do_selection:
            reg2 = RandomForestRegressor(n_jobs=3)
            selector=RFE(reg2,int(hyperparams['nfeats']),step=25)
            selector.fit(X_train, y_train)
            X_train = selector.transform(X_train)
            X_test = selector.transform(X_test)
            selectors.append(selector)
        reg.fit(X_train, y_train)
        regs.append(reg)
        preds = reg.predict(X_test)
        scores.append(mean_absolute_error(preds, y_test))
    return scores, regs, selectors
scores, regs, selectors = pipeline_for_test(fm_list)
print([float('{:.1f}'.format(score)) for score in scores])
print('Average MAE: {:.1f}, Std: {:.2f}\n'.format(np.mean(scores),
np.std(scores)))
most_imp_feats = utils.feature_importances(fm_list[0], regs[0])
```

The preceding code block should produce the following output showing predicted MAE in each iteration and their average. Additionally, it shows the baseline MAE values and statistics about the engine recording cycles:

```
[33.9, 34.5, 36.0, 32.1, 36.4, 30.1, 37.2, 34.7,38.6, 34.4]
 Average MAE: 33.1, Std: 4.63
 1:
MAX(recordings.settings_clusters.LAST(recordings.sensor_measurement_13))
[0.055]
 2: MAX(recordings.sensor_measurement_13) [0.044]
 3: MAX(recordings.sensor_measurement_4) [0.035]
 4: MAX(recordings.settings_clusters.LAST(recordings.sensor_measurement_4))
[0.029]
 5: MAX(recordings.sensor_measurement_11) [0.028]
```

Now let's again try using LSTM to see whether we can reduce the MAE error:

```
X = fm.copy().fillna(0)
y = X.pop('RUL')
X_train, X_test, y_train, y_test = prepareData(X, y)

hidden_neurons = 128
model = createLSTMModel(X_train, hidden_neurons)

history = model.fit(X_train, y_train, batch_size=32, nb_epoch=5000,
validation_split=0.20)
# plot history
plt.plot(history.history['loss'], label='Training')
plt.plot(history.history['val_loss'], label='Validation')
plt.legend()
plt.show()
```

The preceding lines of code should produce the following diagram, in which the validation loss drops below the training loss:

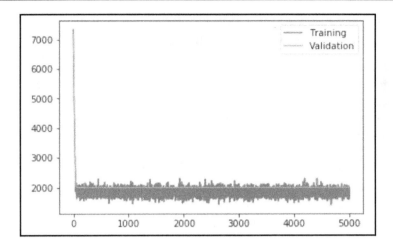

Finally, we can evaluate the model's performance based on the MAE:

```
predicted = model.predict(X_test)
print('Mean Abs Error: {:.2f}'.format(mean_absolute_error(predicted,
y_test)))
```

The preceding code block should produce an MAE of 52.40, which is lower than we experienced in the previous section.

FAQs

In this section, we will cover some **frequently asked questions (FAQs)**, which will help you to extend this application:

1. **Can we use other deep architectures to make predictions in similar IoT settings?**

   Answer: Yes, using other deep architectures could be a viable option. For example, creating a convolutional-LSTM network by combining the predictive power of both CNN and LSTM layers has proven to be effective in many use cases, such as audio classification, **natural language processing (NLP)**, and time-series forecasting.

2. **Sometimes we do not have enough IoT data to train the model flexibly. How can we increase the amount of training data?**

   Answer: There are many ways to do this. For example, we can try to generate the training set by combining all the engines data. For this, the generated CSV files for both training, testing, and RUL would be helpful. Another example might be to try to extend the dataset by adding more samples.

3. **Can I perform anomaly detection in an industrial setting?**

   Answer: Yes, you can. In fact, this is very common in an industrial setting such as production fault identification, real-time time-series anomaly detection, predictive monitoring, and so on.

4. **Where can I get data to perform other analytics in an IoT setting?**

   Answer: Time-series data from some nominal state to a failed state from the **Prognostics Data Repository** can be used for the development of prognostic algorithms. See the following link to learn more about the dataset: `https://ti.arc.nasa.gov/tech/dash/groups/pcoe/prognostic-data-repository/`.

Summary

In this chapter, we have looked at how to develop a DL solution for predictive maintenance using IoT and the Turbofan Engine Degradation Simulation dataset. We started by discussing the exploratory analysis of the dataset before we modeled the predictive maintenance using one of the most popular tree-based ensemble techniques called **RF**, which uses features from the turbine engines as it is. Then, we saw how to improve the predictive accuracy using an LSTM network. The LSTM network indeed helps to reduce network errors. Nevertheless, we saw how to add a Gaussian noise layer to achieve generalization in the LSTM network, along with dropout.

Understanding the potential of DL techniques in all layers of IoT (including the sensors/sensing, gateway, and cloud layer) is important. Consequently, developing scalable and efficient solutions for IoT-enabled healthcare devices is no exception. In the next chapter, we will present a use case that exploits DL for data analysis in all potential stages of its life cycle.

Deep Learning in Healthcare IoT

9

The IoT has diverse application domains, including health and medical care. Use of IoT in healthcare is growing at a dangerously fast pace, and market research shows that the global IoT healthcare market could reach US $534.3 billion by 2025. Most of these applications, including remote and real-time patient monitoring, will generate heterogeneous, streaming, and/or big data. However, analyzing and extracting useful information from this data is a challenging task for medical and healthcare professionals. In this context, **machine learning (ML)** and **deep learning (DL)** models can address the challenge by automated analysis, classification of various data, and detection of anomalies within data. The healthcare industry is extensively using ML and DL for various applications. Hence, the use of ML/DL models in IoT healthcare applications is a necessity for the true realization of healthcare IoT.

In this chapter, we present DL-based IoT solutions for healthcare in general. In the first part of the chapter, we will present an overview of the various applications of IoT in healthcare. Then, we will briefly discuss two use cases where healthcare services can be improved and/or automatized through DL-supported IoT solutions. In the second part of the chapter, we will present hands-on experience of the DL-based healthcare incident and/or diseases detection part of the two use cases. In this chapter, we will cover the following topics:

- IoT and healthcare applications
- Use case one: remote chronic disease management
- Implementation of remote chronic disease management
- Use case two: IoT for acne detection and care
- Implementation of acne detection and care
- DL for IoT in healthcare

- CNN and LSTM in IoT healthcare applications
- Data collection
- Data preprocessing
- Model training
- Evaluation of the models

IoT in healthcare

Globally, health and medical care services are facing tremendous challenges owing to, for example, soaring costs, an ageing population, an increase in the prevalence of chronic and/or multiple conditions, and a shortage of skilled healthcare professionals. In addition, traditional care services relying on average and/or qualitative data and a one-size-fits-all prescribing approach do not work well. In this context, the use of IoT in healthcare services addresses many of these challenges by offering the following features:

- Seamless integration with various existing technologies
- Support of big data processing and analysis
- Personalized services
- Remote and real-time monitoring-based connected healthcare services
- Quantitative data, which offer more effective services than qualitative data
- Interactive and real-time interaction between healthcare professionals and patients
- Ubiquitous access to services
- Efficient management of healthcare resources

All these features of the IoT-based solutions will disrupt the healthcare industry by offering various services. These services can be viewed and served in two different environments:

- Hospital and clinics
- Non-clinical patient environments

The following diagram highlights a few main applications of these two environments and presents a list of potential services in each of the environments:

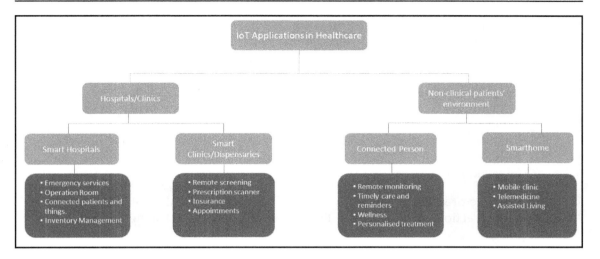

The following are the key subdomains of IoT healthcare:

- **Smart hospitals**: Globally, in both developed and developing countries, hospitals are overcrowded with patients. Also, they have a shortage of resources—including skilled professionals—and equipment. The situation is really bad in rural areas of most countries, where people have limited or no access to healthcare facilities. In this context, IoT-based remote services, such as remote monitoring and telemedicine, can offer access to many basic healthcare services. Also, remote monitoring of elderly patients and those with chronic diseases can greatly reduce healthcare-related costs, and improve quality of life for both patients and healthcare professionals. Smart and connected ambulances can offer on-fleet prompt and emergency services, and reduce emergency services-related incidents. In an operating room, connected doctors (locally and externally), staff, and medical devices can offer a better and smoother operating environment. Also, inventory management in hospitals can be greatly improved through IoT applications.

- **Clinics**: Many people go to a **general practitioner (GP)** practice or clinic for primary care services. These service providers can also benefit from using IoT applications. For example, a GP can view and analyze virtually the patient's pathology report, which saves time for both parties. Importantly, patients will get more time for care-related discussions than information gathering. Clinics can verify insurance coverage for patients in real time. Appointment management in clinics and GP practices is a global challenge. In England, approximately 15 million appointments per year are missed, which costs the **National Health Service (NHS)** millions of pounds. This situation can be improved by IoT-based applications.

- **Non-clinical patient environments**: Two potential application areas of IoT could be connected—the patient and the smart home. Here, the smart home would offer healthcare services to patients anytime and anywhere. Remote monitoring of a prescribed intervention, such as physiotherapy, can be done through a connected patient application. Also, patients can get personalized services, such as reminders to take medication. Offering monitoring and healthcare services to elderly people is a great challenge worldwide. Smart home solutions can improve existing services and offer new services for these highly vulnerable people through fall detection, medication reminders, telemedicine, and general assisted living.

It is clear from the preceding discussion that IoT has huge potential in healthcare domains. In the following section, we will briefly discuss two use cases of IoT in healthcare.

Use case one – remote management of chronic disease

Chronic diseases—including cardiovascular diseases, hypertension, and diabetes—cause over 40 million deaths per year globally. This problem has different dimensions in developing countries and developed countries. In developing countries, people with chronic diseases have limited or no access to many basic health services, including early or on-time detection facilities, which leads to many deaths. On the other hand, in developed countries, medical research has led to a significant increase in life expectancy. This has been achieved by means of, for example, early detection and monitoring of disease. However, in developed countries, including the UK, for every 2 years of increased life expectancy, we gain just 1 year of quality life. Consequently, the proportion of our lives spent with chronic diseases and disability is rising. The cost of managing patients with multiple chronic diseases is trillions of dollars/pounds. Fortunately, IoT-based remote monitoring of patients with chronic diseases can address most of these issues and offer cost-effective services.

Implementation of use case one

We are considering an IoT-based remote patient monitoring application for use case one. The following diagram briefly presents how the IoT-based, remote patient monitoring and management system will work:

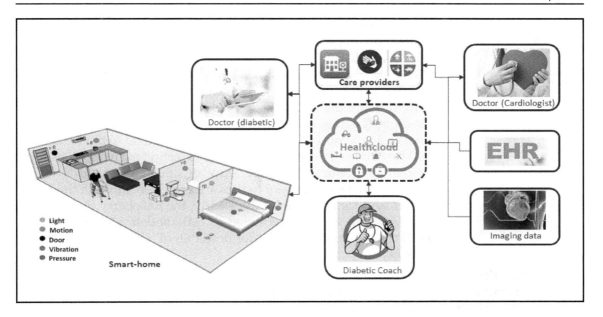

As shown, the IoT-based, remote patient monitoring system consists of three main elements, namely, smart home, care providers, and Health Cloud:

- **Smart home**: This is the heart of the solution, and includes the patient and various devices for the IoT solutions. The smart home consists of the following key components:
  - **Patient**: A patient will be attached to multiple sensors, including an **electrocardiogram (ECG)**, blood pressure sensor, accelerometer, and gyroscope. These sensors will collect physiological and activity-related data and send them to the care providers for necessary and real-time feedback.
  - **Ambient sensing**: Body sensors and wearable devices are not sufficient to cover all of the activities of the patient. Also, patients do not feel comfortable with too many sensors on their body for many reasons, including the need for seamless movement. The smart home will be installed with various ambient sensors, including light, vibration, motion, pressure, and door sensors. These sensors will provide contextual information about the patient.

- **Edge computing platform**: We have various options for this component, for example, a smartphone/tablet, edge gateway, or a Raspberry Pi 3. For this use case, we are considering a Raspberry Pi 3. All the sensors mentioned earlier can be connected to the Raspberry Pi 3. Most will sense the environment and/or patient's activity continuously, and others will be event-driven (for example, the door sensor will be activated if someone opens or knocks on the door). These sensors will send data to the Raspberry Pi 3 for further processing, including detecting events such as high blood pressure or body temperature, or a fall. Finally, this processed data will be sent to the care providers through the home router, and Health Cloud. Importantly, the Raspberry Pi 3 will be installed with various pretrained DL/ML models, including an ECG measurement classifier for detection of any heart-related anomalies.

- **Health Cloud for model learning and data analysis**: The Health Cloud is a cloud computing platform, mainly designed for healthcare-related services, and is mainly responsible for the following:
  - DL model training
  - Data analysis

The model training component will train the necessary DL models for categorizing or classifying a variety of physiological signals from the patient and contextual data to make informed decisions. The Health Cloud will receive various data from the Raspberry Pi 3, and some of them may conflict with each other. In this context, a data analysis tools will analyze and present the data to the healthcare professionals for decision making.

- **Care providers**: Care providers can be hospitals or clinics that provide care services. As many patients have multiple chronic diseases, most need to be directly or indirectly connected with more than one specialized doctor. Once the doctor receives information about the patient and their environment, they will make a decision with the support of other data, including historical data from an **electronic health record (EHR)**. Once the decision has been made, it will be sent back to the patient and, if necessary, a decision will be actuated through the appropriate devices (such as an insulin pump) connected to the patient.

ECG-based health checking of the heart is an essential element of the above use case. In the second part of the chapter, we will describe implementation of the DL-based ECG measurement classification of the preceding use case.

Use case two – IoT for acne detection and care

Acne is one of the world's most common skin conditions. Most people, at some point in their lifetime, are affected by acne. Generally, acne develops on the face and appears as spots (as shown in the following diagram) and oily skin. Sometimes, the skin can become hot or painful to the touch. Acne can manifest as whiteheads, blackheads, pustules, papules, cysts, and nodules. The first three are also known as pimples. Different types of acne need different treatments and care; therefore, detection and automated classification of acne could be useful. Acne can be confused with one of three similar conditions—rosacea, eczema, or allergic reaction—because patients often self-diagnose and treat. Incorrect diagnosis and treatment can make the condition worse. The following diagram shows two examples of what acne can look like:

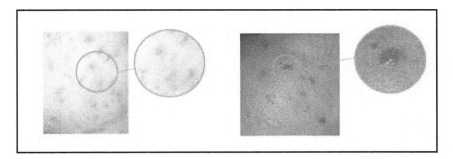

Generally, acne is not only a physical health issue, but also a mental health issue for many affected people. According to research, acne is significantly linked with depression. In a study published in the *British Journal of Dermatology*, researchers analyzing the records of patients with acne between 1986 and 2012 in the UK made a strong claim about the mental health issues these patients. They concluded that patients with acne have a 63% higher risk of developing depression compared with patients who did not have acne.

In this chapter, we will present an innovative solution using IoT and DL modes to address the acne detection/diagnosis problem.

Implementation of use case two

Most people with acne and related skin conditions use a mirror to detect acne and monitor the progress of treatment. Therefore, the innovative idea is to create a smart and connected mirror to help the user detect and identify skin (mainly facial) anomalies, including acne.

The following diagram presents an IoT infrastructure for the implementation of automated acne detection, classification, and care services:

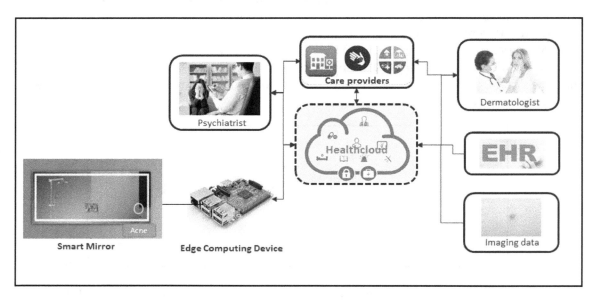

As shown in the diagram, the IoT-based automated acne detection, classification, and care system consists of three main elements—a smart mirror, care providers, and the Health Cloud:

- **Smart mirror**: This is the heart of the solution, and includes the following three components:
    - **Camera**: The mirror features a high-resolution camera embedded in such a way that it will be able to capture facial images. There will be a button in the mirror that will activate the detection process, as a patient might not always be interested or in need of the service. The mirror will also have a small display to present the results and/or suggested treatment for the acne from care providers.

- **Edge computing platform**: We have various options for this component, including a smartphone/tablet, edge gateway, or a Raspberry Pi 3. For this use case, we are considering a Raspberry Pi 3 that will be connected to the camera. Once it receives the images, it will detect any skin-related issue, including acne, with the support of a preinstalled DL model. Finally, the Raspberry Pi 3 will send the detection results, along with the images, to a care provider to obtain treatment suggestions. Also, a model can be incorporated in the Raspberry Pi 3 (not within the scope of this book) that will analyze facial images for potential depression detection and corresponding support from a psychiatrist.

- **Health Cloud for model learning and data**: The Health Cloud is a cloud computing platform mainly designed for healthcare-related services. This cloud platform will be used to train the DL model for the image-based detection and classification of acne and other skin conditions. The Health Cloud is also responsible for updating any preinstalled model in the Raspberry Pi 3 or IoT devices.

- **Care providers**: Care providers can be hospitals and clinics that provide care services. As acne might cause depression, we are considering two potential doctors—a dermatologist for skin-related issues and a psychiatrist for depression-related issues. Once the doctors receive the detected information and images, they will make a decision with the support of other data, including historical images of the patient. Finally, the suggested treatment or feedback will be sent back to the patient.

In the following sections, we will describe implementation of the DL-based solutions required for the aforementioned use cases. All the necessary codes are available in the chapter's code folder.

DL for healthcare

DL models are evolving as the most powerful and effective computing resources for every industry. They are contributing significantly to the industries' value by improving user experience and enabling more informed decision making. Healthcare is one of the key application domains of DL, and DL has been further progressed by the increasing availability of heterogeneous healthcare data.

Unlike many other industries, the health and medical industries are obtaining highly value-added applications in many areas, including research, innovation, and real-world medical environments. Many of these applications are patient-facing (such as early detection and prediction of cancer, and personalized medicine) and others are for improving the user experience in various aspects of healthcare IT. The following diagram highlights some of the application areas of DL in healthcare:

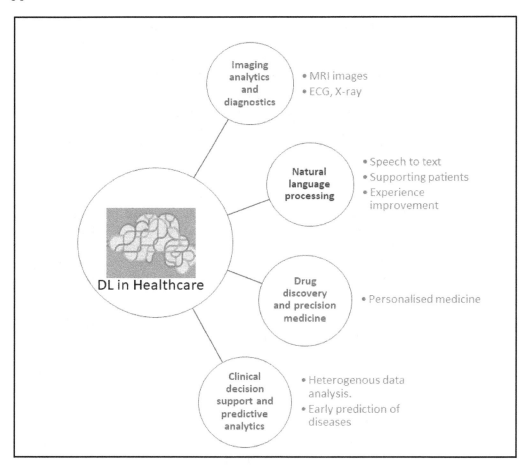

CNN and LSTM in healthcare applications

Healthcare applications generate big data, and they come from heterogeneous sources in heterogeneous formats. A large number of these, including screening and diagnostic data from **magnetic resonance imaging (MRI)**, X-ray, and ultrasound are in image format. Human physiological signals, such as those detected by **electromyography** (**EMG**), **electroencephalography** (**EEG**), ECG, and **electrooculography (EOG)**, are time series data. EHRs include structured (such as diagnosis, prescriptions, and laboratory tests) as well as unstructured (such as free-text clinical notes) clinical data. Also, high-throughput biology, such as genomics, produces high-dimensional data regarding human internal structures. All of this different healthcare data requires the support of ML—especially DL—to extract valuable information and gain insights into any potential issues.

A number of DL models have been used for the analysis of these heterogeneous healthcare data. CNN and LSTMs (RNNs) are the most widely used DL models, as their features work well with most healthcare data types. For example, CNN models are best for image processing and are used for various medical images. By contrast, LSTMs/RNNs are best for most physiological signals, as they have a memory feature to handle the temporal properties of the signals. ECG measurements are one of the key physiological signals in screening for cardiovascular disease. Therefore, the remote patient-monitoring system includes a DL-based ECG signal analyzer for detecting various heart conditions, such as **atrial fibrillation** (**AF**).

Considering the temporal aspect of the ECG signal, we will consider an LSTM for the implementation of the remote patient monitoring system. In addition, we will test a CNN for the ECG signal as a comparison. The IoT-based acne detection and care system will rely on images. Therefore, we will implement this using a CNN architecture. Both of these DL models have been briefly presented in chapters; please refer to those for an overview.

Data collection

Data collection for health and medical care applications is a challenging task for many reasons, including privacy and ethical issues. In this context, we have decided to use two different open source datasets for the two use cases.

Use case one

The ECG dataset for use case one has been collected from 2017 PhysioNet/computing in cardiology challenge. This dataset consists of 8,528 ECG measurements. These measurements were recorded through an AliveCor hand-held device (as shown in the following screenshot), and, interestingly, this is an example healthcare IoT application:

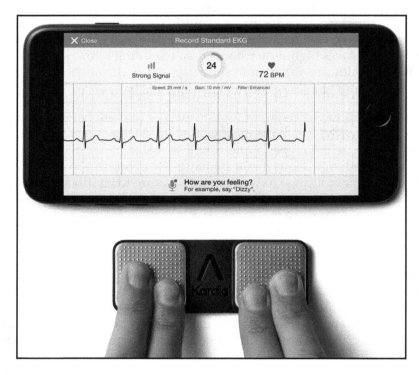

The sampling rate of the ECG measurements was 300 Hz, and noise was removed by band-pass filtered by the AliveCor device. Each recorded measurement is compliant with MATLAB V4 WFDB format, and consists of two files:

- A file with a `.mat` extension that presents the main ECG signal information
- A corresponding header file with a `.hea` extension that contains the waveform-related information of the measurement

The dataset consists of four different classes of signals: normal rhythm, AF, other rhythm, or too noisy to classify. The following diagram presents a visualization of these different classes of the ECG signals:

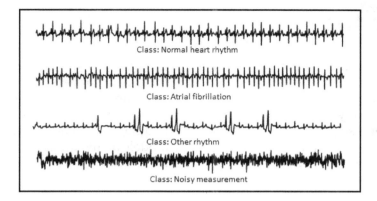

AF is characterized by rapid and irregular beating of the atria and indicates that the heart rhythm is not normal. Other abnormal heart rhythms are considered as the other rhythm class. Finally, any measurements that do not reflect one of the three classes, as they are too noisy to be classified, are defined as a noisy measurement. The DL model-based classifier needs to extract these features in the measurements to classify the signals recorded from the patient, and the corresponding heart-related issues. For a better understanding and real-life implementation, further studies on ECG signals are necessary, which is not within the scope of this book. The following graph presents normal versus AF heart signal measurements:

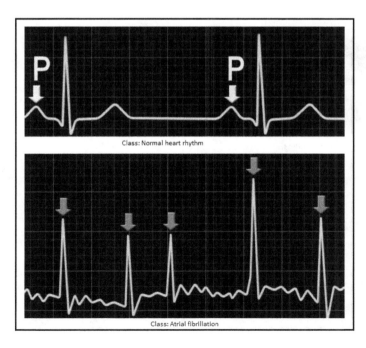

Use case two

For the acne detection and care system use case, we are relying on an image dataset. We have gathered images from the *Dermnet Skin Disease Atlas*, which is an open-source database on various skin diseases. The database contains 23 datasets, each on a different skin disease, and each of the categories (including acne and rosacea) has subcategories. The datasets are not easily downloaded as there are too many pages. We have written an image, or image scraper, using Python's Beautiful Soup module, and we have made the scraper generic so that readers can test their LSTM/CNN models on the different skin diseases. The scraper `image_scraper.py` is available in the chapter's code subfolder, `use-case-2`. To scrap all 23 datasets, run the following command:

```
python image_scraper.py
```

The following screenshot shows the downloaded images folder of all types of skin disease:

Name	Date modified	Type
Acne-Closed-Comedo	08/05/2019 13:58	File folder
Acne-Cystic	08/05/2019 14:00	File folder
Acne-Excoriated	08/05/2019 14:00	File folder
Acne-Histology	08/05/2019 14:00	File folder
Acne-Infantile	08/05/2019 14:01	File folder
Acne-Mechanica	08/05/2019 14:01	File folder
Acne-Open-Comedo	08/05/2019 14:02	File folder
Acne-Primary-Lesions	08/05/2019 14:02	File folder
Acne-Pustular	08/05/2019 14:03	File folder
Acne-Scar	08/05/2019 14:03	File folder
Acne-Steroid	08/05/2019 14:03	File folder
Gram-Negative-Folliculitis	08/05/2019 14:03	File folder
Hidradenitis-Suppurativa	08/05/2019 14:05	File folder
Hyperhidrosis	08/05/2019 14:05	File folder
Milia	08/05/2019 14:05	File folder
Minocycline-Pigmentation	08/05/2019 14:05	File folder
Nevus-Comedonicus	08/05/2019 14:05	File folder
Perioral-Dermatitis	08/05/2019 14:07	File folder
Prominent-Sebaceous-Glands-and-Fo...	08/05/2019 14:08	File folder
Rosacea	08/05/2019 14:10	File folder
Rosacea-Granulomatous	08/05/2019 14:10	File folder
Rosacea-Nose	08/05/2019 14:11	File folder
Rosacea-Steroid	08/05/2019 14:11	File folder
Tes-Cate	08/05/2019 14:11	File folder
testcat-6	08/05/2019 14:11	File folder

Data exploration

In the following section, we will explore the datasets used for the two use cases. These are as follows:

- The ECG dataset
- The acne dataset

The ECG dataset

The following diagram presents a snapshot of the ECG dataset, which includes four classes of data. As shown in the diagram, each of the signals has distinctive features to be exploited by the DL models:

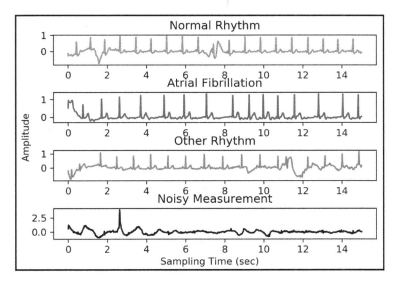

We can generate this exploration result, or similar, using the available code, `ecg_singal_explorer.py`, in the chapter's `use-case-1` code folder.

The acne dataset

We have used the acne and rosacea images dataset. The following screenshot presents a folder view of the dataset, including the number of images in the class. Unfortunately, as we can see, only four of the folders or classes have 100 or more images:

As we are using MobileNet v1 architecture, any class with lower than 100 images might show an error. In fact, we have tested this and found the data size-related error. In this context, we have chosen a reduced dataset, which consists of only four classes of data that have more than 100 images.

The following screenshot shows the reduced acne dataset following exploration:

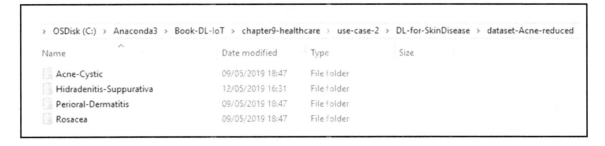

Data preprocessing

Data preprocessing is an essential step for a DL pipeline. The ECG dataset is not ready to be used for model training and validation. The preprocessor for the ECG signals is included in the model training and validation codes, LSTM_ECG.py and CNN1D_ECG.py, respectively. They will run the models after preprocessing .mat input data. However, the acne image dataset is ready to be used for training and validation.

Model training

As we mentioned earlier, we are using LSTM and CNN, particularly 1D CNN, for use case one. For use case two, we are using MobileNet v1. All of these DL implementations support transfer learning that does not require training from scratch to use them in IoT devices.

Use case one

We used an LSTM five-layered architecture for the ECG data classification, as shown in the following diagram:

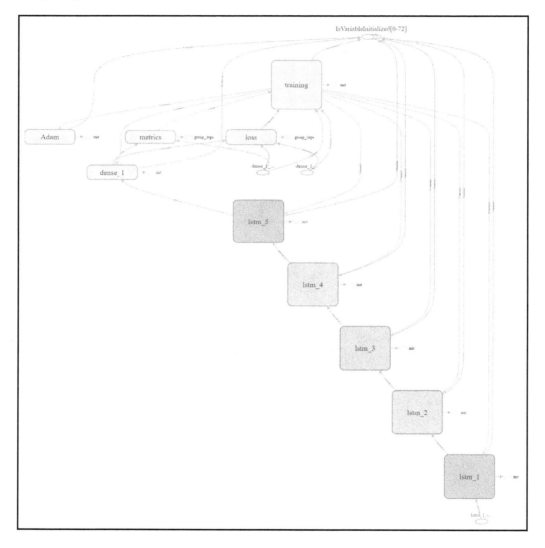

We can train and test the model by running the `LSTM_ECG.py` file available in the chapter's code folder named `use-case-1` subfolder:

```
python LSTM_ECG.py
```

For the ECG data in the remote patient-management system, we also tested and validated a CNN model. The following diagram presents the CNN architecture we used for the ECG dataset. As we can see, the CNN architecture consists of four convolutional layers:

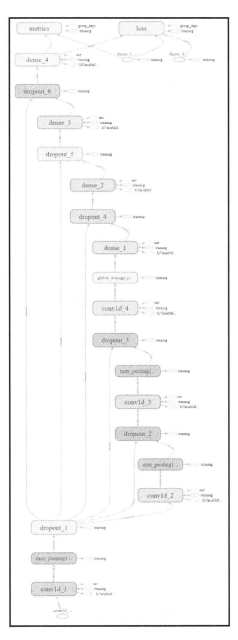

We can train and test the model by running the `CNN1D_ECG.py` file, available in the chapter's code folder named `use-case-1` subfolder:

```
python CNN1D_ECG.py
```

Use case two

We used MobileNet v1 for the second use case. The following diagram presents the architecture of the model:

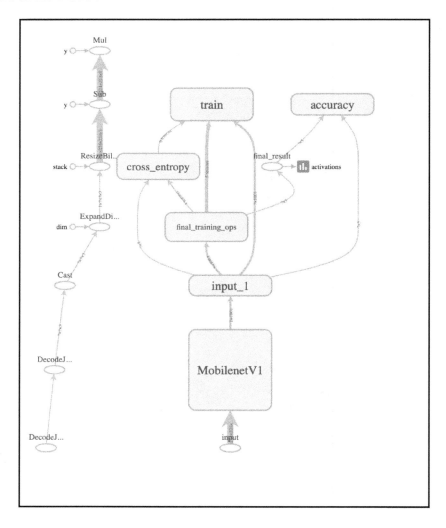

To train and validate the model on the acne dataset, we need to run the `retrain_CNN.py` file available in the chapter's code folder named `use-case-2` subfolder. To train and test the model, we need to just run the following in the Command Prompt.

```
python retrain_CNN.py \
--output_graph=trained_model_mobilenetv1/retrained_graph.pb \
--output_labels=trained_model_mobilenetv1/retrained_labels.txt   \
--architecture mobilenet_1.0_224 \
--image_dir= dataset-Acne-reduced
```

The final two parameters of MobileNet v1 training are compulsory, and the rest are optional.

Model evaluations

We have evaluated three different aspects of the models:

- Learning/(re)training time
- Storage requirement
- Performance (accuracy)

In terms of training time, in a desktop (Intel Xenon CPU E5-1650 v3 @3.5 GHz and 32 GB RAM) with GPU support, LSTM and CNN 1D on the ECG data took more than one hour, and MobileNet v1 on the acne dataset took less than 1 hour.

The storage requirement of a model is an essential consideration in resource-constrained IoT devices. The following screenshot presents the storage requirements for the three models we tested for the two use cases:

As shown, a saved model of LSTM took 234 MB of storage, CNN 1D took 8.5 MB, and MobileNet v1 (CNN) took 16.3 MB. In terms of storage requirements, all of the models, except the current version of LSTM, are fine to be deployed in many resource-constrained IoT devices, including Raspberry Pi 3 or smartphones.

Finally, we have evaluated the performance of the models. In both of the use cases, dataset-wide evaluation or testing has been executed during the training phase in the desktop PC platform/server side, but we can also test them in the Raspberry Pi 3 or any IoT edge computing devices as the models are transferable.

Model performance (use case one)

The following screenshot shows the training and validation result of the LSTM used on the ECG dataset. As seen in the screenshot, the test accuracy is consistently very close to 1.0 or 100%. However, validation accuracy is not great, and is in the range of 50% for the two different runs of the model (100 and 500 epochs). The following screenshot shows how the LSTM model is progressing during the training stage:

```
Epoch 42/100
 - 12s - loss: 0.0260 - acc: 0.9919 - val_loss: 3.2725 - val_acc: 0.4954
Epoch 43/100
 - 13s - loss: 0.0083 - acc: 0.9984 - val_loss: 3.5102 - val_acc: 0.5073
Epoch 44/100
 - 13s - loss: 0.0022 - acc: 0.9997 - val_loss: 3.6529 - val_acc: 0.5033
Epoch 45/100
 - 13s - loss: 0.0020 - acc: 0.9999 - val_loss: 3.7180 - val_acc: 0.4980
Epoch 46/100
 - 13s - loss: 0.0017 - acc: 0.9999 - val_loss: 3.7393 - val_acc: 0.4993
Epoch 47/100
 - 13s - loss: 0.0021 - acc: 0.9997 - val_loss: 3.7430 - val_acc: 0.4941
Epoch 48/100
 - 13s - loss: 0.0092 - acc: 0.9969 - val_loss: 3.6456 - val_acc: 0.4729
Epoch 49/100
 - 12s - loss: 0.0217 - acc: 0.9922 - val_loss: 3.3237 - val_acc: 0.4690
Epoch 50/100
 - 12s - loss: 0.0306 - acc: 0.9904 - val_loss: 3.3988 - val_acc: 0.4650
Epoch 51/100
 - 13s - loss: 0.0094 - acc: 0.9975 - val_loss: 3.4694 - val_acc: 0.4927
Epoch 52/100
 - 12s - loss: 0.0036 - acc: 0.9987 - val_loss: 3.6257 - val_acc: 0.5033
Epoch 53/100
 - 13s - loss: 0.0037 - acc: 0.9993 - val_loss: 3.6225 - val_acc: 0.4742
Epoch 54/100
 - 13s - loss: 0.0022 - acc: 0.9993 - val_loss: 3.6380 - val_acc: 0.4901
```

The following graph, generated through TensorBoard's log file, shows the training accuracy of the LSTM model on the ECG dataset:

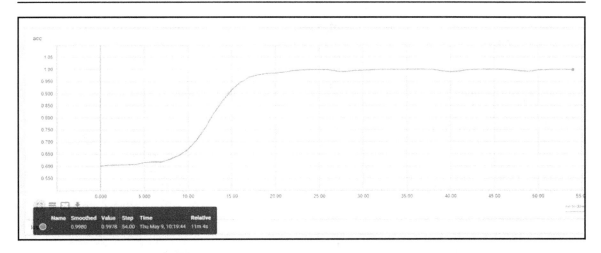

The following diagram presents the confusion matrix of the LSTM model's validation results for the ECG data:

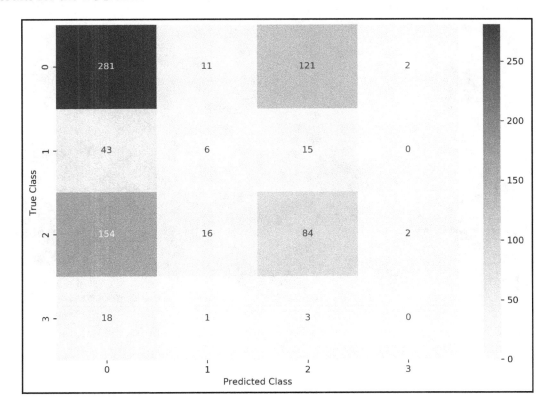

The matrix clearly highlights the fact that the LSTM model is performing poorly on the ECG data. In particular, it is failing to identify most AF measurements (abnormal heart rhythm).

The LSTM's poor performance on the ECG dataset motivated us to test the CNN 1D model on the dataset. The following diagrams present the performance of the CNN 1D model on the ECG dataset. As shown in the diagrams, CNN's one-dimensional model test accuracy is consistently well above 0.96 or 96% (slightly lower than for the LSTM model) and, importantly, its validation accuracies are consistently in the range of 0.82, which is well above that for LSTM. Models with this level of accuracy should be able to classify the correct heart rhythm of the patient in most cases and report accordingly. The following screenshot shows how the CNN 1D model is progressing during the training stage and its final training and validation accuracy:

```
 - 10s - loss: 0.1073 - acc: 0.9634 - val_loss: 0.8192 - val_acc: 0.8394

Epoch 00495: val_acc did not improve from 0.85815
Epoch 496/500
 - 10s - loss: 0.1155 - acc: 0.9623 - val_loss: 0.7955 - val_acc: 0.8406

Epoch 00496: val_acc did not improve from 0.85815
Epoch 497/500
 - 10s - loss: 0.1181 - acc: 0.9618 - val_loss: 0.8229 - val_acc: 0.8488

Epoch 00497: val_acc did not improve from 0.85815
Epoch 498/500
 - 10s - loss: 0.1081 - acc: 0.9634 - val_loss: 0.9242 - val_acc: 0.8406

Epoch 00498: val_acc did not improve from 0.85815
Epoch 499/500
 - 10s - loss: 0.1013 - acc: 0.9643 - val_loss: 0.8431 - val_acc: 0.8394

Epoch 00499: val_acc did not improve from 0.85815
Epoch 500/500
 - 10s - loss: 0.1054 - acc: 0.9642 - val_loss: 0.8921 - val_acc: 0.8288

Epoch 00500: val_acc did not improve from 0.85815
Last epoch's validation score is  0.8288393903868698

(tf-gpu) C:\Anaconda3\Book-DL-IoT\chapter9-healthcare\use-case-1\DeepECG-
```

The following graph, generated through TensorBoard's log file, shows the validation accuracy of the CNN 1D model on the ECG dataset:

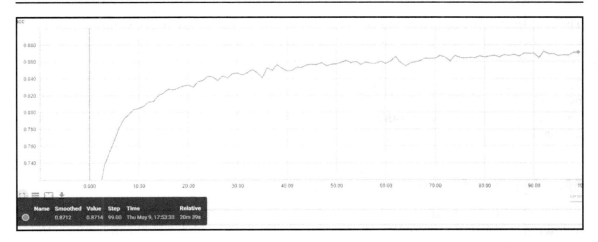

The following diagram presents the normalized confusion matrix of the CCN 1D model's validation results for the ECG data:

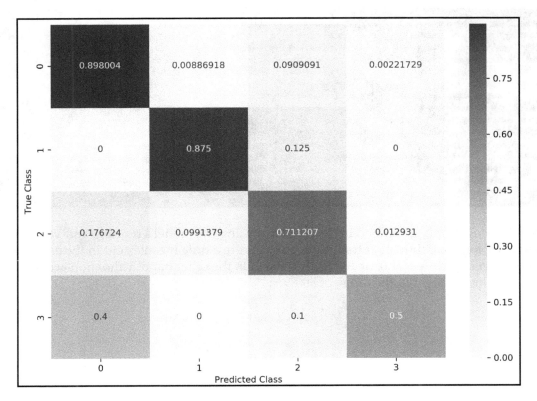

The matrix clearly highlights the fact that the model is performing much better than the LSTM model on the ECG data. Importantly, it is successfully identifying most (87.5%) AF measurements (abnormal heart rhythm).

The CCN 1D model's performance can be improved; it can even be made very close to 100% by making the model's network denser. However, this will make the model complex, and the trained model will need more memory, making it unsuitable for resource-constrained IoT devices.

Model performance (use case two)

We have trained and validated the MobileNet v1 model on the reduced acne dataset. The following screenshot presents the evaluation results of the model. As we can see from the screenshot, training accuracy is 1.0, or 100% in most steps, and final test accuracy is 0.89, or 89%:

```
INFO:tensorflow:2019-05-12 14:29:29.897619: Step 3960: Train accuracy = 100.0%
INFO:tensorflow:2019-05-12 14:29:29.897619: Step 3960: Cross entropy = 0.002337
INFO:tensorflow:2019-05-12 14:29:29.999564: Step 3960: Validation accuracy = 81.0% (N=100)
INFO:tensorflow:2019-05-12 14:29:30.962488: Step 3970: Train accuracy = 100.0%
INFO:tensorflow:2019-05-12 14:29:30.962488: Step 3970: Cross entropy = 0.002503
INFO:tensorflow:2019-05-12 14:29:31.069451: Step 3970: Validation accuracy = 83.0% (N=100)
INFO:tensorflow:2019-05-12 14:29:32.018879: Step 3980: Train accuracy = 100.0%
INFO:tensorflow:2019-05-12 14:29:32.018879: Step 3980: Cross entropy = 0.002206
INFO:tensorflow:2019-05-12 14:29:32.098854: Step 3980: Validation accuracy = 84.0% (N=100)
INFO:tensorflow:2019-05-12 14:29:33.001305: Step 3990: Train accuracy = 100.0%
INFO:tensorflow:2019-05-12 14:29:33.001305: Step 3990: Cross entropy = 0.001930
INFO:tensorflow:2019-05-12 14:29:33.089275: Step 3990: Validation accuracy = 81.0% (N=100)
INFO:tensorflow:2019-05-12 14:29:33.907782: Step 3999: Train accuracy = 100.0%
INFO:tensorflow:2019-05-12 14:29:33.908782: Step 3999: Cross entropy = 0.001757
INFO:tensorflow:2019-05-12 14:29:33.992750: Step 3999: Validation accuracy = 86.0% (N=100)
INFO:tensorflow:Final test accuracy = 89.5% (N=76)
```

The following graph, generated in TensorBoard using the model's training and validation accuracies' log files, show that training accuracies are a little inconsistent in the early steps, and consistently close to 1.0, or 100%, after that. On the other hand, validation accuracies are a little inconsistent in the range of 80-89%:

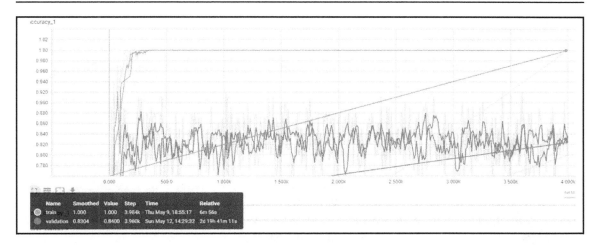

We believe that, even with this inconsistency, the model should be able to detect the type of acne in more than 80% of cases.

Summary

The healthcare industry is adopting ML and DL for various applications. IoT healthcare applications need to adopt ML and DL techniques for the true realization of healthcare IoT. In this chapter, we have tried to show how DL-based IoT solutions can be useful and how they can be implemented in healthcare applications. In the first part of this chapter, we presented an overview of the various applications of IoT in healthcare. Then, we briefly discussed two use cases where healthcare services can be improved and/or automated through DL-supported IoT solutions. In the second part of the chapter, we presented a hands-on experience of the DL-based healthcare incident and/or skin diseases, detection part of the two use cases.

The use of DL in IoT applications is emerging. However, there are challenges associated with DL techniques and IoT that need to be addressed soon in order to get the best results from the integration of these two exciting technologies. In the next and final chapter, we will identify and discuss these challenges. In addition, we will provide a few future directions to mitigate some of the issues.

References

- Bahar Farahani, Farshad Firouzi, Victor Chang, Mustafa Badaroglu, Nicholas Constant, and Kunal Mankodiya, *Towards fog-driven IoT eHealth: Promises and challenges of IoT in medicine and healthcare*, Future Generation Computer Systems, volume 78, part 2, 2018, pages 659-676
- Missed GP appointments costing the NHS millions: https://www.england.nhs.uk/2019/01/missed-gp-appointments-costing-nhs-millions/
- World Health Organization, (September 10, 2017), *Noncommunicable diseases*: http://www.who.int/mediacentre/factsheets/fs355/en/
- MACAELA MACKENZIE, *All the Ways Acne Can Mess With Your Mental Health*: https://www.allure.com/story/how-acne-affects-mental-health-depression
- Vallerand IA, Lewinson RT, Parsons LM, Lowerison MW, Frolkis AD, Kaplan GG, Barnabe C, Bulloch AGM, and Patten SB: *Risk of depression among patients with acne in the UK: a population-based cohort study*, Br. J. Dermatol, (2018) 178(3): e194-e195
- Riccardo Miotto, Fei Wang, Shuang Wang, Xiaoqian Jiang, and Joel T Dudley, *Deep learning for healthcare: review, opportunities, and challenges*, Briefings in Bioinformatics, Volume 19, Issue 6, November 2018, pp. 1236–1246
- Goldberger AL, Amaral LAN, Glass L, Hausdorff JM, Ivanov PCh, Mark RG, Mietus JE, Moody GB, Peng C-K, Stanley HE. *PhysioBank, PhysioToolkit, and PhysioNet: components of a new research resource for complex physiologic signals*, Circulation (2000) 101(23): e215-e220
- AliveCor: https://www.alivecor.com/
- *Dermnet Skin Disease Atlas*: http://www.dermnet.com/dermatology-pictures-skin-disease-pictures/

What's Next - Wrapping Up and Future Directions

10

The use of IoT will be come omnipresent in our life through various applications, including connected healthcare, smart home, and smart city. Although IoT applications are exciting, there are significant scientific and technological challenges to be overcome before they can be fully realized. One of the key technical challenges for IoT is the design and development of **Deep Learning** (**DL**) models that work well in resource-constrained IoT devices or edge/fog computing devices, and those that meet the real-time response requirements. In this final chapter, we shall first present a summary of the earlier chapters, and then use examples to discuss the main challenges faced by the existing DL techniques in their development and implementation of resource-constrained and embedded IoT environments. Finally, we will summarize a few existing solutions and point out some potential solutions that can fill the gaps for DL-based IoT analytics.

The topics that we will cover in this chapter are as follows:

- What have we done in this book?
- Challenges in design and the development of DL models for resource-constrained IoT devices
- Existing solutions to support DL in resource-constrained IoT devices
- Potential future solutions

What we have covered in this book?

Most IoT applications are generating—and will generate—big or fast/real-time streaming data. Analysis of such big data or data streams is crucial to learning new information, predicting future insights, and making informed decisions. Machine learning, including DL, is a key technology for this analysis. The use of DL models in IoT applications for data analysis has been making progress recently. However, an overall application view of DL models in the IoT landscape is missing. In this book, we have made an effort to fill this gap by presenting IoT applications from various domains and their DL-based implementations.

In the first chapter of the book, we presented an overview of IoT, its key applications, and a three-layered, end-to-end view of IoT solutions, which is useful for knowing and applying DL-based data analysis in the IoT ecosystem. We presented an overview of DL and its popular models and implementation frameworks, including TensorFlow and Keras. In the remaining chapters (3-9), we presented various generic services provided by DL models (such as image processing) in different IoT application domains through various use cases. The following table summarizes those chapters in terms of key activities in each chapter:

Chapter Name	IoT Use Cases	DL Models Used	Model Performance
Image Recognition in IoT	• Image-based road's fault detection • Image-based smart solid waste separation	Two implementations of CNN: • Incentive V3 • Mobilenet V1	• Storage requirement suitable for transfer learning. • Training and validation accuracies for both use cases are above 90%.
Audio/Speech/Voice Recognition in IoT	• Voice controlled smart light • Voice-controlled home access	Three implementations of CNN: • Incentive V3, • Mobilenet V1, and • CIFAR-10 CNN with SVM	• Storage requirement suitable for transfer learning. • Training and validation accuracies for use case 1 are around 75% and are around 90% for use case 2.
Indoor localization in IoT	Indoor localization with WIFI fingerprinting	Autoencoder	• Storage requirement suitable for transfer learning. • Validation accuracy around 90% .
Physiological and Psychological State Detection in IoT	• Remote progress monitoring of physiotherapy • Smart Class Room	LSTM and two implementations of CNN: • Simple CNN • Mobilenet V1	• Storage requirement suitable for transfer learning. • Training and validation accuracies for use case 1 are above 90% and around 70% for use case 2.
Security in IoT	• Intelligent Host Intrusion Detection in IoT • Intelligent Network Intrusion Detection in IoT	LSTM, DNN, and Autoencoder	• Storage requirement suitable for transfer learning. • Training and validation accuracies for both use cases are above 90%.
Predictive Maintenance for IoT	Predictive maintenance for aircraft gas turbine engine.	LSTM	• Storage requirement suitable for transfer learning. • Was able to successfully predict maintenance with acceptable mean error rate.
Deep learning in Healthcare IoT	• Remote Chronic Disease Management • IoT for Acne Detection and Care	LSTM, CNN1D, and Mobilenet V1	• Storage requirement of CNNs are suitable for transfer learning, but LSTM struggles. • Validation accuracies for LSTM in use case is around 50%, CNN1D is around 85%. Accuracies for Mobilenet V1 in use case two are around 90%.

As we can see from the table, CNNs and its variants are used in most cases. One potential reason could be that CNN models perform very well on image datasets, and most datasets are either images or can be converted into an image (such as voice data). The model performance presented in the table, as well as in the chapters themselves, are not final performance values; rather, they are indicative performance values, as DL models are sensitive to the structure and size of data. Changes in datasets and/or the structure of the DL architecture may alter DL models' performance. Generally, DL models work well on large datasets with a wide range of features compared to their shallow counterparts.

Deployment challenges of DL solutions in resource-constrained IoT devices

Although the IoT application use cases, presented herein with their DL-based implementations, demonstrate the potential of DL in IoT, there are still some open research challenges in many directions. In particular, research and development support are needed in many areas. A few of the key areas of research and development are dataset preprocessing, secure, and privacy-aware DL, aspects of handling big data, and resource-efficient training and learning. In the following sections, we briefly present these remaining challenges from a machine learning perspective, as well as from the perspective of IoT devices, edge/fog computing, and the cloud.

Machine learning/DL perspectives

Recently, machine learning and DL techniques are being used in various application domains to make informed decisions. However, there are a few challenges that are specific to machine learning and DL. These are as follows:

- **The lack of Large IoT datasets**: Many IoT application domains are adopting DL for their data analysis. Unfortunately, most of these existing works, including this book, rely on datasets for model training and testing that are not from IoT applications and/or real-life applications. One of the consequences of this is that many IoT-specific issues are not significantly reflected in the models. For example, IoT devices are more prone to hardware failure than general-purpose computing devices. In this case, the use of general-purpose computing data in IoT use cases may provide an incorrect prediction of an incident. Furthermore, hardware failure could be reported as a security incident. In addition, most of these datasets are not sufficiently large enough to overcome overfitting.

All these dataset-related issues are an important obstacle to the deployment and acceptance of IoT analytics based on DL. Datasets are a key requirement for the empirical validation and evaluation that the IoT system will work in the real world with no or minimal issues. Accessibility to the available datasets is another big problem that many people are facing, including us in this book. Healthcare and human activity detections are big application domains of IoT; however, their related data is usually copyrighted or under privacy considerations, restricting us from using the data with complete freedom. Many web resources have compiled a general list of useful datasets. A similar type of collection would be of a lot of help to IoT application developers and researchers.

- **Preprocessing**: Preprocessing is an essential step in DL that processes raw data into a suitable representation to be fed into DL models. Unlike many other application areas of DL, this is a challenge in IoT applications as IoT sensor- and/or thing-generated data are in different formats. For example, consider a remote patient-monitoring IoT application. The application needs to use various sensors, and they generate data in different formats. To use that data and make a collective and correct decision about the patient, we need to preprocess the data before applying it to a DL model.

- **Secure and privacy preserving DL**: Security and privacy is the number one challenge for IoT. Consequently, most IoT applications are working on guaranteeing data security and privacy in the end-to-end life cycle of data. Most of the time, IoT big data will be communicated through the internet to the cloud for DL-based analysis and can thus be seen by the people or devices around the world. Many existing applications rely on data anonymization for privacy; these techniques are not hacker-proof. Interestingly, most people talk about security and privacy of data produced by IoT devices, but what about the security of the operations, including machine learning and DL running on that data? In fact, DL training models can also under go various malicious attacks, including **False Data Injection** (**FDI**) or anomalous sample inputs. Through these attacks, many functional or non-functional requirements of the IoT solution could be in serious danger, or they may make the solution useless or even dangerous for the intended target. As a result, machine learning and DL, models need to be equipped with a mechanism to discover abnormal or invalid data. A data monitoring DL model on top of the main model could be a potential solution here. Further research and developments are necessary for security solutions to defend and prevent the DL models against these attacks and make the IoT applications useful and reliable.

- **Big data issues (The six Vs)**: IoT applications are one of the big contributors to the big data generation. Hence, challenges faced by DL for big data are also challenges to DL for IoT. Every feature of IoT big data (the six V's: volume, variety, veracity, velocity, variability, and value) imposes a challenge for DL techniques. In the following points, we briefly discuss their challenges.

- The huge volume of data poses a tremendous pressure for DL, especially in terms of time and structural complexity. Time is a serious concern in a real-time IoT application. The huge amount of input data, its heterogenous attributes, and its classification variability may require a highly complex DL model that may need longer running time and huge computing resources that are not available in most IoT applications. DL models are generally good at handling noisy and unlabelled during model learning. However, IoT's huge volume of noisy and unlabeled data may face issues.

- The heterogeneity (variety) of IoT data formats coming from heterogenous sources and/or devices can be an issue for DL models in IoT applications. This could be a serious problem if these sources conflict with one another. Many IoT applications produce continuous and real-time data, and they need real-time responses, which may not always be possible in IoT devices. Stream-based online learning is a potential solution. However, further research is required to integrate online and sequential learning approaches for DL models to address the velocity issue of the data in IoT.

- The authenticity (veracity) of data in many applications, such as medical care, driverless cars, and the smart electrical grid, is an obligatory requirement that could pose challenges for DL models in IoT. Lack of authentic data could make the IoT big data analytics useless. Hence, data validation and authenticity need to be checked at every level of data analysis. The data variability, such as data flow rates, could cause additional challenges for the online processing of streaming data.

- Finally, having a clear understanding of business value of an IoT adoption and its corresponding big data is essential. However, most decision makers fail to understand that value.

DL limitations

Even with tremendous success in various application domains, DL models have many issues to be addressed in the future. For example, any false claim made by a DL model that is not recognizable by humans is an issue. Lack of regression capability of DL models is an issue for many IoT applications, as they need some kind of regression as their core analysis component. Few works already propose solutions for the regression capability integration within DL models. We need further research in this direction.

The following diagram summarizes the key challenges related to the DL perspective:

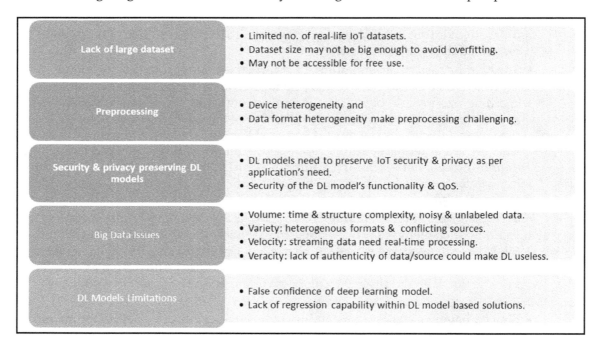

IoT devices, edge/fog computing, and cloud perspective

As we mentioned in `Chapter 1`, *The End-to-End Life Cycle of IoT*, an end-to-end IoT solution consists of three different key components or layers, which mainly includes IoT devices, edge/fog computing, and cloud platforms. All these components have their own challenges in regard to DL implementations. In the following list, we will briefly discuss those challenges:

- **Resource-constrained IoT Devices**: IoT devices are resource-constrained in terms of processors, battery energy, memory, and network connectivity. DL models developed for traditional computers may not be directly useful in IoT devices. Importantly, the training of DL models is not possible in IoT devices as the training process is a resource-hungry operation. For this book, all the DL models' training was done on a powerful desktop computer or the cloud. In some cases, resources are so scarce that a pre-trained model may not run on them for inferencing. As shown in the following screenshot, the two versions of CNN implementations discussed in `Chapter 3`, *Image Recognition in IoT*, for image classification need around 90 MB to store their pre-trained models, and this storage may not be available in many IoT devices. Hence, we need lightweight DL models, especially lightweight pre-trained DL models. A number of existing solutions are available for addressing the IoT device-related issues, and we shall briefly cover these in the next section:

- **Edge/fog computing**: Edge/fog computing is becoming a popular computing platform in IoT solutions, especially for real-time applications, as the data used in these applications does not need to always be moved to a cloud platform. However, this technology is in its early stages and has many challenges, including the following ones:

  - **DL service discovery for devices**: Edge/fog routers or gateways will be distributed geographically, and will offer services to IoT end users/nodes using a specific DL model. For example, a **fog node** may offer image classification services through a CNN, and another nearby node may offer an intrusion detection service using LSTM. In this context, devices need service discovery protocols that can efficiently discover their appropriate data analytics services based on their needs and context.

  - **DL model and task distribution**: Fog computing may rely on a distributed learning approach by sharing the learning responsibility between different fog/edge nodes. This will require some time to split the DL model execution process, as well as their tasks distribution, which could be an issue for real-time IoT applications.

  - **Mobile devices as edge devices**: Smart mobile phones are omnipresent, and are becoming a key element in the IoT ecosystem. However, the dynamic nature of these devices in terms of joining/leaving the network is a challenge for the DL-based analysis services relying on them, as they can leave the network at any time. In addition, their energy usage and other accurate resource-related information needs to be available at the task distributor in order to assign them appropriate tasks.

- **Cloud computing:** The cloud is an essential computing platform for IoT big data analytics. However, its response time and legal/policy restrictions (such as data, which may need to move from a security boundary) can be an issue for many IoT applications. In addition, security and privacy of IoT data during processing and in storage is a concern for many IoT applications.

The following diagram summarizes the key challenges in IoT devices, edge/fog computing, and the cloud perspective:

Resource-constrained IoT Devices	• Limited battery, processing and memory capacity. • Model learning infeasible in most devices. • Inferencing using pre-trained models is infeasible in some cases.
Edge/Fog Computing Challenges	• New discovery protocol needed. • In distributed learning, model execution and task splitting is an issue. • Dynamicity of mobile edge devices.
Cloud Computing Challenges	• Response time and legal/policy. • Security & privacy of user data in the cloud (processing and storage).

Existing solutions to support DL in resource-constrained IoT devices

Generally, DL models require calculations of ultra-large (in the range of millions to billions) numbers of parameter, which necessitates a powerful computing platform with huge storage support, which is not available in IoT devices or platforms. Fortunately, there are existing methods and technologies (this is not used in this book, as we did the model training on a desktop) that can address a few of the aforementioned issues in IoT devices and thus support DL on them:

- **DL network compression**: DL networks are generally dense and require huge computational power and memory that may not be available in IoT devices. This is required even to do the inferencing and/or classification. DL network compression, which converts a dense network into a sparse network, is a potential solution for resource-constrained IoT devices. A number of existing services, including Mobilenet V1 & V2, have tested the technology. For example, the Incentive V3 architecture of CNNs can be compressed from 87.0 MB of storage to 17.0 MB (as we demonstrated in `Chapter 3`, *Image Recognition in IoT*) using the Mobilenet V1 architecture. However, the approach is still not generic enough to be used for all DL models, and a compression technique may need specific hardware in order to carry out the operation.

- **Approximate computing for DL**: This approach works by considering the predictions as part of a range of acceptable values rather than an exact value (such as 95% accuracy), as many IoT applications may not need the exact values. For example, many event detection applications only require the event to be detected, not an exact value of the prediction accuracy of the event. Approximate computing will save energy, but this is not suitable for critical applications (such as medical care) where exact values are needed.
- **Accelerators**: Hardware-based accelerators for DL models have been gaining some research and development attention recently. Special hardware and circuits can be used to minimize memory footprint and improve energy efficiency to run DL models on IoT devices. In addition, software acceleration can be used for this. However, accelerators may not work with traditional IoT hardware.
- **Tinymotes**: Researchers are working on developing tiny-sized nodes that run on batteries and do the DL based on-board data analysis through the support hardware accelerator. These are useful for real-time applications. However, they are for special-purpose DL networks, and security is an issue for them.

Potential future solutions

In this section, we shall briefly discuss a few potential research and development solutions in order to address some of the issues mentioned:

- **Distributed learning**: In this book, the model learning or training were done centrally, but this may not be feasible in many IoT applications. In this context, distributed learning can be a potential solution. However, distributed computing has a security problem, and this can be minimized through *Blockchain-based Distributed Learning*.
- **IoT mobile data**: Smartphones are a key contributor of IoT proliferation. Efficient solutions for mobile big data analysis through DL models can offer better IoT services in various application domains, including smart cities. This area needs further research.
- **Integration of contextual information**: Contextual information is essential for correctly using and interpreting DL-based data analysis. However, it is hard to understand the environmental contexts of an IoT application using IoT sensor data. Ambient sensor data fused with IoT-application sensor data can provide contextual information. Hence, developing DL-based solutions integrated with contextual information could be another future direction.

- **Online resource provisioning in edge/fog computing**: Demand for edge/fog computing resources could be dynamic for real-time data analysis on streaming IoT data. Hence, online or demand-driven resource provisioning is necessary to provide data analysis services for diverse IoT applications. A few proposals are available for this, but they are focused on specific application domains. Further research is necessary for wider IoT applications.
- **Semi-supervised data analysis frameworks**: Supervised data analysis needs a large quantity of labelled data that may not always be available for many IoT applications. Often, we will have more unlabeled data than labelled data. Therefore, a semi-supervised framework could be a better option. A few initiatives are available, and further work is necessary to support the adoption of this solution.
- **Secure DL models**: DL-based data analysis will only be useful if it operates correctly and their non-functional properties (such as trustworthiness and availability) are maintained. However, DL models can be the target of various malicious attacks, making them vulnerable. Very limited research and development is available in this area. This could be a potential research and development direction.

Summary

This is the final chapter, and here we have presented a summary of the earlier chapters, and then discussed the main challenges faced by the existing DL techniques in resource-constrained and embedded IoT environments. We have discussed these challenges from both a machine learning perspective, and that of an IoT solution's components (such as IoT devices, fog computing, and the cloud). Finally, we summarized a few existing solutions, and also pointed out some potential directions for future solutions that can fill the existing gaps for DL-based IoT analytics.

References

- *Artificial intelligence*: `https://skymind.ai/wiki/open-datasets`
- *List of datasets for machine-learning research:* `https://en.wikipedia.org/wiki/List_of_datasets_for_machine-learning_research`
- *Deep Learning for IoT Big Data and Streaming Analytics: A Survey*, M Mohammadi, A Al-Fuqaha, S Sorour and M Guizani, in *IEEE Communications Surveys & Tutorials*, vol. 20, no. 4, pages 2,923-2,960, *Fourthquarter*, 2018
- *Compressing Neural Networks with the Hashing Trick*, W Chen, J T Wilson, S Tyree, K Q Weinberger, and Y Chen, in the Proceedings of the 32nd International Conference on Machine Learning, vol. 37. JMLR: W&CP, 2015
- *Ensemble Deep Learning for Regression and Time Series Forecasting*, in Computational Intelligence in Ensemble Learning (CIEL), 2014 IEEE Symposium. IEEE, 2014, pages 1–6

Other Books You May Enjoy

If you enjoyed this book, you may be interested in these other books by Packt:

Hands-On Artificial Intelligence for IoT

Amita Kapoor

ISBN: 9781788836067

- Apply different AI techniques including machine learning and deep learning using TensorFlow and Keras
- Access and process data from various distributed sources
- Perform supervised and unsupervised machine learning for IoT data
- Implement distributed processing of IoT data over Apache Spark using the MLLib and H2O.ai platforms
- Forecast time-series data using deep learning methods
- Implementing AI from case studies in Personal IoT, Industrial IoT, and Smart Cities

TensorFlow Deep Learning Projects
Alberto Boschetti, Luca Massaron, Et al

ISBN: 9781788398060

- Set up the TensorFlow environment for deep learning
- Construct your own ConvNets for effective image processing
- Use LSTMs for image caption generation
- Forecast stock prediction accurately with an LSTM architecture
- Learn what semantic matching is by detecting duplicate Quora questions
- Set up an AWS instance with TensorFlow to train GANs

Leave a review - let other readers know what you think

Please share your thoughts on this book with others by leaving a review on the site that you bought it from. If you purchased the book from Amazon, please leave us an honest review on this book's Amazon page. This is vital so that other potential readers can see and use your unbiased opinion to make purchasing decisions, we can understand what our customers think about our products, and our authors can see your feedback on the title that they have worked with Packt to create. It will only take a few minutes of your time, but is valuable to other potential customers, our authors, and Packt. Thank you!

Index